# TOP OF THE HILL

# TOP OF THE HILL

Dabo Swinney and Clemson's Rise to Football Greatness

## MANIE ROBINSON

TRIUMPH
BOOKS

Library of Congress Cataloging-in-Publication Data

Names: Robinson, Manie, author.
Title: Top of the hill : Dabo Swinney and Clemson's rise to college football greatness / Manie Robinson.
Description: Chicago, Illinois : Triumph Books LLC, [2018]
Identifiers: LCCN 2018020492 | ISBN 9781629376257
Subjects: LCSH: Swinney, Dabo, 1969– | Football coaches–United States–South Carolina–Biography. | Clemson University–Football–History. | Clemson Tigers (Football team)–History.
Classification: LCC GV939.S5925 A3 2018 | DDC 796.332092 [B]–dc23
    LC record available at https://lccn.loc.gov/2018020492

This book is available in quantity at special discounts for your group or organization. For further information, contact:

**Triumph Books LLC**
814 North Franklin Street
Chicago, IL 60610
(312) 337-0747
www.triumphbooks.com

Printed in the United States of America

ISBN: 978-1-62937-625-7
Design and editorial production by Alex Lubertozzi
All photos courtesy of AP Images

*To Parthenia, Zoe, and Elijah,*
*the star players on my favorite team*

# CONTENTS

# FOREWORD

*"There's something in these hills."*
—Joe Sherman, Class of 1934

EVERY PERSON who is or will be associated with Clemson University will understand exactly what that means when the time is right. You see, Clemson isn't just a place or a university—it almost seems like a life of its own. I've seen people enter this world with orange pacifiers and bibs, and I've seen them exit with a tiger paw pin turned right to the official 30-degree angle on their lapel. It is a unique place here at Clemson, and it takes a special kind of person to help you envision the potential that it holds. I'm not talking about the lakes and mountains that surround the area—no, no, this is about the true spirit of Clemson Football.

There's a man here named Dabo Swinney, who has built everything in his life around the word "faith." If you know his story, then you know he wouldn't be here without it. The day Coach Swinney called me, the man who doesn't promise much made me one promise he knew he could keep: "All I'm asking you to do is take a visit, I promise you won't forget it." He didn't need to sell me on the program, although at the current time there wasn't much to sell. He sat down with me and my parents and told us who he truly was and where he came from. Knowing where he had been and where he was currently spoke volumes about where he was headed. And the work he was willing to put in to get there.

It is easy to talk about wins and accomplishments, but his conversation was different; he spoke about heartbreak, losses, and how he overcame adversity. From my own experiences, I learned that life is about taking hit after hit and still finding a reason to fight. Coach Swinney had been doing that his whole life. Any university I could have chosen would have shaped me into a better football player, but, as I look back, it's hard to imagine who could have contributed to my maturation and growth more than he did. He taught me and my teammates the importance of integrity, perseverance, and community. Playing the game of football will end for us all at some time, but we can only hope the lessons we learn from the game will stay with us forever.

There was one special moment that will forever be engrained in my memory. The date was October 21, 2013, two days after a demoralizing defeat to Florida State. When Coach Swinney called a team meeting, our spirits were deflated and our heads hung low. He stood at the podium with the signature "believe" sign that he carried into every meeting. Without saying a word, he began bouncing a green tennis ball up and down. Eventually, he looked us all in the eye and said, "Men, all we can do is bounce back." He walked around and handed each of us a tennis ball with a tiger paw and the words "Bounce Back" written in bold, black ink. We went on to finish that season strong and bring home our first BCS Bowl Victory in the modern era.

That's the spirit that Coach Swinney embodies, and that is Clemson.

—Tajh Boyd
*Coach Swinney's first quarterback recruit*

# PROLOGUE

A BLANKET OF GRAY covered the sky. Bare trees stood stoically in the light breeze. The temperature rested in the low 60s.

It looked like the middle of winter. It felt like the middle of spring.

Convertibles cruised down College Avenue with the tops back. Dabo Swinney and his family slid through in a classic blue Cadillac. Thousands of friendly faces stuffed the sidewalks and greeted the Swinneys as they coasted.

It was more than a Saturday morning stroll. It was a celebratory parade.

On January 9, 2017, the Clemson University football team captured the national championship in a thrilling tussle with the University of Alabama. Five days later, members of its dedicated and devoted fan base lined downtown Clemson to commemorate the culmination of an enchanting season.

The forecast projected rain. Parade organizers contemplated rescheduling the event. However, Swinney insisted that the celebration adhere to the original schedule.

Not a single raindrop fell. Swinney used the providence as evidence to support a longstanding theory.

"You show up in January, and you get a day like this," Swinney said. "You tell me God ain't a Clemson fan? C'mon, now."

The playful proclamation opened the 30-minute speech Swinney delivered to more than 65,000 fans who filed into Clemson Memorial Stadium after the parade. A stage stretched from the 14-yard line to Death Valley's east end zone. Swinney sat on the front row in a light brown pinstriped suit. He watched proudly as the team's captains rotated to the lectern to share thanks and thoughts on the milestone achievement.

Swinney followed with an elaborate recount of the program's rapid resurrection. He honored past players, coaches, and administrators who forged the foundation on which this championship was built. "One of the things that I really try to pour into these guys is to understand how we got here," Swinney said. "And for those teams that came before this one, what we did was meant for then. What this team did was meant for now. But all of us are a part."

Swinney's emotions overwhelmed him as he thanked his former athletic director, Terry Don Phillips, who had the defiant fortitude to extend an opportunity to a young position coach and then to extend that coach's tenure after a disappointing dip. "There's not a lot of people in this world who have the guts and the conviction to do what they believe regardless of what other people think," Swinney said. "Terry Don Phillips, he's one of those men."

He relayed the doctrine of character, belief, confidence, and commitment that propelled the team through adversity. Those same principles have steered his own life. They now steer the vibrant life of his program.

"Winning the national championship is great," he said. "I've literally dreamed about this. I dreamed about it, and still think I am dreaming. But it's how we won that matters the most to me."

He repeated his signature slogans. His catchphrases could easily be printed under a portrait of an inspiring landscape and hung on the walls of elementary classrooms or hospital waiting areas. Instead, they are plastered on the walls of the team's immaculate facilities and inscribed on the hearts of every player.

He thanked the fans, who traveled to Boston and Miami and Phoenix and Tampa and everywhere in between. They flooded those cities with vibrant orange threads, thunderous cadence count cheers, and tiger-paw-stamped two-dollar bills, one of Clemson's countless beloved traditions. He thanked his support staff. He thanked graduate assistants. He thanked the cleaning crew.

Against a backdrop of orange, purple, white, and gray, Swinney painted a picture of jubilance, relief, and faith. He trumpeted the competitive and cooperative spirit his team exemplified along that championship journey. On a campus, in a state, amid a climate encroached by divisive discourse, Swinney desired for that same spirit to extend well beyond his locker room.

"I truly hope that through what this team has done that we can give a lot of people hope out there," Swinney said. "Greatness is for all of us. If you truly believe, you can do anything. You can dream big, man. I'm talking about extravagant dreaming."

Dreaming propelled Swinney through an arduous upbringing. It forced him to walk out of the bleachers and walk on the football team at the University of Alabama. It compelled him to leave a lucrative, secure career to pursue his passion in an equally lucrative but severely less secure field. It equipped him with more confidence than he may have deserved. It bolstered him in the face of adversity. It heartened him against his critics. It transformed him from an undistinguished novice to an influential forerunner.

Dreaming thrust Swinney from the depths of dereliction to the top of the hill.

# 1

# THAT BOY FROM PELHAM

DABO SWINNEY is too polite to correct folks when they mispronounce his name. He is too Pelham to go by William Christopher. That is the regal name his parents, Ervil and Carol, gave him when he was born on November 20, 1969, the third boy in the family after Tracy and Tripp. As a nickname, Carol wanted to call the youngest of her three sons "Chris." However, Chris's 18-month-old brother Tripp had no interest in trying to pronounce that. He referred to his baby brother as "That Boy." When filtered through the diction of a toddler and the dialect of Alabama, "That Boy" sounds like "Dǎbo." With a short *a* and an abrupt inflection.

Swinney admits that he did not know his name was William until the third grade. The peculiar moniker suited him. It signified his family ties, his deep Pelham, Alabama, roots. And just like Swinney, once you encountered the name, you would not easily forget it. Carol recognized Dabo's signature grit immediately. "The first time I ever laid my eyes on him, he had his little fists up," Carol said. "I laughed and said, 'Uh-oh, he's going to be a fighter.'"

Takes one to know one.

Before her second birthday, Carol was afflicted with polio. During the 1940s, polio killed or paralyzed more than 500,000 people worldwide each year. Carol was admitted to the Birmingham Crippled Children's Hospital and remained there for 11 years. She was temporarily paralyzed and stricken by scoliosis. At one point, polio disfigured Carol's body so severely that her head could touch the side of her feet. Doctors presumed she would never walk normally.

After 10 years of treatments, two surgeries, and one determined spirit, Carol walked out of that hospital. She even became a majorette in her high school marching band.

During her lengthy treatment, Carol was isolated from her family. Her childhood was far from normal, even farther from easy. She wanted desperately to create a normal, pleasant life for her own children. She dreamed of the storybook life complete with the dog and white picket fence.

Two weeks after she graduated from Woodlawn High School in 1962, Carol married Ervil. Seven years and three sons later, her dream of a loving, thriving home had bloomed into fruition. Dabo was two years old when his family moved from Birmingham to the burgeoning suburb of Pelham. The Swinneys settled on a two-story house on Ryecroft Road. The Swinney home became the hub for neighborhood children and the stadium for sandlot football games.

Ervil operated a successful washer and dryer repair service. At one point he ran three locations, including one in the M&M Hardware shop in Alabaster, just south of Pelham. Ervil regaled the regulars with tall tales and trademark quips. Carol flourished as a stay-at-home mother. She volunteered at her children's schools and even served as a substitute teacher. The Swinneys' life played out like the script of a classic family sitcom.

The dream series was interrupted in 1984, when Tripp was involved in a terrifying car crash, one block from the Swinneys' home. Tripp was 16 and sustained severe head trauma and memory loss. Carol guided Tripp through photo albums like they were bedtime story books. She hoped to trigger Tripp's suppressed memories, but he recognized no one in the pictures. He did not even recognize Carol as his mother. After several months of painstaking but imperceptible progress, Tripp celebrated a breakthrough. The doorbell rang at the Swinney home. The family's pet poodle began to bark. And Tripp was instantly annoyed.

"Shut up, Peppy!" Tripp hollered.

Tripp's recall of the dog's name prompted an optimistic inquiry from Carol.

*"Do you know this dog?"*

*"Yeah, that's Peppy."*

*"Do you know who I am?"*

*"Yeah, you're Mom."*

The family rejoiced at Tripp's recovery. However, during that same period of triumph, Ervil wrestled with an economic recession. His business eventually accumulated more than $250,000 in debt. The threat of bankruptcy pushed Ervil to the edge. Alcohol pushed him over.

"He was a good dad, but when he would drink it wasn't good," Dabo said. "He was mean. It was something he struggled with for a long, long time in his life, and it affected everything. It affected his business and his family. Ultimately, it took him to the bottom."

Ervil disappeared for days randomly on drinking binges. Carol and Dabo drove around town looking for him. Sometimes, they ended their searches unsuccessfully, but thankful that they did not have to encounter Ervil while he was drunk.

Dabo quickly learned to escape whenever the pungent aroma of alcohol crept through the door with his father. He retreated to his backyard or crawled through the upstairs window to sit on the roof. He occasionally sought refuge in the family car or at a friend's house.

"I can remember many nights crawling out the window, crawling up on my roof, and just crying and hoping that it would end soon," Dabo said. "Fighting. Screaming. Things being broken. Police coming to my house."

The old, delightful Ervil usually returned by the next morning. Carol attempted to stabilize her family through this destructive cycle. Her oldest two sons, Tracy and Tripp, had moved out of the family home. Dabo was a sophomore at Pelham High School. He and his mother watched crestfallen as unpaid bills collected in the mailbox. Ervil could no longer afford the $60 mortgage payment.

The bank foreclosed on the Swinneys' home. Their family unit was fractured.

"I always told my boys, 'Tough times don't last. Tough people do,'" Ervil said in 2009, during an interview with Ron Morris of *The State*. "Then, I didn't practice what I preached. I let tough times get to me. I just wasn't doing the right things. That's all. I've never done anything minor league. If it's anything, it's major league. When it came to screwing up, I did it major league."

Ervil moved into a mobile home behind the hardware store. Carol and Dabo rented a condo, but after merely three months, they were evicted. Before then, Carol's only job was mother. Now that she and Dabo were out on their own, she picked up a position at a department store, but the $8 per hour wage was not sufficient. They moved in with friends. Dabo slept on makeshift mattresses on floors. He and his mother were essentially homeless. Nevertheless, Dabo remained an honor student and a standout athlete. He also took the first steps of his walk in the Christian faith.

Dabo began attending Fellowship of Christian Athletes gatherings at Pelham High. On February 3, 1986, the featured speaker was University of Alabama wide receiver Joey Jones. Swinney was so moved that day that he professed his commitment to Jesus Christ.

Christian salvation did not eliminate Dabo's troubles. However, his fresh understanding of faith, devotion, and sacrifice helped him process his pain and maintain a positive outlook. "When I got saved, I thought life was going to be good. That's when life became the worst," Swinney said. "Within a year, it became as bad as it had ever been. We lost our home. My parents got divorced. We moved into a place. We got evicted. I'd go live with friends. I had a car, lost a car. That's the greatest lesson I've had in life—trust the Lord and do the very best you can in making decisions. Just because you're a Christian doesn't mean life's going to be gravy. It's all about having peace and happiness on the inside."

Dabo graduated from Pelham and enrolled at the University of Alabama in 1988. He attended Alabama football games that fall. He sat anxiously in the stands at Bryant-Denny Stadium. After each game, wonder stirred inside of him. By the third game, that wonder transformed into resolve. He turned to his longtime girlfriend, Kathleen, and confidently proclaimed, "I can do this."

Alabama closed that season with a 9–3 overall record. The Crimson Tide was ranked No. 17 in both the Coaches and Associated Press polls. Yet Dabo Swinney, a straggly, 170-pound freshman, believed he belonged on that field.

"Most people don't believe," Dabo said. "Most people, they want you to fail. They get excited to see you struggle. They get excited to see you not have success. That's the world we live in. It's really sad that people have so much joy in somebody not being successful. But I've never been afraid to fail. I've never been afraid to put myself out there, because I believe in myself, and that's what I've learned as a human, is that, if I have my eyes on the right things and I believe in myself, I'm going to make it. That doesn't mean it's going to always go right, but I'm going to be successful."

Swinney joined more than 45 other aspirants the following January during a strenuous walk-on tryout program. He reported to strength and conditioning coach Rich Wingo, in a heated weight room at 5:30 AM, three days each week. After two months of grueling tests, only two men remained standing. Dabo was one of them. He earned a spot on the scout team as a wide receiver.

"They'd put us all in jail today, for that program," Dabo said with a smile. "It was surreal for me to finally be in the room and to be introduced to the team. I always tell everybody I was a 'crawl-on.' I was one notch below a walk-on. I crawled on the field out there. They didn't invite me to come out. But to get to go out that spring and be a part of the Crimson Tide was unbelievable for me. I mean, I was one of those kids who watched *The Bear Bryant Show* every

Sunday, and every time Alabama was on TV or on the radio, I was listening. I'd fight you in school if you talked bad about them."

That summer, while enduring his first training camp with the football team, Dabo continued a side hustle he had worked successfully for years. He cleaned gutters in large, affluent neighborhoods around Pelham and Birmingham. "Man, I'm the best gutter cleaner out there," Dabo said. "I started cleaning gutters when I was 14, me and Les Daniels, my buddy. We couldn't drive at the time, so we'd carry a ladder and a blower and a rake. All the big houses were in a place called River Chase, and we'd just knock on people's doors and clean their gutters and got really good at it."

Dabo cleaned gutters like he did everything, with tireless energy. He developed a rapport with many of his customers, and before long, he did not need to randomly knock on any doors.

"People just expected me to show up, and I did," Dabo recalled. "It's just what I needed to do. It was a great way to go make some money. It was good times, man, a lot of fun. I still, even now to this day, I ride around and look at people's gutters, man. I should go knock on their door and clean it up."

That particular summer, the gutter cleaning enterprise did not yield quite enough to cover Dabo's share of the rent and utilities and his tuition, books, and fees. As the start of the 1989 fall semester neared, Dabo waited anxiously for the Pell grants and student loan funds to arrive. He went to Coleman Coliseum on the edge of campus to retrieve his class schedule. Instead, he received disappointing news from the bursar.

"Tuition at the time was like $1,100 a semester," Dabo recalled, "and she said, 'You've got to pay 50 percent by tomorrow or your schedule's canceled.'" That was only half of Dabo's problem. He also owed his landlord, Mr. Cotton, approximately $400.

"I was expecting to get my check that day, and I was going to pay him off and be good to go," Dabo said. "I went home, and I just remember sitting in my little apartment, going, 'You know, I guess you've just got to go home. You've got to do what you've got to do.'"

Dabo called his mother to relay the predicament.

"We just cried on the phone, and I told her, 'Listen, I'll just come home, and I'll work this semester and maybe I can come back in January," Dabo said. "I had no answers. A thousand dollars, at that time, that might as well had been a million for me. I was devastated, because I'd put all this work in. I was going to be a redshirt freshman. But I really didn't have anywhere to turn. I got on my knees. I prayed and just had peace about it."

Dabo walked to the mail center at his apartment complex. He opened his box and pulled out a stack of envelopes and flyers. He returned to the apartment and unloaded the stack on the coffee table. He noticed a Discover card envelope peeking from behind the pizza coupons. Dabo curiously opened the envelope and found a letter announcing the new Discover Checks program for current cardholders. He was immediately skeptical.

"There were two checks attached to it, with perforated edges. Two checks. It gives me chills to even think about right now," Dabo said. "You've got to understand. I didn't have a checking account. I operated in cash only, because at that time, we'd had some problems in my family of checks being written and things like that, and I was just scared of a checkbook. I thought it was a scam. I didn't know what it was. But it said, 'If you've got any questions, call 1-800-DISCOVER.' So I called 1-800-DISCOVER."

A pleasant customer service representative answered. Dabo explained the letter he had just opened. "She says, 'Oh, yeah, yeah, that's a new program. You just use it like a check, and you just write it for anything you want, just like a normal check," Dabo recalled. "And I said, 'There's only one problem here. I don't have a Discover card.'"

The customer service representative was puzzled. She asked for Dabo's social security number, punched it into her computer, and searched for his account information.

"She pauses, and she comes back and she goes, 'Oh, I'm sorry, Mr. Swinney, your card was returned. We sent it to a faulty address.' I'm kind of panicking, because I was thinking it might've gotten sent to somebody, and now I'm in debt or something, but she said, 'Just give me your correct address, and I'll be sure to send it out there to you.'"

Dabo stuttered in disbelief. He could not yet process what the lady on the phone was telling him. "I'm like, 'Wait a minute! You mean I've got a Discover card?' And she said, 'Yeah, because of your grades. It's a student program, and you qualified for it,'" Swinney recalled.

"I said, 'Well, what's my credit limit?'"

"She said, 'A thousand dollars.'"

"I went nuts. This lady is probably telling this story somewhere in America right now. I went crazy. I'm like, '*Whaaaaaat?!*'"

Stunned, Dabo asked the lady again to ensure he did not hear wrong. He asked her once more to ensure he was not dreaming.

"I said, 'Now, wait a minute. You mean—what do I do again?'" he recalled.

"She said, 'You just write it for whatever you want.'"

"'Oh, my God! You've got to be kidding me.'"

Dabo thanked the lady, hung up the phone, and then picked it back up to call his mother again. "I had chills on me. I said, 'Mom, you're not going to believe this.' And I told her the story, and we're both crying on the phone," Dabo said. "I hung the phone up. I got on my knees. I'm just thanking God."

Dabo returned to Coleman Coliseum. He tore one of those checks off the back of that letter. He wrote it for $550 to the University of Alabama. Then, he ventured directly to Mr. Cotton. He tore off the second check and wrote it to cover his rent. "I'm $1,000 in debt, but I'm good to go," Dabo said. "Then, about a month later, I got my Pell grant, I got my student loans, and then I never had that problem again. You live, and you learn."

The Pell grants and loans were not the only reason Dabo avoided that same predicament. The former crawl-on inched closer to earning a scholarship. In 1989 he climbed to the periphery of the receiver rotation. Alabama rolled to a 10–2 record and won a share of the Southeastern Conference championship. Alabama lost the Sugar Bowl to Miami and then lost its head coach, Bill Curry, to Kentucky. Among the departing assistants was Dabo's first position coach, Tommy Bowden.

Alabama replaced Curry with Gene Stallings, who had played for legendary coach Bear Bryant at Texas A&M University and been a member of Bryant's first coaching staff at Alabama in 1958. Stallings replaced Bowden with Woody McCorvey, who initially relegated Dabo to the scout team.

"I swear to you Woody McCorvey didn't know my name, and I had just been through a spring and a summer with him." Dabo said. "I hadn't sniffed the field."

Alabama dropped four of the first seven games of the 1990 season, and the receivers dropped enough passes to make McCorvey rethink his depth chart. In addition, Alabama lost its top two receivers, Craig Sanderson and Prince Wimbley, to injury in consecutive games against Florida and Georgia. McCorvey needed to either motivate his starters to tighten up or find an alternative. At the start of a practice during the ninth week of the season, McCorvey figured he could possibly achieve both of those objectives through Dabo.

"I'm over there on the scout team getting ready to do my daily job, and, out of the blue, Coach McCorvey, he starts calling my name over from the other field," recalled Dabo, who immediately began to retrace his steps to ensure he had not done anything to draw McCorvey's ire.

"Did I miss class? Was I late? I'm trying to think, *What did I do?*" Dabo said. "He might not have said it this nice, but he said, 'Dab, I need somebody who can catch the football. I'm going to give you a chance today. If you catch the ball, I'm playing you this

Saturday.' Now, I don't know if he was trying to fire them other guys up or not. He, to this day, won't admit it. That's my opinion. But that was my big break and my opportunity, and I took it and ran with it."

Dabo earned a spot on the travel squad for the road trip to Mississippi State that week. Alabama returned from Starkville with a 22–0 victory. Two games later, during a 45–7 win against Cincinnati at Legion Field in Birmingham, Dabo caught his first pass. It was an 18-yard gain.

Dabo did not catch another pass that season, but he caught the eye of Stallings. He considered offering Dabo a scholarship, but he would not concede it easily. "He's like a father. He's a mentor, been a great role model and a leader for me," Dabo said of Stallings. "He instilled a lot of great qualities and toughness and work ethic. When I kind of broke through and actually kind of became a first-team guy for a little while and I thought I was going to get my scholarship right then, he told me I hadn't earned it."

Alabama finished that season with a 7–5 overall record. The Crimson Tide snapped a four-game losing streak in the Iron Bowl against Auburn. After the season, Stallings awarded Swinney that scholarship.

Dabo shared the news with his mother, whom he had persuaded to move to Tuscaloosa with him that summer. Carol was hesitant to agree. First of all, she asserted that no young man needed his mother cramping his college days. Second of all, Unit 81 at the Fountainbleau Apartments only had two bedrooms. Dabo's friend, Chris Donnelly, claimed one. Yet Dabo convinced Carol to share the other room. Dabo pushed his bed against the wall to optimize space. He wedged a broomstick in the closet to give them a second rack to hang clothes.

"You just do what you've got to do, first of all, but I loved having my mom there," Dabo said. "It was a little different at first, but again, when you're in the middle of situations in your life, you just make the best of it. That's kind of how I've always lived my life, and that's what I try to tell people. Just make the best of it. That's what the happiest people in the world do. They don't have the best of everything. They just make the best of everything. That's to me what true peace and happiness is all about."

Carol kept her job as a retail sales clerk at a Parisian department store in Birmingham. On off days, she cooked for Dabo and his friends. The runaway favorite dish was chicken and dumplings, with a little peach cobbler for dessert. Carol and Dabo shared the same bed until they moved into a three-bedroom house.

"When you're in the midst of that, sometimes it's very hard to keep that perspective and focus on the future because you get caught up in some tough moments," Dabo said. "But my mom was great. I think that it gave me a drive, because I was driven to graduate. I was driven to create a better path for my family, for my brothers, for my dad, for my mom, and I didn't want to be a part of the problem. I wanted to be a part of the solution. I wanted to exhaust the moment that I had from a relationship standpoint, networking, academically. I didn't want to just get my degree. I wanted to excel. I wanted to be on honor roll. I wanted to be an All-SEC academic guy. I wanted to get my master's. I wanted to arm myself because I was sold out that if I get my education, then my life can be better, and if my life can be better, my family's life can be better."

Dabo earned three varsity letters and closed his career with seven receptions for 81 yards. He garnered SEC Scholar Athlete and Academic All-SEC honors twice. Alabama swept through Dabo's senior season in 1992 with a perfect 11–0 record. The Crimson Tide defeated Florida 28–21 at Legion Field in the first ever SEC Championship Game. Alabama proceeded to the Sugar Bowl to face Miami. The Hurricanes had won their previous 29 games, including the 1991 national championship. Dabo earned a starting role in the game and helped Alabama shock Miami 34–13. The victory earned Alabama its first national championship since 1979.

"We were just a heavy underdog. It was probably 12 points or more going into that game, but we had just a resolve," Dabo said. "We had an incredible chemistry. We had great leadership on the team. We had a selflessness, and we just had this drive to get it done. We all knew that that moment right there would be something that would bond us forever. That '92 team, just because it had been so long to get Alabama back on top, was pretty special to be a part of."

Dabo graduated with a degree in commerce and business administration in 1993. He was the first member of his family to earn a college degree. His father, Ervil, was there to watch him walk across the stage to receive it.

Dabo matured spiritually during his college career. He exhibited the Christian principles of sacrifice and faith, but above all, Dabo discovered the power of forgiveness. He learned that it is not benevolence for the offender. It is freedom for the offended.

"I did not have a great relationship with my dad from the time I was probably 14 to 27 years old. We dealt with a lot of things," Dabo said. "The good news is prayer works. If my family can be healed, then anybody's can, because I promise you, they were deep, deep wounds."

The hardships Dabo endured shaped him. They motivated him. They drove him toward greatness. While he would have preferred to learn through different circumstances, Dabo valued the lessons. They helped him seize responsibility for his life. That eliminated the need to blame Ervil or harbor any hurt.

Dabo forgave his father. Ervil escaped the grasp of alcoholism and committed to the Christian faith. He and Carol reconciled as friends. Ervil met his second wife, Phyllis, in 1997. Carol married Larry McIntosh in 1998.

Dabo and Kathleen were married in 1994, and as their own family grew, Dabo's fractured family reassembled. The Swinney and the McIntosh crews gathered to celebrate birthdays, holidays, and football games, often at Dabo and Kathleen's home.

In 2007, when Ervil was diagnosed with lung cancer, he stayed with Dabo and Kathleen while he underwent treatments. Dabo relished the late nights he spent with his father in his basement. He appreciated Ervil's interaction with his grandchildren. Dabo was thankful that his three sons could see the jovial, wise man Dabo grew up admiring, not the troublesome villain that alcohol made him.

Ervil fought valiantly through a second bout with cancer before passing away on August 8, 2015. His friends found him slumped over sitting in a chair in that old M&M Hardware Store. He was scheduled to travel to Clemson the next day to visit Dabo for training camp.

Ervil found his final resting spot in a place that always brought him peace. Where his jovial spirit flowed. Where his son, who blossomed into one of the most prominent coaches in college football, could retreat in the off-season and simply be a regular "ol' boy from Pelham" listening adoringly as his father held court with his signature stories. Swinney keeps four voicemails from his dad saved on his smartphone. He pulls them up occasionally just to hear his dad's voice again.

"My dad was a great man. I loved my dad. He had some demons that he fought, and it was tough to have to see some of those things as a kid," Dabo said. "For a long time, I didn't think there was any hope. But God works on everybody, and in His own time. God put our eyes in front of our head, not behind, for a reason. I am very thankful for my upbringing. I think everything that I dealt with had great clarity on what the purpose of my life was. I just believe that God doesn't save you from things. He saves you through them."

# 2

## DAB AND KATH

THE INTERIOR of Kathleen and Dabo Swinney's home could fill an hour-long HGTV special. The décor is carefully calculated. The furniture flows fluidly. Countless photographs line the walls, tables, desks, and appliances. They illustrate the memorable milestones in the family's history. But there is one particularly "precious" photo that perfectly depicts the enchanted, enduring relationship Kathleen and Dabo have shared.

Kathleen Bassett is wearing a vibrant blue dress with a bright red belt. She is holding a small bouquet of flowers affixed by a matching blue bow. The flowing curls in her hair flip just above her shoulders. Dabo is sporting a light-colored patterned jacket, a white shirt, and a brown necktie. His bangs hang down over his raised eyebrows. His left arm is stretched to embrace Kathleen gently on her shoulder.

Dabo keeps a copy of that photo in his office. It is framed with a more recent photo of Kathleen and Dabo posed in precisely the same manner at a football game. Many observers can stare at that photo and never notice the attire. They would be enthralled by the broad smiles Kathleen and Dabo have stretched across their faces. They would be charmed by the exuberance and innocence in their eyes.

The photograph is a candid shot from the River Chase Middle School dance in 1982. Dabo nervously passed a note to Kathleen to ask her if she would accompany him to the social event. By that time, Kathleen had known Dabo for five years. They met when Kathleen was in the first grade. Dabo was in the second grade.

Their friendship blossomed when Kathleen's older sister began dating Dabo's oldest brother.

"I'd go over to her house. She'd come over to my house. I'd go with my brother. She'd come with her sister," Dabo recalled. "We'd just hang out and play together. We were always such great friends."

Then, once the two reached middle school, Dabo and Kathleen decided to take their friendship to the next level. Kathleen checked the "yes" box and returned the note to Dabo.

"We started 'going together,'" Dabo said with a laugh. "That's what you did back then. So we 'went together' for a little while."

Their magical romance cooled over the next year. Momentarily.

"I'll never forget that day," Dabo said. "We had had that long Christmas break, and it's not like we had cell phones or social media. You just didn't see each other for three weeks. I just decided along the way that, 'You know, I just don't want a girlfriend right now. I just want to be great friends.' It was one of the worst days, because we ate lunch together. I told Kath, 'You know, we're such good friends. I just think I don't really want a girlfriend right now.'"

Dabo initially feared that he would anger Kathleen and lose her friendship completely. The opposite occurred. "She was just like, 'Oh, it's okay. It's okay. It's not a problem. It's not a problem,'" Dabo recalled, mimicking Kathleen's sugary, Southern soprano drawl.

Kathleen speaks with a warm intonation and calming cadence that could cut through the thickest tension. Her voice can soothe disappointed quarterbacks and disconcerted linebackers. It can assure apprehensive mothers that they can entrust their sons to Clemson's program. It matches her warm and calming character.

"That's just been her spirit," Dabo said. "She's always been the sweetest person in the world."

Thus, when Dabo revealed that he wanted to scale back their relationship, Kathleen was unfazed. She exhibited her easy-going compassion, but she was also confident that their romance would rekindle at the appropriate time. "We always kind of liked each other," Kathleen said, "and when I was old enough to date in high school, we did."

Kathleen and Dabo's first official date was in 1987. Dabo escorted Kathleen to dinner in Hoover, about 30 minutes from Pelham. "I had 10 bucks," Dabo said. "We went to eat. She ordered fried cheese. It was the first time I ever heard of fried cheese."

Kathleen obliged Dabo's modest budget with a dinner order of mozzarella sticks and water. "I'm sure he was thinking, *What is she ordering?* Kathleen said. *"But, hey, it's only three dollars."*

After completing the gourmet meal, the couple continued to the movie theater to watch *Summer School* starring Mark Harmon. "So we are watching this movie, and it is like 10:45, and we are a good 25 minutes from [Kathleen's] house," Dabo recalls. "I mean, it is like the best part of the movie. It didn't even start 'til 9:45, and she says, 'I have to be home by 11:00.' I'm like, 'What?'"

Dabo tried his best to zip back to Pelham. He was not as worried about encountering a police officer along the highway as he was Kathleen's parents. "We did not make it," Dabo said, "and I think she was grounded for the next weekend."

Despite the regrettable conclusion to their first date, Kathleen was inclined to continue dating Dabo. That was the first example of her abiding support for him. She displayed it in far more serious situations through the remainder of their high school days.

Dabo's father lost the family business, then lost control of his alcohol use. The family lost its home. Ervil and Carol Swinney lost their marriage. Dabo lost the family structure he had relished. He did not want to lose his friends. Thus he attempted to hide his hardships from his closest companions, including Kathleen.

Kathleen's home was comparatively stable. Her parents were formally educated. Dabo's parents never attended college. He thought revealing the dysfunction in his family would suddenly illuminate these discrepancies to Kathleen and push her away from him. However, as Dabo escaped his father's drunken wrath and bounced from home to home, Kathleen pushed closer. She revealed that caring, calming spirit.

"I think that may have brought Dabo and I even closer," Kathleen said. "It didn't matter to me. We just had this bond."

"She was always there. She was a part of me and encouraged me to believe in myself," Dabo said. "When I was living at a friend's house, she didn't care. When I didn't have a car, she didn't care."

Kathleen was there when Dabo got his first car. She was there for him when he lost it. "I didn't have a car when I went to college," said Dabo, who enrolled at the University of Alabama in 1988. "After that first year, I went to a little Toyota place in Birmingham. They had, like, a first-time buyer's program. So I bought a black, five-speed Nissan Sentra."

Dabo immediately drove the car to Kathleen's house.

"I pulled up, and she was so happy for me, because I drove her car everywhere," Dabo recalled. "I said, 'It looks like a BMW, doesn't it?' I was so proud of that car."

Dabo returned to Tuscaloosa for classes, but on the weekends, he would drive that Sentra back down to Birmingham and join a couple of his friends to clean gutters around the nearby neighborhoods. The extra money helped him cover rent, utilities, gas, and fried cheese.

"I'd had the car a little over a month," Dabo said. "I go home, I pull into Les Daniels' driveway. My buddy Alex was behind me. He had the truck. I pull in there. I throw it into second gear and get out."

Dabo began walking toward the truck when his friend Alex began frantically pointing toward him. Dabo turned around and discovered that his car had shifted out of gear and was slowly creeping forward down the slightly sloped driveway. Dabo sprinted to the driver's seat but quickly determined that he could not stop the car from inside. He darted in front of it and attempted to impede it from creeping further toward the cliff at the end of the driveway. Alex could not tell if Dabo was aware of his waning margin.

"Swinney!" Alex shouted, as the car slid over the ledge.

"I just barely—I just dive and flip, and I'm down in the woods. I'm rolling," Dabo said. "I'm going down, and my car goes down the cliff in this backyard and T-bones into a tree. And I'm like, 'This ain't happening.'"

Les Daniels' father summons a tow truck to fetch the car out of the woods. Dabo's beloved ride mended in a body shop for several months.

"For the next year, I'm making payments on a car every month that I don't even have," Dabo said. "That sucker had so much Bondo [body filler] when I got it back. But once I got it back, I drove it until I couldn't drive it no more."

Kathleen supported Dabo through his calamity. She also backed him in his audacity. She joined him at the University of Alabama in 1989. That previous fall, they sat together in the stands at Bryant-Denny Stadium to watch football games. She quickly noticed something stirring inside of Dabo.

"He was absolutely miserable," Kathleen recalled. "And he said right there that he was going to walk on to the team that spring."

Some folks may have dismissed Dabo's proclamation as foolhardy. Kathleen urged him forward. She encouraged him as he advanced through the grueling tryout process. After he made the team, she returned to the stands to watch him play.

Dabo and Kathleen both graduated from Alabama with bachelor's degrees in 1993. Kathleen earned hers in elementary education, while Dabo earned his in commerce and business administration. He cleaned gutters for another summer before joining Alabama head coach Gene Stallings' coaching staff as a graduate assistant.

Dabo moved from the tiny apartment in which he shared a bed with his mother. He, his mother, and his friend Chris Donnelly rented a three-bedroom house in Coventry toward Alberta City.

"We each had our own room. That was big-time," Dabo said with a smile.

On August 19, 1993, Dabo asked Kathleen to meet him to grab a quick bite to eat. She arrived dressed comfortably in her workout clothes. Dabo pulled the car into a fancier restaurant than Kathleen expected, The Cypress Inn, but he assured her that she was not underdressed. After dinner, Dabo convinced Kathleen to join him for a walk to Denny Chimes, the bell tower on the south side of the quad at the center of the Alabama campus.

As the bells began chiming for the 10:00 o'clock hour, Dabo crouched to one knee and asked for Kathleen's hand in marriage. Stunned but touched, Kathleen accepted Dabo's proposal. They married the following year.

"I think that sometimes in life the greatest asset that you have is hope and potential," Swinney said. "That's what I always tell people with my wife. She married me because of my potential. That's for sure. She was very patient, great perseverance, and she saw some potential in me."

The Swinneys' first few years of marriage were blissful but not bountiful. As a graduate assistant, Dabo worked long hours grinding for Coach Stallings while also pursuing his master's degree in business administration. He earned less than $500 per month. Kathleen graduated with a master's degree in education and began her career as a school teacher. She also moonlighted occasionally at Shelton State Community College.

"We ate SpaghettiOs every night, and we loved it," Kathleen said. "We were young and full of energy, and it was great."

Dabo's mother, Carol, had moved out of the small house she shared with her son and into her own apartment in a nearby complex. Dabo ensured they remained roommates in spirit. On the first Valentine's Day alone in her apartment, Carol came home and found a single red rose, a carton of candy, and a small card. The inscription read: *Happy Valentine's Day to my #1 V'tine! Thank you for all that you sacrifice to see that I have everything. You are truly a special person to all. I love you, Mom!*

Carol still has that card to remind her of the simple joys that can prevail through tough times.

"We were happy," Carol said. "We were peaceful."

"I've always found a way to have a positive attitude," Dabo said. "What's the alternative, to be miserable? To think that things can't ever change?"

Dabo was rewarded for his positive impact on the Alabama program in 1996, when Coach Stallings hired him as a full-time assistant. Dabo's former position coach and mentor Woody McCorvey had been promoted to offensive coordinator. Dabo was placed in charge of wide receivers and tight ends. Alabama won the Southeastern Conference West Division championship that season.

After defeating rival Auburn 24–23 in the Iron Bowl at Legion Field in Birmingham, Coach Stallings announced his retirement. Defensive coordinator Mike Dubose was promoted to head coach. Dubose retained Dabo and allowed him to focus solely on wide receivers. McCorvey was elevated to assistant head coach.

Ann McCorvey helped Kathleen adjust to the life of a coach's wife, in part by sharing some baking recipes, which Kathleen used to prepare treats for Dabo's players. Kathleen even traveled with Dabo on the final week of recruiting periods. She would sit with him in hotel rooms to help him craft the schedule for the next day of visits. She would occasionally walk laps around the high school tracks while Dabo was inside presenting his pitch to prospects.

In 1998 Kathleen was forced to resign from her de facto position as Dabo's traveling administrative assistant. Exactly five years after Dabo proposed to Kathleen, the Swinneys welcomed their first son, Will. He was born in Tuscaloosa. Kathleen took a leave of absence to stay home with her newborn. She intended to return to teaching. "Then I got pregnant again nine months later," Kathleen said with a laugh.

Drew was born 17 months after Will. Kathleen did not return to teaching. While she managed the home and children, Dabo helped Alabama compile a 21–15 overall record from 1997 to 1999. Alabama won the SEC championship in 1999 and lost an overtime thriller 35–34 to Michigan in the Orange Bowl.

Alabama opened the 2000 season ranked No. 3 in both the Coaches and Associated Press polls. It fell to No. 13 after opening the season with a 35–24 loss to UCLA at the Rose Bowl in Pasadena, California. Alabama slipped to No. 15 the following week after a 28–10 victory against Vanderbilt, but a 21–0 loss to Southern Mississippi at Legion Field dropped the Crimson Tide out of the top 25. Alabama salvaged a little bit of optimism with consecutive victories against South Carolina and Ole Miss. However, Alabama dropped its next two games, which included a 10-point loss at rival Tennessee and then a two-point loss to Central Florida in Bryant-Denny.

On homecoming.

Four days after that defeat, Alabama athletic director Mal Moore announced Dubose would resign at the end of the season. Alabama lost its final three games to rivals Louisiana State, Mississippi State, and Auburn.

The embarrassing losses were not the only thing that cost Dubose his job, and subsequently the jobs of his staff members. In May 1999 Dubose held a press conference to deny rumors and reports of improper conduct with a female secretary. He later admitted that he misled school officials and authorities in his denial. The school paid $360,000 to settle the sexual harassment claim.

The NCAA also scrutinized Alabama during an investigation into the recruitment of Albert Means, a defensive tackle from Trezevant High School in Memphis, Tennessee. Means was one of the most highly coveted defensive players in the country. He chose Alabama over Arkansas, Georgia, Kentucky, Michigan State, Ole Miss, and home-state team Tennessee. Means played in seven games, with four starts, as a freshman in 2000.

In January 2001 the Memphis newspaper, the *Commercial Appeal*, reported that Alabama booster Logan Young paid Trezevant head coach Lynn Lang $200,000 to steer Means to Alabama. A preliminary letter of inquiry arrived from the NCAA the next month. Lang later testified in federal court that he accepted $150,000 from Young, who was convicted and sentenced to six months in federal prison. The NCAA eventually punished Alabama with five years of probation, a two-year bowl ban, and lost scholarships.

Means denied any knowledge of the wrongdoing. Alabama released him from his scholarship, and he closed his career at the University of Memphis. But Dabo's affiliation with Mike DuBose and this recruiting scandal left him without a soft place to land.

"I didn't leave the profession. I couldn't get a job," explained Dabo, who admitted he initially was a little naïve about the duration of unemployment.

He proclaimed to Kathleen that several teams would desire his services, considering his record as a winner and a recruiter. He pursued a job at Notre Dame. The Fighting Irish had recently lost their receivers coach Urban Meyer, who left to become head coach at Bowling Green. Stallings and Moore called Notre Dame head coach Bob Davie to recommend Dabo, but Davie offered the position to Joker Phillips.

Dabo was disappointed but not disillusioned. He turned his attention toward his young family. Will was three years old. Drew was two. They removed some of the anguish Dabo felt knowing he would have to spend at least one year away from the game.

"It had been a difficult time," Dabo said. "I just decided, 'I'm going to take this season off and kind of regroup and really spend some time with my boys.'"

Then Dabo received a call from a former coach offering him a job. But not in coaching. It was Rich Wingo, the former strength coach at Alabama. He offered Dabo a position at AIG Baker, a commercial real estate development firm in Birmingham. Dabo was reluctant. The real estate game was foreign to him, and he had no intentions of doing anything other than coaching. Wingo convinced Dabo to try the firm for one year. His starting salary was $80,000 before bonuses.

When Swinney pulled off for his first day on the job, Kathleen stood in the driveway, holding Will and Drew with tears streaming down her face. Dabo would be making more money than he did coaching at Alabama. But a full bank account is meaningless if the heart is not fulfilled. Kathleen knew this was not his calling. They both hoped it was only temporary.

"He'd come home and say, 'What am I doing? I should be coaching,'" Kathleen said. "There was such a void there."

Nevertheless, Dabo excelled at AIG Baker. He approached his new role with the same intensity and attention to detail that made him an exceptional coach. He studied traffic and demographic data like playbooks and formation charts. He put names to faces and developed genuine relationships just like he did on the recruiting trail. He set a vision for potential tenants just like he would for a facilities construction plan. Then he followed through on his contracts and delivered on his promises.

"I learned a lot, traveled the country, learned new things with this company, met a lot of new people, and had great success doing something outside of coaching," Dabo said. "But the best thing is it really made me a better coach, and it really gave me an appreciation that I didn't have. I always thought I was a good coach and loved what I did. The passion for coaching and teaching and impacting people's lives, I just couldn't find anything to fill that void, even though I was working a nine-to-five job, at home on the weekends. I was making more money than I had ever made, but that's not why I got into coaching."

Dabo would periodically receive calls from his former players at Alabama. The reminders of those relationships reconfirmed his desire to mentor young men.

"He definitely missed football," Kathleen said. "He was great at what he was doing, but he had a longing to be back. His heart was with coaching kids. We prayed about it and knew, if the timing was right, it would come back around."

Dabo asked God to present him with another opportunity to operate in his passion or fill his heart with an equally fulfilling fervor. "I would pray a specific prayer every day," Dabo said. "'God, I'm passionate about coaching and teaching, and that's what I want to do, but if that's not your plan for me, then I pray that you keep that door closed.'"

Dabo believed God responded to his supplication in February 2002, although then Swinney did not recognize the sign. He drove from Birmingham to Anderson, South Carolina, to represent AIG Baker on a shopping center project. His hotel was approximately a 20-minute drive from the Clemson University campus. Swinney had never visited Clemson before, but he heard about its picturesque splendor from former colleagues who had coached and played at Clemson. In 2002 Swinney's first position coach at Alabama, Tommy Bowden, had just finished his third season as Clemson's head coach. While he was nearby, Swinney called his former coach to see if they could meet and catch up. However, Bowden was out of town. One night during his weeklong visit, Swinney decided to drive to Clemson anyway.

Swinney pulled around to the east side of Memorial Stadium. He parked his car to take a picture of the Clemson football relic, Howard's Rock, which sits on a pedestal at the top of The Hill near the east gate. Swinney looked out over the field known as Death Valley. Former Presbyterian College coach Lonnie McMillan equated Clemson's home turf to that infamous scorching California desert in 1948, after his team lost five consecutive games in Clemson by a combined score of 244–0.

"I remember calling my wife, saying, 'Hey, guess where I am?'" Swinney said. "'I'm in Clemson. I'm at Death Valley. I'm looking at The Rock. I'm at the top of that hill, and it's steep.' That was a cool experience."

Swinney did not realize then that one year later he would be back in Clemson posing for photos by Howard's Rock with his entire family. He would stand in that same spot but in a much different role.

Meanwhile, back at Alabama, Dubose's replacement Dennis Franchione steadied the program through the infractions and sanctions. Alabama finished the 2002 season with a 10–3 record. It was inhibited from accepting a bowl invitation, so Alabama culminated the season on November 30 with a visit to Honolulu to play Hawaii. Five days later, Franchione left to become the head coach at Texas A&M.

Mal Moore filled the vacancy with Mike Price from Washington State. Shortly after accepting the position, Price contacted Dabo to offer a spot on his staff as tight ends coach. Dabo accepted the offer in principle, but the deal could not be formalized until after Price coached his former team in the Rose Bowl. Dabo was thrilled about the opportunity to return to coaching, but when Price returned to Tuscaloosa, he informed Dabo that he wanted to hire a more experienced assistant coach. He offered the job to Sparky Woods instead.

Dabo again was disappointed. But this time, the closed door prevented him from walking into another mess. In April, rumors surfaced that Price, while in Pensacola, Florida for a pro-am golf tournament, spent hundreds of dollars at a strip club. Price reportedly lost his credit card, and an unidentified woman found it and charged $1,000 worth of room service on it. The next month, Alabama rescinded Price's contract. He was dismissed before ever coaching a game.

Before Swinney could get the sigh of relief completely out of his mouth, his phone rang again. This time, it was Tommy Bowden with more than a reciprocated request for lunch. He informed Dabo that he needed a replacement for longtime Clemson assistant Rick Stockstill, who became the offensive coordinator at East Carolina. Bowden asked if Dabo was interested in the position.

Despite his urge to return to coaching, the decision was not simple. The Swinneys were finally stable. They were finishing up construction of their dream home, a 6,400-square foot manor in southeast Birmingham. Kathleen was pregnant with their third child. Their entire family was in Alabama. In addition, Bowden suffered at least five losses and finished with a 4–4 record in the Atlantic Coast Conference in each of the previous two seasons. Terry Don Phillips was in his first academic year as Clemson's athletic director and could easily clean house and tailor the program to match his vision. Bowden could not offer any job security.

Also, Dabo had to compete for the position with T.J. Weist, another former Alabama receiver who played for Bowden and was then Western Kentucky's offensive coordinator. Dabo had never been a coordinator, but Weist had never been a shopping center leasing agent. Dabo knew how to sell, and he had never known a product so well. He was selling himself. He convinced Bowden. He had a harder time convincing the folks back in Birmingham.

"I had a bunch of people calling me and saying, 'Are you crazy?'" Swinney recalled. "'You can't take that job. You're going to walk away from this? You're going to walk away from that? He's going to be fired in six months, and you're going to be without a job again. You just built this house, and your wife's pregnant and you're going to take the grandkids from all the family.'"

Swinney did not disregard the merit of those concerns. He prayed that God would offer him further confirmation. He believes he received it during his visit to Bowden, shortly after he landed in Greenville, South Carolina.

"I got off the plane and I didn't really know where I was," said Swinney, who hopped in the car with his chauffeur to make the hour-long drive from the airport to Clemson. A few miles down the highway, Swinney spotted his sign. "We just barely get on the Interstate, and there's this big ol' sign that says, 'Pelham Road.'" It was an exit sign to one of Greenville's bustling thoroughfares. It was the confirmation Swinney sought.

"I said, 'I'm from Pelham, Alabama, so this place can't be that bad,'" Swinney recalled.

Bowden offered Swinney the position with a starting salary that was $5,000 more than Swinney's target figure. The Swinneys placed a "For Sale by Owner" sign in the front yard of their dream home. It sold in two days. To a family from South Carolina.

"When I came up here I just knew this was where I was supposed to be," Dabo said. "Without a doubt, God wanted me in Clemson, South Carolina."

Once again, Dabo chased after his dream with Kathleen running right beside him. "She's been there every step of the way, and I'm not here without her," Dabo said. "She's just been a rock for me, very blessed to have the wife that I have, that I met in the first grade."

Shortly after they arrived in Clemson, the Swinneys welcomed their third son, Clay. As a coach's wife, Kathleen deemed it fitting that all her children were boys. Will, Drew, and Clay prepared her for the 100 other young men she mothers each season.

"I'm always in 'boy mode,' with three of my own and then the players who miss their moms," Kathleen said. "I just have a very strong passion for them. You just can't help but love a frightened and excited 18-year-old who comes to school to play football."

Dabo no longer had the set schedule and open weekends, but Bowden encouraged the fathers on his staff to bring their children to the workplace. The two older Swinney boys frequented practices, and Kathleen continued her ritual of baking for players. But when she picked up Will and Drew or delivered her cookies at the practice fields, she learned not to observe too closely. She would get defensive of her other "sons" who were wearing pads.

"There were times when Dabo would get on them, and I'd just be mortified," Kathleen said. "I'd tell them after practice, 'I'm so sorry he yelled at you.' And they would tell me, 'It's okay, Mrs. Swinney.'"

"Typical Kath," as Dabo would say. Kathleen still carried that same smile she held that evening at the River Chase Middle School Dance. She has stood cheerfully and steadfastly by Dabo's side. In the darkest of times, she has been his light. Pulling someone through their hardships and pushing them toward their potential requires strength, humility, and devotion. Kathleen has gladly given that to Dabo. When she needed him most to return that gesture, Dabo did not blink.

In 2003 Kathleen's older sister, Lisa, was diagnosed with breast cancer. She underwent a double mastectomy and chemotherapy. The treatments overpowered the cancer, but she discovered that she carried a mutated BRCA gene linked to the disease. She implored her sisters to get tested for the gene. Kathleen did not heed Lisa's plea right away, but then she thought about what her sister had endured. She concluded that neglecting to pursue this knowledge would be an affront to Lisa's honor. In 2005 Kathleen went to genetic counselor for testing. She discovered that she carried the gene.

According to her doctors, Kathleen had a 90 percent chance of developing breast cancer. Kathleen could begin taking a medication that could potentially decrease the risk or she could undergo a double mastectomy to virtually eliminate it. At the time, Kathleen was 34 years old. Lisa was diagnosed at 38. Kathleen did not want to take any chances. She did not want to waste any more time.

"Even though it took me a year to get tested, I knew when I left there," Kathleen said. "I told Dabo, 'I have to have a mastectomy.' If somebody said it's almost a 90 percent chance of rain, you're probably going to take your umbrella."

A few months later, amid the football season, Kathleen underwent surgery. Through the entire ordeal, from preliminary doctor's visits to follow-up assessments, Dabo ensured that he was there to hold Kathleen's hand whenever she needed to reach for his.

"There are so many bigger things out there than a football game," said Dabo, who maintained family as his chief priority.

He was delighted to be back working in the role for which he profusely prayed. He was also thriving at Clemson. The Tigers finished the 2003 season with a 9–4 record and a Peach Bowl victory against Tennessee. The 2004 season was marred by five losses and an appalling bench-clearing brawl with the rival South Carolina Gamecocks. Clemson rebounded with an 8–4 record in 2005. Clemson suffered through three consecutive gut-wrenching losses during the first half of the schedule, including overtime nail-biters against Miami and Boston College and a 31–27 edging at Wake Forest. Clemson responded by winning six of its last seven games, including the Citrus Bowl against Colorado.

Yet Dabo often wondered if chasing his dream cost too much. His sons were in grade school and began participating in various activities, many of which conflicted with Dabo's practice and recruiting schedules. Dabo did not want to miss those moments, nor did he want to place the burden of managing the home all on Kathleen.

"I almost got out of coaching," Dabo said. "They were little, and they were playing ball. And I was gone all the time. I remember being down in Florida, calling home, and Will had just hit a home run. Drew was doing this. Clay was crying. Kath is going, 'Aww.' And I'm gone for like four weeks. I just felt like I was sacrificing my family. I just told Kath, I said, 'Kath, I can't do this anymore.' And I came home."

Dabo gathered Will, Drew, and Clay for a family meeting. The three boys sat on the edge of the bed with their tiny feet dangling against the comforter. "They're just looking at me," Dabo recalled. "And I just told them, 'Listen, I just want y'all to know, y'all are the most important thing in the world to me. I love y'all, and your dad can do a lot of things. And I'm going to get out of coaching, and I'm going to get a job where I can coach your teams and be home on the weekend. And I just don't want to miss this opportunity to be a great dad."

Dabo had thought long and hard about what he would say that evening, but he had not thought much about how his sons would react. "When I got done with my big speech, they look at me and go, 'But, Daddy, if you're not a coach, we won't get to know the players and we don't get to ride the bus,'" Dabo recalled. "All of a sudden God used my kids to speak to me. I was focused on the things that we didn't get to do. God used my kids to get me to focus on the things that we do get to do and that they got to do. So that was a life-changing moment for me. It really was. So, through these boys' mouths and their experiences that they had had, they started telling me, 'Dad, we love you being a coach. And Mom videos anyway. She videos it.'

"From that point on, I said, 'You know what? I've got to change my perspective here. You can be a great coach and be a great father and be a great husband. You can be all those things. You don't have to sacrifice all those things to be a great coach."

Kathleen optimized the boys' time with their father and accommodated Dabo's hectic schedule as much as she could. "Kath is a great mom," Dabo said. "She makes it easy for me. She takes care of a lot of things that I just don't have time for. She gives me every opportunity that there is to be around my kids, whether it's just coming up and having dinner with me in my office or bringing them by to practice, or whatever—coming to the ballgames, being at the hotel on Friday nights. She makes sure that they're around. There's nothing more important to me than being a good dad. I look at those little boys every day, and it's an awesome responsibility as a father to be a good example to your children, to discipline them when they need to be disciplined, to praise them when they need to be praised, to tell them you love them.

"And it's okay to say you love somebody. It's okay to cry. I just think that's important, and there are so many kids out there who don't get that from their fathers. I think that is one of the main problems we have in this country, poor parenting. Just about everything bad in this country you can probably trace back to poor parenting somewhere along the way. It becomes a cycle.

"I just want these kids to grow up to be good citizens. I want them to be good husbands and then good fathers. I hope that I'm planting seeds in them that will grow and bloom somewhere down the road, and they'll remember their dad, remember the good times we had, remember the quality of life, the quality time we had—maybe not necessarily think about what we didn't have or what we weren't able to do but just cherish the moments that we did have."

That is the principle that has guided Dabo's life, that sustained his charmed romance with Kathleen. They did not ponder Dabo's harsh upbringing. They did not ponder the meager means with which they commenced their marriage. They did not ponder the wrecked car or the steady diet of SpaghettiOs. Kathleen and Dabo could not be deterred by a frustrating job search. They could not be daunted by breast cancer.

They outlasted all the doubt and overpowered all the struggle, simply by cherishing what they have. "We didn't know any different," Kathleen said. "It hasn't been necessarily easy, but we wouldn't change anything."

# 3

# LIGHTNING STRIKES TWICE

A BUSINESS CARD rests on the desk inside of Dabo Swinney's office. On the back of the card is a hastily scribbled contract:

*I, C.J. Spiller, agree to visit CU on the 13th of Jan. 06.*

Clifford Spiller Jr. has been told that he first held a football at five years old. It was kindergarten picture day, and the photographer brought several items for children to hold as they posed for the picture. A man tossed a football toward Spiller, and he caught it. That was the first indication that Spiller was a natural performer with the ball in his hands and with the cameras flashing.

He dominated Pop Warner leagues in Lake Butler, Florida. As he matured and advanced to Union County High School, his dominance did not wane. He rushed for 5,511 yards through his high school career, including 1,840 yards and 30 touchdowns in his senior year. He was named a first-team *Parade* All-American and was ranked as the No. 1 prospect in Florida by several recruiting publications. Spiller also won the state track and field championship in the 100- and 200-meter dash. He was coveted by college programs from across the country but was expected to sign with one of the home-state powers—the University of Florida or Florida State University.

That did not deter Dabo Swinney. He was in his third season as the wide receivers coach and recruiting coordinator at Clemson University. Apparently, he had not been there long enough to realize that Clemson had little success pulling five-star recruits out of the Sunshine State, and thus had no business pursuing Spiller. Yet, against that conventional caution, Swinney was in Lake Butler ready to challenge Urban Meyer, who was then the head coach at Florida, and legendary Florida State coach Bobby Bowden, who also happened to be his boss' father.

Spiller did not know much about Clemson before he received that initial call from Swinney. But he was comfortable defying the norm. He grew up a Seminoles fan in deep Gator territory. Lake Butler is approximately 30 miles north of the University of Florida campus. Florida finished with a 9–3 record in 2005, Meyer's first season in Gainesville. The Gators ran a dynamic spread option offense, and in December, a few weeks after pounding Florida State 34–7, Meyer secured a commitment from one of the most highly touted quarterback recruits—Tim Tebow. There appeared to be no way any school could drag Spiller out of the Swamp.

Blinded by his own confidence, Swinney did not see it that way. He called Spiller each week and focused on building a genuine relationship. "Man, oh, man, it didn't take me long to realize this kid was much more than a good football player. He was a special and unique person," Swinney said. "I don't think many people gave Clemson much of a chance. I was just trying to get him to take a visit."

Swinney convinced Spiller to add Clemson to his lists of official visits. But he did not want to leave Lake Butler without some form of assurance. He jotted the makeshift agreement on the back of his business card. Spiller signed it. Swinney exuberantly returned with promising news for Tommy Bowden, trusting that Spiller was a man of his word.

Spiller honored his pledge and traveled to Clemson alone. It was the only visit he made without his mother, Patricia Watkins. Shortly after he arrived in Clemson, after gazing over the lake, seeing Death Valley rising into the skyline, meeting with coaches, touring the sprawling campus, interacting with running back James

Davis, who stayed on campus during a free weekend to host Spiller, and feeling that family vibe, he called his mother. He told her he felt at home at Clemson.

"He told me before he left that day, 'I'm about 99 percent sure I'm coming to Clemson,'" Swinney recalled. "And I was like, 'Really?' And he said, 'Yeah.'"

Swinney was not as shocked as he was by the Discover Card customer service representative, but just like that day, he had to ask Spiller again to ensure he was hearing everything correctly.

"You sure you're still 99 percent?"

"Yes, sir."

Swinney and Tommy Bowden traveled to Lake Butler the following Sunday to secure Spiller's commitment. They sat down in Spiller's living room with his family that evening. "I'm thinking we're going to end this thing," said Swinney, who grabbed Spiller for an aside.

"You're still coming to Clemson?" Swinney asked.

"Yeah, I'm coming," Spiller said. "But I just don't want my mom to know."

Swinney worried that Spiller had changed his mind but, out of respect and anxiety, was reluctant to tell Swinney.

"Why don't you want your mom to know?" Swinney asked.

"Well," Spiller said, "I want it to be a surprise."

Swinney was briefly reassured. He trusted Spiller, and this time, he did not feel compelled to pull out a business card. He drove back with Bowden, who knew Clemson could not celebrate the coup just yet.

"We're sitting there going, 'Unbelievable. C.J. Spiller just committed to us,'" Swinney recalled. "But Urban's coming in Monday. Bobby Bowden Tuesday. He's still got to visit Florida State. We've got a week and a half before signing day. It was the longest 10 days of my life. He told me he was coming, but he had to take these other visits. I had a couple of other running backs that we had the opportunity to sign. I said, 'C.J., what do you want me to do? If you're not coming, I need to know. I don't want to miss out on a good player. He said, 'You don't have to take them. I'm coming.'"

On Signing Day, Wednesday, February 1, 2006, Spiller stepped to a lectern inside the Union County High auditorium. Spiller's smooth bone white suit popped against the Florida orange and blue balloons decorating the scene. He delivered a touching six-minute speech. He thanked the people who influenced him, encouraged him, and guided him to that point. He looked up from his manuscript, paused, exhaled deeply, and said, 'Now, what everyone's been waiting on. In the fall of 2006, I will enroll at Clemson University."

A muted golf clap spread through the room rife with Gators fans. As Spiller reached to the adjacent table and grabbed a purple Clemson cap, the ovation began to amplify as the attendees disregarded their own astonishment and disappointment to applaud a young man who had performed and represented that community with class.

Back in Clemson, there was no slow build.

"It was a complete eruption. It probably registered on the Richter scale in Clemson, South Carolina," Swinney said. "It was a shocker to everyone because they just thought he was going to go with Florida or Florida State. I wasn't surprised, but I was overjoyed and relieved that he said it publicly. That was the first time he'd said it publicly."

The aftershock of Spiller's earth-shattering announcement quaked loose the preconceived complacency at Clemson. The Tigers did not need to wait in line behind anyone on the recruiting trail. Spiller dug the first trench in the briskly flowing pipeline Clemson established in Florida. Clemson eventually pulled five-star recruits from every neighboring state and then stretched its recruiting net to the Pacific coast. That growth was initiated by Spiller's fortitude to forge his own path—and his courage to recommit to that decision a year later.

Spiller rushed for 938 yards and averaged 7.3 yards per carry as a freshman. He scored 12 touchdowns from scrimmage. He dazzled Clemson fans when he embarrassed defenders with the grace of a matador in the open field and the speed of a world-class sprinter. Davis and Spiller became known as "Thunder and Lightning," and the duo struck often. Davis rushed for 1,187 yards and 17 touchdowns that season. He averaged 5.8 yards per carry as the primary interior bruiser.

Clemson ranked fifth among NCAA Division I Football Bowl Subdivision (FBS) teams in rushing offense, with an average of 217.9 yards per game. It was 12th in scoring offense with 32.7 points per game. The Tigers were also ranked in the top 20 in total defense, rushing defense, pass-efficiency defense, sacks, tackles for loss, and points allowed. Nevertheless, those statistics did not translate into more than eight wins. Clemson notched victories against No. 10 Florida State and No. 13 Georgia Tech and peaked at No. 11 in the Coaches Poll. Then Clemson plummeted out of the top 25 after losing two consecutive games to unranked foes Virginia Tech and Maryland. Clemson closed the regular season with a 31–28 home loss to South Carolina.

By that point in Bowden's tenure, an eight-win season was slightly better than par. He averaged seven wins per season through the previous seven years at Clemson. Conversely, at that same point, Florida held a 12–1 record, a Southeastern Conference championship, and a spot in the Bowl Championship Series National Championship Game against Ohio State. Spiller could not travel home to Lake Butler for the Christmas holiday, as Clemson prepared for the Music City Bowl against Kentucky.

Clemson lost that game, and Spiller returned home to celebrate the New Year. His daughter, Shania, arrived earlier in 2006. Spiller savored the quality time he spent with her, his mother, and his friends. He felt the tug of his hometown once again. Then he watched Urban Meyer hoist the crystal ball on the Coaches' Trophy after Florida smashed Ohio State 41–14 to claim the national championship.

Before Spiller arrived back on Clemson's campus, media outlets in Florida were reporting that, upon his arrival, he would inform Bowden and his staff that he planned to transfer to Florida. Patricia Watkins asserted that her son called her that morning to relay those intentions.

But shortly after he made it back to Clemson, his mind reverted to everything that convinced him to sign with the Tigers a year earlier. He had turned off his cell phone during that trip to impede the deluge of unsolicited advice that poured into his voicemail.

"I really wasn't interested in any phone calls on my way back to Clemson. I had a lot of people telling me what I should do," Spiller said. "Transferring had nothing to do with football. It had more to do with family matters. Once I thought about things and the opportunities I had coming in the future, I thought it would be best to stay here at Clemson."

Spiller turned his phone back on and called his mother to share his decision. Watkins was initially upset and critical of Clemson's coaches, including Swinney. Like any mother, she missed her son and wanted to protect him. She was convinced that Bowden had coaxed her son into changing his mind. But after a conversation with Swinney and Bowden, Watkins eventually cooled. She recognized that it was Spiller's decision, and she supported it. She visited her son in Clemson shortly after he returned and attended the football team's banquet.

"She was just being a mom," Spiller said. "She wanted me close."

Spiller could understand his mother's instincts. Although he was comfortable again at Clemson, he still longed to be closer to his daughter. "It isn't fair for her, but I knew that when I was getting into this," said Spiller, who was able to adjust his spring class schedule to facilitate more long weekends. He used those respites to return to Lake Butler as often as possible to see Shania.

Swinney was also contemplating returning home. After the bowl loss, he explored the possibility of becoming the head coach at the University of Alabama-Birmingham. He contemplated the idea of coaching home games at Legion Field, where he had often watched the Crimson Tide. However, UAB passed on Swinney in favor of University of Georgia offensive coordinator Neil Callaway.

West Virginia coach Rich Rodriguez called Swinney to offer him a position on his staff—at Alabama. Four years earlier, Mike Shula replaced Mike Price as the Crimson Tide head coach. Shula compiled a 26–23 record, but Alabama was ordered to vacate 16 of those victories after the NCAA sanctioned the entire athletic program after it determined that athletes exploited their scholarship benefits to obtain free textbooks for other students. Beyond the scandal, under Shula, Alabama never finished higher than third in the SEC West Division. After the Crimson Tide lost the 2006 Iron Bowl to Auburn, athletic director Mal Moore dismissed Shula.

Moore offered the position to Rodriguez, who informed Swinney that he planned to accept it. However, Rodriguez reneged on his decision and returned to West Virginia, his alma mater. Moore instead hired Nick Saban, who was plodding through a disappointing tenure with the Miami Dolphins. After he arrived in Tuscaloosa, Saban extended a similar offer to Swinney, but this time, Swinney would have the title of co–offensive coordinator. Swinney was pleased with his contributions to Clemson over his four years there. He considered the offers to return home and the significant pay raise he would enjoy. But, at that time, he was not familiar with Saban and was eager to welcome the recruits he had secured in that signing class. Swinney concluded that he had more to accomplish at Clemson. Bowden rewarded Swinney's decision with a multi-year contract extension and the title of assistant head coach.

During the 2007 season, Swinney mentored receiver Aaron Kelly, who led the Atlantic Coast Conference with 83.2 receiving yards per game. "Lightning" continued to electrify Death Valley. Spiller amassed 2,104 yards and 15 touchdowns from scrimmage through the next two seasons. He also returned three kickoffs for touchdowns. Clemson closed the 2007 season with a 9–4 record and an overtime loss to Auburn in the Chick-fil-A Bowl.

The 2008 season opened with promise.

Clemson started the season ranked No. 9 in both the Associated Press and *USA Today* Coaches Polls. Clemson appeared in the preseason top 10 merely five times through the previous 50 seasons.

Clemson appeared in the preseason top 25 three times through Tommy Bowden's previous nine years as head coach. The Tigers finished only one of those seasons in the top 25. That was in 2000, when the Tigers compiled a 9–3 overall record behind dazzling dual-threat quarterback Woodrow Dantzler. It was Clemson's first season with more than eight victories since 1993.

But in 2008 Clemson welcomed back Spiller and James Davis and solid standout defenders Kavell Connor, Crezdon Butler, and Michael Hamlin. Clemson also signed the No. 1–rated recruit, Da'Quan Bowers, a defensive end from Bamberg, South Carolina.

For Bowden, expectations had never been higher. Media members projected a Bowden-coached team to win the Atlantic Coast Conference title in 15 of the previous 17 preseason polls. But it was Tommy Bowden's father, Bobby, who served as Florida State's head coach for 34 seasons.

Florida State ruled the conference for more than a decade. It won the ACC title in 12 of its first 14 seasons in the league. But in 2008, another Bowden captured the league's favor. "I've been telling everyone who has asked me that Clemson has the best talent in the conference. I mean, they're really loaded," Boston College coach Jeff Jagodzinski said in July during the ACC Kickoff media event in Greensboro, North Carolina.

Other ACC coaches echoed the acclaim.

"No surprise at all. Zero surprise," Miami coach Randy Shannon said after discovering the preseason poll results. "Have you seen their roster?"

The adulation can set a team up for a spectacular season, but it can also set a team up for embarrassment. Preseason praise is always inflated. It is based solely on conjecture. No one can truly assess the composition and caliber of a roster. No one can accurately project how new pieces will fit into the puzzle. No one can predict injuries. No one can predict outcomes.

Preseason polls should be used for nothing more than fun fodder for Monday morning debates around the office. Yet they are the barometer by which all assessments are calibrated. Every subsequent loss and victory is measured by that initial gauge. It negotiates the appropriate amount of grace or condemnation teams are granted for each loss.

It is a clever trap set up by perception. It set up the dismantling of Clemson's program.

Clemson opened the 2008 season where it closed the 2007 season. In the Georgia Dome. Instead of Auburn, Clemson faced Alabama, Auburn's Iron Bowl nemesis. Alabama was ranked No. 24 in the preseason AP poll and essentially 26 in the Coaches Poll. But Alabama was optimistic that the Crimson Tide could finish much higher. Nick Saban was in his second season as head coach, and the Crimson Tide was beginning to turn. The Chick-fil-A Kickoff matchup against No. 9 Clemson provided a chance for Saban to notch his first signature win at Alabama.

It was not even close.

Alabama manhandled Clemson 34–10. Alabama quarterback John Parker Wilson tossed two touchdowns and ran for another. Alabama amassed 239 rushing yards on 50 attempts. It possessed the ball for more than 41 minutes. Clemson possessed the ball for less than 19 minutes. Clemson converted one of nine third-down attempts and netted 188 yards of total offense. Davis and Spiller combined for 20 yards from scrimmage. That paltry figure can be attributed partly to Alabama's defense, but the majority of the performance can be attributed to the emphasis of Clemson offensive coordinator Rob Spence. Spiller and Davis combined for eight carries. Conversely, quarterback Cullen Harper attempted a pass on 34 of Clemson's 48 plays. He was sacked on three other snaps.

"We got smashed," said Swinney, who was then in his sixth season at Clemson. "We just got physically whipped. That was a long night, long ride back to Clemson."

Clemson plummeted to No. 22 in the Coaches Poll and completely out of the AP poll. It followed with a decisive win at home against Division I Football Championship Subdivision (FCS, formerly known as I-AA) opponent The Citadel. The next week, Clemson enjoyed a 27–9 win against a mediocre North Carolina State team. It then followed with a win against another FCS foe, South Carolina State. Alabama defeated its next three opponents by an average margin of 27.7 points. As the Crimson Tide climbed into the top 10 of each poll, Clemson's 3–1 start did not seem as catastrophic as it was initially portrayed.

Then Clemson lost to Maryland.

Clemson capitalized on the three turnovers Maryland donated in the first half. The Tigers led 17–6 at halftime in front of an announced crowd of 81,500 in Death Valley. Despite the circumstances, Maryland coach Ralph Friedgen was not worried. He was not intimidated by Clemson and he wanted to ensure that his players were not either.

"I don't know if they expected me to get on 'em or not, but I didn't," Friedgen said. "I just got the team together, and I said, 'This is where we're at. We really can't play any worse than we have, but we're only down by 11.'"

The merciful message worked. In five drives after halftime, Clemson gained 92 yards. The fact that it was not 93 revived the frustration that Clemson fans hoped they had left in Atlanta. Clemson trailed 20–17 and faced fourth-and-1 from the Maryland 40-yard line with less than six minutes remaining. By that point, Davis and Spiller had combined for 244 rushing yards. Nevertheless, on this pivotal play, Spence entrusted Harper with a quarterback sneak. Maryland halted the attempt and claimed possession with 5:36 remaining. Clemson did not touch the ball again.

"As a coach, you're disappointed that you let 80,000 people down," Bowden said of Clemson's fans. He added that he was pleased with his staff's performance but not with the results. Bowden had 10 days to prepare for Clemson's next game, but he felt no need to make any major alterations.

Then Clemson lost to Wake Forest.

Clemson traveled to Winston-Salem on a Thursday night and forgot to pack its offense. The Tigers compiled 198 yards, averaged 3.4 yards per play, and scored on only one of their 12 possessions. Clemson had stumbled to the edge of the cliff. The Wake Forest loss pushed the Tigers over the edge.

"At 3–3 you're going to struggle to see who your leadership is," Bowden said, not knowing how true those words would be a few days later.

On that ensuing Monday morning, Clemson athletic director Terry Don Phillips beat Bowden into the office at the McFadden Building. Phillips asked Bowden to meet to discuss the status and outlook of the program. Phillips did not intend to dismiss Bowden, at least not that day. But he wanted to respectfully inform Bowden of where he stood. Phillips and Bowden agreed that the current standing was not acceptable. Bowden had pulled the program out of the rut of mediocrity. Clemson finished in the top 25 in four of his first nine seasons. He reached a bowl in eight of those nine seasons. The lone outlier was the 2004 season that ended with the nasty brawl with rival South Carolina. Players threw punches. They threw helmets. They threw insults. And they threw away their postseason. With that ugly display behind them, the Tigers could at least enjoy another victory against the Gamecocks. Bowden held a 7–2 record against South Carolina. That body of work appeared strong enough to withstand a dismal start. In addition, in the previous December, Bowden brokered a four-year contract extension that would award him a $3.5 million buyout.

Nevertheless, Phillips contended that, after a decade, a conference championship, or at least a divisional title, was a reasonable demand. He intended to impress that expectation upon Bowden that morning. He expected Bowden to accept that challenge and profess his intentions to revamp the offense. After the Wake Forest loss, Bowden announced that sophomore Willy Korn, a homegrown star from Byrnes High School in nearby Duncan, South Carolina, would replace Harper in the starting lineup. He expected the conversation to be spirited. It was. But the outcome was not what he expected.

Bowden responded to the ultimatum with a startling suggestion. He proposed that the best solution was for him to step down. Immediately.

Phillips was surprised, but he accepted Bowden's resignation. He also considered Bowden's recommendation that his wide receivers coach and recruiting coordinator should be his interim replacement. Phillips shared Bowden's esteem for Swinney. Whenever he visited practices, he observed Swinney pressing his players, promoting toughness and relentlessly demanding effort. When Phillips would roam the halls of the McFadden Building across the parking lot from the practice fields, he would see those same players huddled in Swinney's office.

"Seeing those things over a period of time made me think he was a leader," Phillips said. "It was obvious Dabo genuinely cared about his players. They didn't look at him strictly as a coach."

Phillips left his final meeting with Bowden and gathered the assistant coaches to inform them of the resignation. He then summoned

Swinney to his office. "If you know Terry Don, you know he's not a man of many words. He doesn't say a whole lot.," Swinney said. "I went into his office really expecting for him to just say, 'Hey, do the best you can do.'

"But his message to me was, 'Hey, look, I've watched you for five and a half years, and I think you're ready for this job. I'd love to see you get the job, but you're going to have to win some games. For the next seven weeks, I want you to be the head coach. I don't want you to be the interim head coach. I want you to do whatever you think you need to do to fix this. I'm going to support you. And at the end of this, you're going to get an interview. Regardless of whether you win one or win them all, you're going to get an interview for this job. I'm going to hire the best guy for the job. But I want you to know, I've watched you. You would be a great fit here.'

"I was really shocked by that, to be honest with you, because again, you know, he's just kind of an old-school guy. So I tell people all the time, just be great at whatever you're doing because you never know who's paying attention. You never know. I go into the meeting with one mentality, and I come out of the meeting with this empowered attitude and confidence."

Swinney exercised his newfound authority immediately. He left Phillips' office, walked down the hall, and relieved Rob Spence of his duties as offensive coordinator. He reassigned tight ends coach Billy Napier to quarterbacks. Napier was an All–Southern Conference quarterback at Furman University in Greenville, South Carolina, in 2001 and 2002. Napier also took over the role of primary play-caller. Swinney promoted graduate assistant Jeff Scott to wide receivers coach. His father, Brad Scott, was also on staff as associate head coach and offensive line coach.

"First of all, you've got a lot of emotion involved. I mean, there's a ton of emotion," Swinney said. "You go from one of them to the leader of them, and there's a lot of dynamics involved there.

You've got different groups, and you've got a whole football team who did not come there for you to be their coach."

Swinney galvanized the staff and the team around their unified objective. It was more than winning games. It was about preserving their dignity and refusing to be intimidated by the circumstances. In that preamble, he fortified a standard of accountability, among coaches and players.

"You've got to push all that aside and get everybody to understand that it's bigger than any one person," Swinney said. "At the end of the day, you have an opportunity to send a message that you're not going to quit, that you're going to stand up and compete and do what's best for your school and your program."

Phillips did not promise Swinney anything beyond the six games remaining in the regular season, but he assured Swinney that he would receive a fair shot to remove that interim tag. He embarked on a six-game audition, engulfed by emotion but eager to seize the opportunity.

"He called me on that Monday, and I just burst into tears for so many reasons," Swinney's wife, Kathleen, said. "I could sense Dabo's anxiety. Not in a bad way, but there were so many emotions."

Swinney channeled those emotions into long, sleepless workweeks. His objective was not simply to guide the plummeting plane to a softer landing. He wanted to tilt the nose of that plane back upward. "Friday morning before we played Georgia Tech, my first game as an interim, [associate athletic director] Bill D'Andrea calls me and wants to take me to the [Board of Trustees] meeting," Swinney recalled. "I didn't want to go. I didn't really know any of them. It was at 7:00 o'clock. I hadn't slept all week. He said, 'They just want to wish you well. You might need to come.'

"So I get up and I go to this board meeting, and I walk over to the room, and they were all great. One of the board members said, 'We're very committed here, but we just want to be great academically and athletically, like Georgia and Florida and Michigan.'

"I couldn't help it. The Alabama just came out of me. I was trying to keep my mouth shut but I couldn't do it. I figured right then, *Well, I'm probably not going to get this job, but I'm going to say it anyway*. I said, 'Sir, I do not want this to be disrespectful, but that is not my vision for Clemson at all. I want for all those other schools to want to be like Clemson.' Since the first time I stepped foot on this campus in 2003 as an assistant, I have truly seen and believed in the greatness and potential of Clemson University."

The first step toward Swinney's objective was reestablishing Spiller as the nucleus of the offense. Swinney knew what kind of player Spiller was. He knew what kind of leader Spiller was. He knew what kind of game-changer Spiller was. He knew, if he had any chance to salvage this season and retain his new role, he needed to let Lightning out of the bottle.

Through the first six games of the season, Spiller averaged 9.5 touches per game. Through the first five games he played under Swinney's leadership, that rate increased to 15.3 touches per game. Before Bowden's departure, Clemson averaged 15.3 points per game against FBS competition. Under Swinney and Napier's command, that average increased to 24.3 per game.

The transition did not start that efficiently. Clemson dropped Swinney's first game as head coach, 21–17, to Georgia Tech. Clemson led 17–14 by the end of the third quarter, but the Tigers' first three possessions of the fourth quarter ended in two three-and-outs and a fumble. Georgia Tech surrendered the ball back to Clemson with merely three seconds remaining. Harper's last desperate pass was intercepted. The loss was Clemson's third against ACC competition. It narrowed the margin for error even more. Clemson would need to sweep through the remainder of the ACC schedule to preserve any shot at the Atlantic Division championship.

Swinney notched his first victory as head coach the following week, with a 27–21 win at Boston College. Clemson had not defeated Boston College since it joined the ACC in 2005. Spiller caught six passes for 105 yards, the most receiving yards a Clemson running back has recorded in a game.

Florida State dashed Clemson's hope for a division championship the following week in Tallahassee. Clemson bolted to an early 10–0 lead by the 7:43 mark of the first quarter but could not maintain the margin. To Swinney's credit, neither he nor the team abandoned the season. With three games remaining, bowl eligibility was still within reach. Clemson returned home to Memorial Stadium and pounded Duke 31–17. It followed with a 10-point victory at Virginia. Swinney's final audition was against rival South Carolina. The Gamecocks were already road weary from the 56–6 drubbing they suffered at Florida the previous week. That loss knocked South Carolina out of the top 25. But Swinney was in no position to offer pity. He recognized how critical a victory against South Carolina would be, not only to ensure Clemson's frustrated fan base at least kept its bragging rights in the rivalry for another year but also to ensure he kept his job.

"I had a good feeling, because we'd had a little bit of success, had some mojo going," Swinney said. "If we win the [South Carolina] game, it's probably going to be hard for them not to at least give me a chance. Maybe it's a one-year contract, I don't know. I didn't really care."

Clemson players supported Swinney with their most impressive performance of the season, considering the circumstances. Clemson claimed a 24–0 lead before South Carolina even drove past the Clemson 45-yard line. Once again, the Tigers posted no points in the fourth quarter, but this time it was not from lack of efficiency. It was because they did not need to. James Davis capped the 31–14 victory in the third quarter with his third rushing touchdown of the game.

"They thoroughly beat us," South Carolina coach Steve Spurrier said. "We just got smashed. You can sugarcoat it all you want. That's a team that should have won the ACC, or could have won the ACC, I should say."

Fans chanted Swinney's name during the final moments of the game. Offensive lineman Thomas Austin and wide receiver Tyler Grisham were among the players who hoisted Swinney on their shoulders and triumphantly carried him onto the field. Swinney hoped that verbal and visual support indicated that he had done enough to remove the interim tag from his new title, but those were not the folks Swinney needed to convince. He needed the approval of Phillips and the Board of Trustees.

He received it swiftly. The next day, Clemson reached an agreement in principle to name Swinney the head coach. He had impressed Phillips with more than the four victories he directed. Swinney reinvigorated the players and the fan base. He established a new gameday tradition, Tiger Walk. Instead of unloading the bus directly in front of the Death Valley locker room area, players disembark at Perimeter Road and march nearly 200 yards across a parking lot through a throng of fans. He invited students to visit and observe practice. More than 1,000 students accepted his offer and even attempted field goals, fielded punts, and punted against a live rush. Swinney's exuberance permeated through the program. He ignited unbridled optimism in the midst of despair.

"By the time we got to South Carolina, I had done a national search, talking with some sitting head coaches as well as coordinators," Phillips said. "Under some difficult circumstances, Dabo did a real good job of salvaging that season, and I kept coming back to him. I had seen the situation he'd been placed in, how he handled it, how the kids reacted to him, the gain in attendance, the way he organized things. It was small things like that, cumulatively, that made me believe he could do it."

Phillips had served as a college athletics administrator since 1980. Swinney's first contract as head coach may have been his easiest negotiation. It awarded Swinney an $800,000 salary for his initial season. That would be considered a significant discount in today's coaching market, but then it far exceeded Swinney's desires.

Swinney earned approximately $500 per month 13 years earlier as a graduate assistant at his alma mater, Alabama. He could survive on water and SpaghettiOs. He might have agreed to coach that first season for free if Phillips had asked.

"I told him to just leave me on the contract I'm on. 'I'm making more money than I've ever made. I'm good,'" Swinney recalled. "I didn't even read the contract. I just signed whatever he put in front of me. I was a pretty cheap investment. I told him that. Because I wanted to get the program going. What are you going to do with all that? I had no idea. I had never had that kind of money, had never even dreamed about it."

What he had dreamed about was leading a program, not simply to hold the title and wear the whistle. He relished the opportunity to sculpt young men, inspire a community, and have a lot of fun winning.

Swinney was formally introduced on Monday, December 1, 2008. He struggled to hold back tears as he opened his speech. He subverted his emotions with his trademark humor. He composed himself and stared through a series of comforting pauses. He knew how much pain, perseverance, and prayer propelled him to that point. He would not rush those moments of reflection and gratitude.

"There is only one reason that an ol' boy from Pelham, Alabama, is sitting in front of you today, and that's the grace of God. To be the head coach at Clemson, that doesn't just happen," Swinney said. "The very first time that I decided to park in the head coach's parking spot—because I was hesitant to do that—it was that Thursday of that week. It was about 5:30 that morning. It was pitch black. Wasn't anybody there. I pulled in that parking spot, and my lights hit the curb. I'd never parked in that spot before. I don't even know if it is the official head coach spot, but that's where he always parked. I pulled in that spot, and the curb had No. 88. That was my college number, and it was just kind of like God saying, 'I got your back. Hang in there.' Things happen for a reason. I think God has a plan for everybody, and this is his plan for me."

That day, Swinney also laid out his plan for the program. It was simple. To recruit at a high level, graduate players at a high level, and win at a high level. He exuded confidence that he could achieve all three. He disregarded the critics who had already denounced the hire.

Many detractors argued that Clemson passed over candidates who were more experienced and thus more qualified than Swinney. Phillips' decision was lumped into a puzzling off-season. Tennessee hired Lane Kiffin, coming off a 1–3 record and midseason firing from the Oakland Raiders. Auburn hired Gene Chizik, coming off a 2–10 record with Iowa State. At that time, Swinney seemed like the biggest risk of the bunch. Yet, when asked if he thought Clemson was gambling on him, Swinney did not hesitate to respond.

"No!" he exclaimed plainly. "If you are asking me, it's a pretty good bet. I don't mean that in an arrogant way. I'm confident in my abilities and always have been. I believe in myself."

During that introductory press conference, D'Andrea ceremoniously slipped an orange blazer over Swinney's shoulders. By conventional sartorial standards, the sleeves were a little long and the torso was a bit too wide. But for a 39-year-old dreamer from Pelham, Alabama, it fit perfectly. For a football program longing to restore its fading glory, Swinney fit perfectly.

# 4

## ALL IN

DABO SWINNEY realized his dream in 2008. Many other hard-working folks had their dreams shattered that year. The economic downturn devastated countless small business owners. Syd Smith was among the recession's casualties.

Smith operated Square One Image Solutions, a printing company that specialized in the impossible. Smith printed photos on dry erase boards. He superimposed panoramic shots on curtains. He wrapped graphics cleanly around oddly configured booths.

He commissioned his first job for Clemson University in 2003 and maintained the relationship even after he was forced to shut down Square One. That allowed him to acquire his most loyal customer.

Dabo Swinney.

When he was designated Clemson's interim head coach midway through the 2008 season, Swinney asserted his intent to exhaust every moment through the remainder of the schedule. He assembled the team for a meeting. He frankly articulated that no player in the room owed him anything. He acknowledged that, although he may have built strong relationships with many of them during their recruitment, they ultimately signed with Clemson to play for Tommy Bowden, not Swinney. He offered to honor players' scholarships until the end of the year if they desired to transfer.

Then Swinney looked over the room solemnly and declared his demand for each one of those players who chose to stay. For the remaining six games, he expected them be "all in." He wanted his 52 players to train, study, prepare, and play like he planned to coach, with the unbridled abandon of a poker shark pushing all his chips to the center of the table.

"I'm all in, everything I've got," Swinney told his players before warning them that if they could not match his commitment then they should not even bother attending practice later that afternoon.

The next day, Tuesday, October 14, Swinney contemplated a way to commemorate that analogy. Smith received a call from former Clemson associate athletic director Robert Ricketts. "He said, 'Syd, Dabo would like to know if we could get poker chips,'" Smith recalled. "I started laughing, and I asked, 'By when?'"

"He goes, 'By Friday.'"

Smith scrambled to procure the materials and equipment. He worked feverishly and produced 200 wooden chips with Clemson's signature tiger paw logo stamped on one side. Swinney distributed the chips to his players prior to their next game. They dropped the chips into a bucket before they entered the field to signify their "all-in" commitment.

Swinney has developed that slogan into an organizational mantra. He developed the tradition into a brand. Smith has helped him keep his chips stacked high. He updated the design and adjusted the materials, and through the duration of Swinney's tenure, he has worked feverishly to meet Swinney's work orders.

The new tradition endeared Swinney to Clemson fans. Clemson football revels in routine. The Tigers' revered rituals inject an unrivaled mystique on each gameday. Outside of Death Valley and outside of context, Clemson's pregame entrance would feel like a waste of time and gas. Players exit the locker room the west end of the field. They drop their chips in the bucket and load two charter buses that escort them around the perimeter of the stadium to the east end zone. Players unload the buses at the top of a steep hill that has been left untouched through several stadium renovations and expansions. Perched at the top of that hill just inside the east gate is a large pedestal. On the top of that pedestal sits a rock. It was a souvenir 1919 Clemson graduate S.C. Jones excavated from Death Valley, California. Jones gave the rock to legendary Clemson coach Frank Howard, who used it as a doorstop in his office for a few years. Finally, in 1966, after tripping over the rock, Howard asked Gene Willimon, executive secretary of the Clemson booster club, IPTAY, to discard it. Instead, Willimon mounted the rock atop the hill. The next season, as a motivational tactic, Howard told his players that the rock had supernatural powers and would invigorate them if they rubbed it before they entered the field. But he warned them with his own version of "all in": "If you give me 110 percent effort, you can touch it," Howard told them. "But if you ain't gone give me 110 percent, then keep your filthy hands off of my rock."

The Death Valley crowd erupts when the first players appear at the top of the hill and hover over the rock. The band breaks into the fight song. A cannon fires. Hundreds of orange balloons are released. The players pour down the hill and onto the field. In 1985 sportscaster Brent Musburger dubbed Clemson's entrance the "most exciting 25 seconds in college football."

Swinney met Frank Howard at his mother's 40th birthday party. A native of Barlow Bend, Alabama, Howard played for Wallace Wade at the University of Alabama from 1928 to 1930. In his final season, the Crimson Tide logged an undefeated record. Howard and Swinney's parents shared a mutual friend, Bobby Hayes, who served as the mayor of Swinney's hometown, Pelham, Alabama, for more than two decades. Howard attended the surprise birthday party as Hayes' guest. Swinney keeps a photo of his parents dining with Howard.

Swinney did not learn about Howard's Rock until much later, in 1990, his redshirt sophomore year at Alabama. When Gene Stallings became Alabama's head coach, he hired former Clemson assistants Woody McCorvey, Bill Oliver, and Ellis Johnson, and former Clemson players Danny Pearman and Chip Davis.

"I knew about Clemson because of Danny Ford and Frank Howard, but I didn't really understand the concept of the Rock and the Hill," Swinney said. "I can remember Chip Davis and Danny Pearman kind of vividly describing it to me. 'We rub the Rock and run down the Hill,' and I'm going, 'Really?' All I ever knew was Alabama, and we just came out of the tunnel. That was kind of a unique concept for me."

Swinney understood Davis and Pearman's esteem for the tradition once he visited Clemson. "Immediately—literally the moment I got here—it was just one of those things," Swinney said. "It's a very iconic thing, and there's just so much history and tradition. Then you start talking to former players, and there's a pride that comes from that experience."

Yet, through his first five seasons on Tommy Bowden's staff at Clemson, Swinney never experienced the exhilaration of the illustrious entrance himself. "Tommy put me in charge of the captains, so I never ran down the Hill. My gameday, I would always take the captains out, and we would wait on the team to come down," Swinney said. "So I always watched it. Every single time for almost six years as an assistant, I was just like, 'Wow, that is so cool.'"

Swinney's first week as interim head coach was frantic. He had so many meetings to attend and plans to draft. He worked nearly nonstop. It did not occur to him until that Friday that he would finally get to participate in the "most exciting 25 seconds in college football."

"That was a very emotional experience for me. Just an honor from all the people who have done that," Swinney said. "I was just like, 'Wow! I can't believe I'm getting to do this.'"

Moments before kickoff against Georgia Tech, the buses cruised around the stadium. Swinney hopped off at the top of the Hill and trotted to the pedestal. He spread his arms and smiled like he was preparing a bear hug for a friend he had not seen in four years. He cupped the sides of the Rock with both hands and bent over the pedestal.

"I just gave it a big ol' kiss," Swinney recalled with a laugh.

When the cannon fired, Swinney sprinted wide open ahead of his players to the center of the field. He turned to extend his hands to greet players as they jogged by him.

"It was a special moment, and it has been ever since," said Swinney, who has preserved enough of his athleticism to ratify another pregame tradition. He has sprinted ahead of the pack before every game. He has avoided calamitous injury, and no player has outrun him yet.

"It never gets old," Swinney said. "It's a magical moment every time."

Other Clemson traditions travel a little easier than Howard's Rock. Clemson fans do not need a gameday to perform a cadence count chant:

*1, 2, 3, 4*
*1, 2, 3, 4*
*C-L-E-M-S-O-N*
*T-I-G-E-RRRRRRR-S*
*Fight Tigers*
*Fight Tigers*
*Fight! Fight! Fight!*

Clemson fans will break into the chant at a moment's notice, in tailgates, in between plays, and in bars, airports, weddings, and restrooms. Another traveling tradition, the $2 bill, exhibits the chip the Clemson fan base carries on its collective shoulder, doggedly daring one of its rivals to even look at it.

In 1977 Georgia Tech announced that, after that season, it would no longer play Clemson. It would instead schedule William & Mary. "We weren't going to any bowl games at that time, so it was our big game of the year," said George Bennett, a 1955 Clemson graduate and former IPTAY executive director. "We were taking

15,000 to 17,000 people down there for that weekend. Our people would actually go down on Wednesday, and wives would shop and all that stuff and stay in those fancy hotels."

Bennett schemed a tactic to show Georgia Tech the economic boon it would eliminate from its city. IPTAY encouraged fans to pay for all their expenses in Atlanta that weekend with $2 bills. "We covered the city up with $2 bills," Bennett said. "The *Atlanta Journal Constitution* wrote articles about it, and the waitresses in the restaurants were talking about it, and the cab drivers and bellhops."

The next year, Clemson fans repeated the tactic but began stamping orange tiger paws on the bills. That tradition has continued for every road game Clemson plays.

Swinney's "all-in" chips fit seamlessly into Clemson's culture of creative customs. He added more traditions, like Tiger Walk. Fans pull away from their tailgates momentarily and line the parking lot outside of the west end zone facility to greet players and coaches as they march in jackets and ties to the locker room. He also tightened the Victory Walk during warm-ups. Players and coaches stand abreast across the 20-yard line, lock arms, and march to the end zone. Swinney started videotaping the tradition to ensure that players took it seriously and executed it properly through the goal line. Fans cheer for that 15-second demonstration of solidarity like it is a 65-yard touchdown. In Clemson, tradition is part of the playbook.

"There's an energy here that I think is a way of life that's kind of lost in other places, to be honest with you," Swinney said. "I think our fans enjoying tapping back into that every time they come. It's one of the greatest gameday environments you could ever imagine."

From the onset, Swinney understood the importance of imagery and messaging. Rekindling the fire in the fans would help him stoke the flames behind his players. That enthusiasm breeds optimism. That optimism facilitates focus. The vision crystallizes for everyone involved. They can look toward a common target. When he took over the program, Swinney was not yet certain where it was headed, but he knew his first objective was to get everyone moving in the same direction.

The day after Clemson athletic director Terry Don Phillips introduced Swinney as the full-time head coach, defensive coordinator Vic Koenning resigned. Koenning said Swinney alerted him that his job status was not certain. "Maybe the best word is *disappointed*," Koenning told Bart Wright of the *Greenville News* that December. "I have no issues with Coach Swinney. What he did for that football team and the university was tremendous. He healed some wounds that had been open and were a little sore. He brought some focus to the team and got everyone pointed in the same direction."

Koenning's praise for Swinney contradicted some of the fiery speculation that began to circulate on the Internet alleging friction between Swinney and Koenning. "He has every right to shape his staff the way he wants to, and I have no hard feelings or problems with what he did," Koenning said. "I do think we had a pretty good defense, and I think the statistics will speak for themselves on that, so sure, it was disappointing. The thing people may not understand is that in this profession, this sort of stuff happens all the time."

Koenning landed a job at his alma mater, Kansas State. Swinney assigned linebackers coach David Blackwell and defensive line coach Ron West to call plays in the ensuing bowl game. Clemson allowed 361 yards and 26 points in the five-point loss to Nebraska in the Gator Bowl. That was 66 more yards and 10 more points than the Tigers averaged through the previous 12 games under Koenning.

Ten days later, Swinney filled the defensive coordinator vacancy with Kevin Steele, a Dillon, South Carolina, native, who had coached for 27 years under Nick Saban at Alabama, Bobby Bowden at Florida State, Tom Osborne at Nebraska, and Johnny Majors at Tennessee. Steele was also assigned to coach linebackers.

Blackwell, a Greenville, South Carolina, native, initially moved to defensive tackles. Swinney retained Chris Rumph to coach defensive ends. In March, Blackwell left Clemson before accepting an offer to become the defensive coordinator at South Florida. Swinney filled that vacancy with Dan Brooks, who had coached the previous 13 seasons under Phillip Fulmer at Tennessee.

Swinney hired former Clemson assistant Charlie Harbison to replace Koenning as secondary coach. Harbison coached at Clemson from 1995 to 1997 under Tommy West. He then coached at Alabama, Louisiana State, Alabama again, and Mississippi State.

Swinney retained offensive line and associate head coach Brad Scott from the previous staff. He promoted Brad's son, Jeff Scott, from offensive graduate assistant to receivers coach. Jeff Scott, a Clemson graduate, opened his coaching career as the head coach at Blythewood High School in a northeastern suburb of Columbia, South Carolina. He directed Blythewood to a state championship in his first year and the school's first year in the South Carolina High School League. Jeff Scott coached the next season at Presbyterian College before returning to Clemson to serve on Tommy Bowden's staff.

Swinney also hired another Clemson graduate, Danny Pearman, to coach tight ends and offensive tackles. Swinney forged a relationship with Pearman in 1990 when Swinney was a redshirt sophomore at Alabama and Pearman was a graduate assistant. They coached together in Tuscaloosa from 1993 to 1997, when Pearman left to coach tight ends and tackles at Virginia Tech. Pearman also served as a special teams assistant under Virginia Tech head coach and special teams guru Frank Beamer. Pearman coordinated special teams at his three subsequent stops—North Carolina, Duke, and Maryland. However, Andre Powell, whom Swinney retained to coach running backs, also retained his role as Clemson's special teams coordinator.

Ron West was reassigned to an administrative role, but, less than a week after Swinney announced the hiring of Steele, West accepted an offer to become co–defensive coordinator and linebackers coach at the University of Tulsa.

Swinney completed his first staff with his former position coach, mentor, and friend Woody McCorvey. He was hired as an administrator, to serve essentially as Swinney's chief of staff. Before coaching Swinney at Alabama, McCorvey coached tight ends and then receivers from 1983 to 1989 at Clemson under Danny Ford. McCorvey knew Clemson, and he knew Swinney.

Swinney and his new staff began game-planning for the 2009 season without knowing if his prize pupil would remain on campus for another school year. Running back C.J. Spiller had just closed an impressive junior season, in which he netted 1,065 yards and 10 touchdowns from scrimmage and 705 yards and a touchdown on kickoff and punt returns. Spiller even tossed a touchdown pass in 2008.

He had one remaining year of eligibility. His backfield companion, James Davis, was graduating. He also had received a favorable early-round draft projection from the National Football League advisory board.

Spiller's daughter, Shania, was living with her mother back in his hometown, Lake Butler, Florida. The reward of a lucrative NFL contract would grant Spiller the resources to support Shania and her mother much more effectively than he could in school. Turning professional would also streamline Spiller's schedule and allow him to optimize his time with Shania. All the signs were directing Spiller out of Clemson, but he had already proven his penchant for defying preconceptions.

He did not rush the decision. Nor did he offer updates through his deliberation. Davis visited Spiller and his family in Florida during that Christmas holiday. Davis and Spiller's mother, Patricia Watkins, discussed Spiller's pending decision, but Spiller did not discuss his leaning with either of them.

"She asked me, 'You know what he's going to do, right?'" said Davis, who responded quickly. "He hasn't told us anything."

Davis agonized through the process a year earlier. He remained at Clemson for his senior season and earned his degree. He wanted Spiller to make the same decision and experience the same gratification of a senior campaign and a graduation. Yet he did not pressure and pester his friend. Davis knew it was the toughest decision of his life.

The deadline to declare for the draft was January 15. Spiller utilized almost every second of that time before making his decision. The Clemson sports information department scheduled a press conference for 3:00 that afternoon in the McFadden Auditorium. By 2:45, Swinney did not even know what Spiller would decide. A few minutes later, Spiller walked up to Swinney's office dressed in a sharp black suit, an orange shirt, and a matching necktie. He sat with Swinney to discuss his decision. As he waded through his thought process, tears began to pour down his face. His heart was overflowing. His mother wanted him to turn pro. He wanted to stay and complete his degree. He wanted to spend more time with his daughter. He wanted to enjoy the spoils of seniority on campus.

He could not do it all. He could not have it all. He could not please everyone. He had to muster the courage to please himself. While media members, coaches, and players sat anxiously in the packed auditorium, Spiller composed himself. He wiped his eyes, looked at Swinney, and said, "I'm ready."

Spiller entered the auditorium and walked toward the stage with a stoic face. He opened the conference by offering some insight on how difficult the decision had been. Not in determining what to do. But in attempting not to let anyone down. Much like his announcement on signing day three years earlier, Spiller wasted no time transitioning to the announcement.

"And for the year of 2009, I'll be here at Clemson University."

A forceful cheer exploded from the rear of the room, where coaches and players had congregated. Initially, Spiller did not smile. He did cry. He rocked slightly in his chair. He relaxed his eyes and scanned the room. As the ovation continued to swell, Spiller licked his lips and cracked a grin. He was at peace.

"When you make a decision, you have to go with your heart," Spiller said. "My mom, she wanted me to go pro. There was a lot crying, but I told her there was something that didn't feel right in my heart about me leaving. A lot of guys start things, but they don't really finish. I didn't want to be labeled as one of those guys."

Swinney was ecstatic. His first season would be anchored by an All-American Heisman Trophy candidate. "If there's one thing I know about C.J. Spiller, he is his own man," Swinney said that day. "We just signed a 10-star recruit. Everything starts with C.J., for sure."

Swinney was not kidding.

Spiller started the 2009 season with a roar in Death Valley by returning the opening kickoff 96 yards for a touchdown. He rushed four times for 12 yards in the first half as Clemson mounted a 30–7 lead. Yet Spiller's light day appeared to be well-deserved rest, considering Clemson's comfortable advantage and that the Tigers would travel to Atlanta the following week to face their rival, No. 13 Georgia Tech. However, Spiller's load was lightened by the turf toe injury he suffered in the first half. Spiller battled through the nagging injury and logged 177 carries through the next 10 games. Clemson lost three of its first five games, falling to Georgia Tech, Texas Christian, and Maryland. A six-game winning streak vaulted the Tigers into the top 20 in the polls.

Spiller rejoiced in the Senior Day festivities in his final game at Memorial Stadium. Seniors were introduced individually at Howard's Rock just before kickoff. They galloped lightly down the hill to greet Swinney. Spiller closed that day with 97 yards from scrimmage, a touchdown, and a rousing walk-off reception. With 1:06 remaining and a 34–21 lead over Virginia, Swinney allowed the play clock to run and allowed Spiller and fellow star senior Jacoby Ford to linger off the field for the last time. Spiller stretched his hand to acknowledge the crowd. A chant of "C.J.! C.J.!" boomed across the stadium.

In addition to the Spiller sendoff, fans also celebrated as Clemson clinched its first Atlantic Coast Conference Atlantic Division championship. In 2004 Miami and Virginia Tech left the Big East Conference to join the ACC. Boston College followed the next year and increased the league's membership to 12 teams. The conference organized divisions for football. Clemson was assigned to the Atlantic Division with Boston College, Florida State, Maryland, North Carolina State, and Wake Forest. The Coastal Division included Duke, Georgia Tech, Miami, North Carolina, Virginia, and Virginia Tech. Clemson finished higher than third only once through the first four seasons of divisional play. Yet, in his first season, Swinney led Clemson to its first appearance in the ACC Championship Game.

Clemson would face Coastal Division champion Georgia Tech at Raymond James Stadium in Tampa. The Yellow Jackets had edged Clemson 30–27 in Atlanta back in the second game of the season. Both teams closed the regular season with disheartening losses to their unranked in-state rivals. Georgia knocked off Tech 30–24 in their annual Clean, Old Fashioned Hate game, while South Carolina defeated Clemson 34–17 in Columbia in the Palmetto Bowl. But once the Tigers arrived in Tampa, their eyes were pinned to the prize. They pursued the program's first ACC championship since 1991.

Three days before the game, Spiller was named the ACC Player of the Year. He validated that selection against Tech. On the fourth snap of the game, Spiller rushed 40 yards to the Tech 19-yard line. He capped the drive three plays later with a three-yard touchdown plunge. Tech responded with a field goal on the ensuing drive and claimed the lead on its next possession, as Jonathan Dwyer rushed for a four-yard touchdown. Clemson quarterback Kyle Parker threw an interception on Clemson's next play. Tech capitalized with a 23-yard field goal drive that ate 7:40 off the clock. Spiller rushed five consecutive times on the next possession and scored on a 41-yard sprint. Clemson's extra-point attempt failed. Georgia Tech answered with another field goal and led by 16–13 at halftime.

The second half progressed much like the first. Whenever Spiller led a touchdown drive, Tech responded. Clemson inhibited Tech from scoring on only two of its six possessions after halftime. One stop was a fourth-down stand, when Clemson stuffed Tech quarterback Josh Nesbitt for no gain on a sneak.

On the next drive, Spiller hastened a touchdown drive with a 54-yard run. Clemson reclaimed the lead at 34–33 with 6:11 remaining, but, once again, Tech responded. The Yellow Jackets manufactured a 13-play, 86-yard drive in 4:45. Clemson thwarted the two-point-conversion attempt, but Tech led 39–34 with 1:20 remaining. Clemson mustered just eight yards on its next four plays, and Nesbitt took a knee as time ran out (Clemson's second "stop" of the second half). Spiller did not touch the ball again.

He finished with 301 all-purpose yards, including 233 rushing yards and four touchdowns. He became the fifth player in NCAA history to compile more than 7,000 all-purpose yards. He tied the record for career kickoff-return touchdowns.

Spiller joined former Southern Cal running back and 2005 Heisman Trophy winner Reggie Bush as the only players in college football history to amass 1,500 kick return yards, 500 punt return yards, 1,000 receiving, and 3,000 rushing. Spiller notched 20 touchdowns that covered at least 50 yards, a higher career total than Bush and fellow explosive Heisman winners Tim Brown and Raghib "Rocket" Ismail recorded.

The Heisman is not a career achievement award. Yet Spiller, his teammates, his coaches, his sports information directors, his family, and his fans contended that he had achieved enough in 2009 alone at least to be named a finalist and receive an invitation to the presentation ceremony in New York City. However, the invites were sent to

Alabama running back Mark Ingram, Stanford running back Toby Gerhart, Texas quarterback Colt McCoy, Nebraska defensive lineman Ndamukong Suh, and Florida quarterback Tim Tebow. Spiller finished sixth in the Heisman voting with 223 points, 167 behind Tebow. Ingram won the award with merely 28 points more than runner-up Gerhart.

Spiller closed his career with 172 all-purpose yards and a rushing touchdown on 20 touches. Clemson defeated Kentucky in the Music City Bowl. Spiller did not leave Clemson with the Heisman. He did not win a conference championship. He did not play in a Bowl Championship Series bowl. However, he did leave Clemson with a lasting legacy. He also left with a degree in sociology.

As Spiller walked across the stage to shake the university president's hand, the Clemson board of trustees rose to lead a standing ovation. "The ovation was very special," Swinney said. "I can't remember going to a graduation anywhere and seeing the board of trustees recognize a student-athlete like that. It certainly shows the level of respect C.J. has."

Spiller was the first in his family to earn a college degree. He proceeded to the NFL Draft, where he was selected ninth overall by the Buffalo Bills. Although he would be heralded as the pioneer of Clemson's recruiting pipeline, he hoped to be remembered just as much for pioneering a new standard of academic achievement for his family.

"This was the No. 1 goal on the list, to graduate," Spiller said on his graduation day. "This was the main reason I came back. This was to show that coming to college wasn't just about football, but about getting a degree. I always knew I could do this. It was tough, but I knew I had to stick to it. I never thought about giving up."

# 5

---

# MR. FIX-IT

DABO SWINNEY is too competitive, too confident, and too stubborn to surrender to circumstance. When life gives him lemons, he makes lemonade, lemon drops, lemon pepper chicken, and lemon meringue pie.

Swinney carried his chronic optimism into the 2010 season. Where analysts and observers saw holes in the roster, Swinney saw opportunity for growth. Sophomore Andre Ellington and junior Jamie Harper were expected to fill the void in the backfield after the graduation of All-America running back C.J. Spiller. Quarterback Kyle Parker returned after starting all 14 games in 2009. Senior left tackle Chris Hairston returned to anchor the offensive line. Veteran receivers Xavier Dye, Terrance Ashe, and Marquan Jones also returned. In addition, DeAndre Hopkins, a Clemson native and product of Daniel High School, joined the rotation as a freshman.

All-America safety DeAndre McDaniel returned to lead the secondary, which also included standout corner Marcus Gilchrist. The defensive line included future NFL draft picks Da'Quan Bowers, Jarvis Jenkins, Brandon Thompson, and Andre Branch. The line and secondary were expected to help Clemson protect and develop a young corps of linebackers.

Swinney did not anticipate a need to improvise to make that lemonade. He appeared to have the lemons, sugar, water, pitcher, spoon, glass, and straw. "We have the ingredients of a good football team," Swinney said in September just before the season opener. But despite his ardent efforts to craft a recipe, despite how carefully he mixed those ingredients, despite how vigorously he stirred, the 2010 batch of Swinney's lemonade turned out bitter.

Clemson won its first two games, a pair of snoozers at home against North Texas and Presbyterian. The Tigers amassed 93 points in those two games and traveled to No. 15 Auburn on September 18 with confidence.

Parker steered a 12-play, 76-yard drive on Clemson's opening possession. He tossed an eight-yard touchdown pass to Harper. Chandler Catanzaro added the extra point. Catanzaro, a redshirt freshman from Greenville, South Carolina, overtook veteran place-kicker Richard Jackson on the depth chart during fall camp. Catanzaro accepted a preferred walk-on offer out of tiny, private Christ Church Episcopal School. Yet he exhibited a little of Swinney's determined spirit to capitalize on the uncertain opportunity. "I remember meeting with him and telling him that I wasn't coming to Clemson just to be another kicker," Catanzaro said. "I was coming to leave a legacy and break records."

Catanzaro kicked a 42-yard field goal with 8:19 remaining in the second quarter to lift Clemson ahead of Auburn 10–0. Clemson extended the advantage to 17–0 on a five-play, 40-second touchdown drive that culminated with a 24-yard pass from Parker to Harper. Clemson sullied a nearly flawless first-half shutout by allowing Auburn to produce a field goal in the final 17 seconds of the half. Yet, through Auburn's first seven possessions, Clemson inhibited their running backs Onterio McCalebb and Michael Dyer from reaching the end zone. Clemson intercepted eventual Heisman Trophy–winning quarterback Cam Newton twice during that span.

Newton only attempted six more passes after that point. He completed five of them. Two of those completions were touchdowns, including a 78-yarder to Terrell Zachery that capped the 21–0, third-quarter barrage Auburn unloaded to eliminate Clemson's seemingly comfortable margin. Even excluding that deflating chunk play, Auburn still averaged more than nine yards per snap in the third quarter.

Clemson tied the game at 24 on its first drive of the fourth quarter. Harper and Ellington combined for 52 yards on six touches on the possession. Ellington scored on a two-yard run. Catanzaro added the extra point. Neither team advanced deeper than the opponent's 44-yard line through the remainder of regulation. Clemson limited Auburn to four yards on the opening overtime possession. Auburn settled for a field goal. Wes Bynum drilled a 39-yarder.

Napier and Swinney schemed an effective play on Clemson's first overtime snap. As Parker rolled right, receiver Jaron Brown slipped behind Auburn defensive back Zack Etheridge. Brown stood wide open in the end zone. Parker lobbed the ball over Etheridge's out-stretched arm but also inches outside of Brown's reach. Clemson drove to the Auburn 8-yard line, before Auburn stiffened on third down. Clemson settled for a field goal, and Catanzaro pushed the 26-yard attempt through the uprights, seemingly sending the game into a second overtime. However, center Dalton Freeman was flagged for an illegal procedure penalty for double-clutching the ball on the snap. Clemson retreated five yards, and Catanzaro lined up for a 32-yard attempt. The kick hooked wide left. Jordan-Hare Stadium erupted in celebration. Catanzaro was devastated.

He laudably faced the media after the game. With his hair disheveled and his eyes glazed from tears, Catanzaro fielded tough but fair questions. "The snap and the hold were great. I hit it good. I kept my head down. I just pulled it just a tad, I guess," Catanzaro said, shaking his head. "When adversity hits you, you've got to turn around and hit it right back."

"I knew when that happened it was going to be the lowest part of his life," Chandler's father, Joseph Catanzaro said. "All of us were upset. I remember telling him that this was going to hurt for a while and that that was okay, that he would get through it and that

I had all the confidence in him to make this the beginning of a great story."

Catanzaro converted all 20 of his extra-point attempts through the remainder of the season. He missed seven of his next 19 field goal attempts, four of which were inside 40 yards. Yet he converted six of his last seven attempts.

After the heartbreaking setback at Auburn, Swinney reiterated his optimistic outlook for the team. "I think we have a chance to be a good football team," he said. "I think we have the ingredients."

However, Clemson appeared to be missing one element to complete the recipe for success. It lost four its next seven games by an average margin of 5.8 points. The Tigers notched a 27–13 win against rival Georgia Tech only to follow it with a 10-point output and a six-point loss at unranked Boston College. A familiar narrative returned to national telecasts, regional print, and local radio. It resurfaced on message boards, around water coolers, and after Sunday School.

It had started during Tommy Bowden's paradoxical period as Clemson's head coach. He would lead the Tigers to landmark victories and follow with inexplicable losses. In 1999 Clemson defeated No. 22 Virginia by 19 points and then followed with a 20-point loss to unranked Virginia Tech. In 2000 Clemson opened with an 8–0 record, vaulted to No. 5 in the Coaches Poll, lost to unranked Georgia Tech at home, and then took a 54–7 beating at Florida State. In 2001 Clemson opened 4–1, climbed to No. 13, and was promptly embarrassed 38–3 by North Carolina on homecoming. In 2004 Clemson knocked off No. 11 Miami in South Florida and followed with a loss to unranked Duke in Durham. In 2006 Clemson opened 7–1, ascended to No. 11, and then dropped consecutive games to unranked Virginia Tech and Maryland. In 2008 Clemson opened the season No. 9 in the polls before its season-opening, 34–10 drubbing against Alabama.

It became known as *Clemsoning*. Swinney despised the term. It discounted the difficulty of winning and the joy of each victory, regardless of how high or low the opponent is ranked. It was also part of the toxic taint that permeated through the fan base and the program. It spread the disease of disbelief. Swinney was allergic to that, but he had to acknowledge Clemson's blemished reputation. He had to recognize the truth in the mistrust.

"We are what we repeatedly do. Excellence, then, is not an act, but a habit." That powerful phrase is often attributed to ancient Greek philosopher and scientist Aristotle. However, American philosopher Will Durant first wrote those words in his book *The Story of Philosophy: The Lives and Opinions of the World's Greatest Philosophers*, first published in 1926. The adage resonated with American philosopher Dabo Swinney in 2010. He understood that Clemson would be what they repeatedly did, but he also understood that they would do what they repeatedly believed. He could not transform Clemson into a championship program until he transformed the culture. He could not change the product until he changed the process.

Swinney countered the perpetual pessimism with his own series of Pelham Proverbs:

*Best is the standard.*
*Don't let anybody walk through your mind with dirty feet.*
*Control what you can control.*
*Championships are won when no one is looking.*
*Greatness never goes on sale. You must pay the full price.*
*To be an overachiever, you have to be an over-believer.*
*The only disability in life is a bad attitude.*
*If you're going to be great, you can't ever be satisfied.*
*There is no elevator to greatness, you have to take the stairs.*

*Let the light that shines in you be brighter than the light
that shines on you.*

Whether one considers them corny or clever, Swinney's adages
elucidated the caliber of character and commitment he expected
from his players. Those phrases positively reinforced Swinney's
vision. He demanded passionate performance and preparation—
in the stadium, in the classroom, and in the community. Swinney
shrewdly realized that greatness is intentional. If he could convince
these young men to invest supreme effort in every task, the desired
results would emerge.

Before they could become champions, the Tigers had to adopt a
championship mentality. Champions celebrate their victories when
the lights are brightest, but they earn them when the lights are off.
Champions maximize the moment, whether they are playing Florida
State and Stanford or Savannah State and Furman. Champions maintain their composure and conviction through triumphs and trials.

"Best is the standard," Swinney said. "Sometimes, I'll get on
my guys, when we may not have quite the practice we want or we
might not quite do what we need to do. I say, 'We'll just change
that. We'll just make it, "Good enough is the standard," or, "Pretty
good is the standard."' Somewhere along the line, I think that was
kind of the mentality that creeped into Clemson. It's not about
being the best. It's about being your best. We're not here to compare ourselves to other people. If you're doing the best you can,
you can live with whatever results you get."

That philosophy helped Swinney sustain his belief, even after
Clemson closed the regular season with a 29–7 loss to rival South
Carolina at home. Clemson suffered consecutive losses to South
Carolina for the first time since 1969–1970.

For South Carolina, the 2010 season was the climax of the drastic
transformation Steve Spurrier initiated when he became the Gamecocks' head coach in 2005. When he arrived in Columbia, Spurrier

encountered the same issue Swinney encountered in Clemson. South Carolina needed a cultural makeover. Spurrier needed to inject that same diligent commitment and broaden the Gamecocks' scope of success. When Spurrier first walked into the South Carolina coaches' locker room, he noticed several signs on the wall that read "Beat Clemson." He walked over to the players' locker room and saw them scattered over the wall there as well. Spurrier ripped them all down. He explained to his players that no game matters more than any other, because no game requires less effort and focus than any other.

"It's a big game, but it's not the only game we play all year," Spurrier said of the rivalry. "Every game is a big game, really. Our record at the end of the year counts every game the same."

The attitude adjustment helped Spurrier elevate the South Carolina program to its most successful epoch. In 2010 the Gamecocks notched nine regular-season victories for the first time since 1984. They also won their first Southeastern Conference East Division championship.

For many Clemson fans, South Carolina's success exacerbated the anguish of the Tigers' 6–6 record. However, as he walked off Frank Howard Field for the final time that season, Swinney remained encouraged. "I knew we were on the right track more than ever, because of how our guys competed," Swinney said. "Even though we didn't see the results that year, our culture was really taking root. It takes toughness to be the best. It takes toughness to continue to believe sometimes when there's doubt. It takes toughness to stay the course."

Swinney was not certain his boss, athletic director Terry Don Phillips, shared his assurance. As he walked back to his office that evening, his wife, Kathleen Swinney, greeted him with a hug and a worried look.

"I could tell something was wrong. She said, 'Terry Don's in your office,'" Swinney recalled. "In my mind, I'm going, *Welp, it was a fun two years. God never says 'Oops.' I guess he has another plan for me.* But I had a peace because I knew I was doing the best I could do. I had no regrets."

Swinney proceeded to his office and found Phillips sitting under the muted glow of a single bulb. It looked like the set for a *Godfather* film, and Swinney suspected his character would not survive the scene. "It's kind of dark in there, and Terry Don's sitting on the couch," Swinney recalled. "I open up the door, and he says, 'Sit down.'"

"Dabo, I'm gonna tell you something. I know you're disappointed. I know it's a tough time," Phillips said. "There's going to be negativity. There's going to be some criticism. There's going to be this and that, but here's what I want you to know—I'm more confident right now, at this moment, that you're the guy for this job, that you're going to be successful, than I was before I hired you. That's all I got to say. If you need me, you call me."

The man of few words spoke directly to Swinney's vision, directly to his heart. Swinney knew his success or failure would also be used to assess Phillips. Removing Swinney's interim tag tagged Phillips for intense scrutiny. "I knew he had a lot of pressure on him too," Swinney said. "You talk about toughness. It took some toughness. That's what that word represents."

Clemson closed 2010 with a 31–26 loss to South Florida. It was South Florida's first bowl win against a major conference representative. It was Clemson's first losing season since 1998. In the locker room after the game, Swinney gathered his players and reiterated his belief. He was still confident that he was driving the program in the right direction, but he needed to make sure he had the right passengers along for the ride.

"I'll fix it. I'll fix it," Swinney said. "I'm going to do everything within my power to make sure that I get us better as a football team and that this never happens again."

Two days after leaving that locker room, Swinney dismissed offensive coordinator Billy Napier and running backs coach Andre

Powell. Napier held the coordinator title, but Swinney intervened and overrode plays when he deemed it necessary. Through the first year of that system, Clemson averaged 362.4 yards and 31.1 points per game. Through the next season, those averages dropped by 30 yards and seven points point game.

Two days after Napier and Powell were fired, defensive ends coach Chris Rumph left to join Nick Saban's staff at Alabama. Swinney hired Duke defensive coordinator Marion Hobby to replace Rumph. Hobby coached Clemson's defensive line in 2005, after assisting David Cutcliffe at Ole Miss and before coaching on Sean Payton's staff with the New Orleans Saints. Hobby earned first-team All-SEC honors in 1989 as a senior at Tennessee.

Swinney facilitated another homecoming for his new running backs coach. Swinney hired one of his former players, Tony Elliott. When Swinney became Clemson's wide receivers coach in 2003, he immediately identified with Elliott, then a senior who had blossomed from walk-on to team captain. Like Swinney, Elliott's childhood was unsettled by undue hardship.

When he was four years old, a truck struck Elliott as he stepped into the street outside the salon in Watsonville, California, where his mother, Patricia, worked. Emergency surgery narrowly saved his life, but after a lacerated spleen, four broken ribs, and a broken arm, Elliott had to learn to walk again.

Shortly after Elliott's recovery, his parents separated. Patricia Elliott absconded from Tony's abusive, alcoholic father in the middle of the night, carrying nothing more than her two children and a fraction of their wardrobe. The three of them were living on the streets of Los Angeles, California, when they befriended Sandra Aguilar. In 1982 Aguilar's husband, Phil, founded Set Free Worldwide Ministries. The church welcomed anyone but declared its mission to "go where the pizza man don't deliver" and minister to struggling families, ex-convicts, and recovering addicts. Elliott, his mother, and his sister, Brandi, moved into the Aguilars' home and became members of the church. Patricia Elliott worked in the church daycare. She eventually divorced her husband and married Wayne Williams, who sang in the church choir.

Patricia, Tony, and Brandi found a happy normal. On June 11, 1989, the family took its normal drive to church. "I didn't have a seatbelt on. Typical nine-year-old. Don't want to go to church," Elliott recalled. "I'm in the back all by myself. We had a little Volkswagen bus. We were just going to church—the same route we always take."

Not far from the church, at the intersection of Sycamore Street and Harbor Boulevard in Anaheim, a driver ran the red light and smashed directly into the side of the Volkswagen. The van tumbled several times before resting on its roof. Elliott quickly freed his sister and stepbrother as they hung upside down in their car seats. Williams' leg was severely injured, but he pulled himself out of the car. Then he and Tony discovered Patricia, lying motionless on the street. The impact of the collision thrust her halfway through the van's windshield.

Bystanders gathered around the accident, but no one assisted the family. Williams told Tony to run for help. Tony sprinted through a nearby park to the church. He ran into Sandra Aguilar and frantically tried to explain what happened. "My mom's in the street! My mom's in the street!" he yelled. Sandra noticed the blood on Tony's shirt. Paramedics finally arrived on the scene, but Patricia died in the ambulance. Tony never saw his mother again.

Tony lost that happy normal. He and Brandi moved back in with their father, and through the next three years, chaos became Tony's new normal. Tony found no assistance in confronting or channeling his grief. Volatile anger stirred inside him. He dismissed school, joined a gang, stayed out until after midnight. Robbed. Fought. Not for survival, but for "no reason at all."

His uncle, Carrol, pulled him out of that turmoil. He moved Elliott and Brandi with him to Atlanta. Carrol insisted that the children attend school and enforced a strict curfew. "You go to school.

You come home and do your homework, and you're in bed by eight o'clock," Elliott said. "You go from being like a high school kid at 12 to being like an eight-year-old at 13."

The structure stabilized Tony, but the long hours Carrol worked made it difficult for him to provide Tony and Brandi the attention and care they needed. Tony and Brandi returned to their father, but a few months later, Jerome Elliott wound up in jail. Brandi moved back to Atlanta with an aunt. Tony moved to James Island, South Carolina, with another aunt. Once again, Tony thrived in a stable home. He stayed out of trouble and filled his report cards with A's and B's. He also enjoyed a fleeting fascination with football.

"It kind of was a substitute for the dysfunction," Elliott said. "Football was my safe haven. But I had some experiences with football where I wanted to quit, and I did."

After high school, Elliott proceeded to the Air Force prep school for one year. He declined appointment into the Air Force Academy and then worked at a grocery store and then on a construction crew to raise money for college. He enrolled at Clemson in the spring of 1998 and covered tuition with a combination of the money he saved, grants, and loans.

He was content with focusing solely on pursuing an engineering degree, until a friend convinced him to walk on to the football team. Elliott rekindled his passion for the game and earned a varsity letter in each of his first three seasons. He produced a 3.55 grade-point average and graduated in December of 2002 with a degree in industrial engineering. He considered forgoing his final year of eligibility. He knew his playing time would be limited behind eventual NFL signees Derrick Hamilton, Airese Currie, and Roscoe Crosby. Yet he decided to return to relish one more year with his teammates. The coaches rewarded his commitment with a scholarship. He was named team captain, and in a team survey conducted by the *Anderson Independent Mail*, Elliott's teammates designated him the most respected player.

Two months later, Swinney arrived, with exuberant energy that further validated Elliott's decision. Swinney admired Elliott's toughness and work ethic. He found a place for Elliott in the rotation. Elliott notched 23 receptions, 286 yards, and a touchdown that season.

"He gave me an opportunity," Elliott said. "He loved all his players, regardless of where they came from. I look at him as one of the father figures, because of the absence of a father in my life."

"I'm just so happy he came back, and I had the opportunity to coach him," Swinney said, "because he made my life better."

After the season, Elliott accepted a position with Michelin North America, a short drive from Clemson's campus in Pendleton. "I didn't have that desire to stay with [football] after I graduated," he said. "The folks at Michelin were great. They already had a plan in place for me to go overseas to learn the business."

Like Swinney, Elliott spent two seasons out of football, working a lucrative position but knowing something was missing. Before he relocated to Michelin's headquarters in France, Elliott was urged again to return to his safe haven. "Things were going well. I had a great boss. Life was good," Elliott said. "But I felt like I was empty. I just wasn't fulfilling my purpose."

To quell the urge, Elliott volunteered as an assistant coach at Easley High School. "Through that experience, I learned this is really what I believe my purpose is," Elliott said, "to use my testimony and my story to help inspire."

In 2006 Elliott pursued a position on Buddy Pough's staff at South Carolina State University. Pough needed a wide receivers coach. Initially, he had little interest in hiring an engineer. Elliott had no college coaching experience, but he did have a strong reference. It was from Clemson assistant coach and former South Carolina head coach Brad Scott. Pough served on Scott's staff at South Carolina for two seasons.

"He thought so highly of Tony," Pough said. "We'd taken some coaches in the past from Clemson upon their recommendations. We brought Tony in as more of a developmental guy, coaching-wise, more than anything."

Pough soon realized that he did not hire an engineer. He hired a coach, one with a bright mind and an even brighter future. "He was just a top-notch guy, a real mature guy, an attention-to-detail guy," Pough said. "From the first day, it was obvious he wouldn't be here very long."

Pough was correct. Elliott spent two seasons at State before Bobby Lamb hired him to coach receivers at Furman University, a tradition-rich FCS program in Greenville, South Carolina. Pough and Lamb both instantly recognized that Elliott's passion for people compensated for his lack of coaching experience.

"We had a couple of guys who really needed a lot of nurturing," Pough said. "Tony just spent unbelievable amounts of time making sure that those guys had all the attention they needed."

"Tony Elliott is a better person than he is a football coach," Lamb said. "That's saying a lot, because he's an outstanding coach. It's incredible how many young men would come by his office and visit with him and tell him about their problems."

Adam Mims was one of those young men.

"He may be the best thing that ever happened to me," said Mims, who was a sophomore receiver at Furman when Elliott arrived. "He corralled me and got me on the right track," Mims said. "He just did everything the right way. You can do nothing but want to emulate that."

Through three seasons under Elliott's guidance, Mims compiled 187 receptions for 2,313 yards with 12 touchdowns. Mims graduated from Furman with a collection of school records and a degree in health and exercise science.

Elliott was one of two coaches Bruce Fowler retained when he replaced Lamb at Furman in December 2010. But like Pough, Fowler could not keep Elliott long. Elliott remained in close contact with Swinney after leaving Clemson. They were together the previous year at a coaches' convention in Los Angeles. During a break in the conference, Elliott asked Swinney to join him for a drive to Anaheim. Elliott pulled the car to an intersection. He shifted the car to park and pointed.

"Right there, that's where my mom died," Elliott told Swinney.

"It just kind of took my breath away," Swinney said. "I was so moved that he wanted me to be there for that."

A year later, Swinney invited Elliott and his wife, Tamika, to dinner at his home. It was not for a casual meal with good friends. It was a job offer.

"Tony, what do you think about being my running backs coach?" Swinney asked.

"Are you serious?" Elliott said, before breaking down in tears.

Swinney could have delivered the offer over the phone. He could have asked Elliott to come to his office. But Swinney does not believe in coincidence. A year earlier, as Elliott pointed out the location of the most tragic moment of his life, Swinney looked up. He saw the street sign. Sycamore Street. He took it as a sign of divine intervention. He knew at that moment, one day, he would hire Elliott. And he knew exactly where he would do it.

"Tony, do you know what my address is?" Swinney asked Elliott.

Before coming to Clemson, Swinney and his wife, Kathleen, constructed their dream home in Birmingham, Alabama. They built an exact replica of it in Clemson. On Sycamore Drive. "I wanted to hire you here," Swinney told Elliott, "so what was a terrible moment in your life on Sycamore can now be one of the greatest moments of your life on Sycamore."

Elliott excelled as a devoted mentor and teacher. His return to Clemson required him to become a more devoted student. He would be coaching a position he never played in college. He prudently sought counsel from more seasoned running backs coaches. He adopted new drills and then adapted them to his coaching style.

"He would always come up with really good ideas," Lamb said. "He was always trying to learn and absorb everything he could."

Nevertheless, considering Elliott's background and expertise was at wide receiver, one of his first pupils at Clemson was initially skeptical of his new position coach. "When he came in, it was kind of like a draw fight in a Western," recalled McDowell, then a sophomore running back at Clemson.

McDowell said his skepticism quickly faded during his first conversation with Elliott. "I could tell he puts his all into not only coaching, but being a father figure, being a person you can look up to," McDowell said. "He cares about the person as a player, as a man, as a whole."

"He's a bright, bright guy," Pough said. "He's got the credentials. The things he does, he's done everywhere."

"I knew he was destined for big things," Mims said. "I'm not surprised by anything great that's happened to him."

Swinney ventured outside the Clemson family and outside the box to find his new offensive coordinator. Swinney introduced Elliott and Hobby in a press conference on January 13, 2011. Another man with an unfamiliar face sat between them wearing a bright orange Oxford shirt with a white Clemson logo embroidered just above his left front pocket. He sat alert with his back stiffened against his seat and his hands in his lap.

But he did not sit still.

Energy exuded from him before he spoke a word, and when he did, it was clear that things were going to be drastically different in Clemson.

"What can the fans expect to see out of this offense?" a reporter asked.

The man leaned in and grinned.

"Well, we've got several hours here, so let's all get comfortable," he said. He then relayed his plan for a fast no-huddle spread offense dedicated to running the football. In the context of college football convention, the concept sounded oxymoronic. But this man desired a Smashmouth Spread. He wanted to overpower opponents in the trenches and open wide lines for the counter, zone, power, and toss. The rushing attack would enable an effective play-action passing scheme that would test secondaries downfield. It could stretch the field from sideline to sideline and from end zone to end zone.

"There's a lot of teams in this country that are going to spread the field from sideline to sideline, but there are very few teams that try to put stress on a defense going vertical," he said, before asserting that, under his guidance, Clemson would develop an identity, or at the very least, a specialty. The offense would master something, even if only one thing.

"You get good at what you do," he said. "You don't trick people. You line up, and you play your style of football."

He professed his demand for a tough, physical unit. He expressed confidence that Clemson could compose a roster that would execute his scheme and contend for a conference championship immediately. He spoke with a no-huddle intensity. His words raced out of his mouth with a clear country inflection, but it was not the Upstate South Carolina drawl familiar to Clemson fans. It was a distinct Texas twang.

This man, Chad Morris, is a native of Edgewood, Texas. And he is Texas from the tips of the hairs standing up on the back of his neck to the core of his electric soul. He graduated from Texas A&M with a degree in mathematics and a minor in statistics. He used that background to specialize in accumulating Texas-sized numbers. Morris spent 16 years coaching football at Texas high schools. Considering the resources and community devotion in the Lone Star State, its high school league could be reasonably classified as NCAA Division IV. Morris won 82 percent of his games. He notched three state championships and steered teams to three other state final games.

Morris served as the offensive coordinator at the University of Tulsa in 2010. Tulsa increased its total offense average by 23.3 percent to 505.6 yards per game, its scoring average by 41.5 percent to 41.4 points per game, and its win total by 100 percent from 5–7 to 10–3.

Morris' numbers did not speak from themselves. They screamed out. They caught Swinney's attention. He previously knew he wanted a faster tempo and a more forceful attack. But he did not yet know Morris. He already learned that chemistry among the staff can be more important than coaching expertise. He needed to ensure that Morris would mesh well with the personalities in the offices, in the locker room, and in the community. He sought the opinion of Gus Malzahn, who then was the offensive coordinator at Auburn. Malzahn won three state championships coaching high schools in Arkansas. He forged a close friendship over the years with Morris as they swapped ideas.

"I just called Gus to kind of get his take on him," Swinney said. "It was a pretty simple conversation. I didn't know Chad, and obviously he kind of gave me some confirmation on who he was as a person. I was more interested in that. I think you hire good people first. There's a lot of good coaches out there. I always tell people, 'Good coaches are a dime a dozen. Good coaches who are good people, good husbands, good fathers, who love their players and are passionate about doing things in a way that I believe is important, that pool gets real small.'"

On February 2, Swinney announced that Brad Scott was retiring from coaching but had accepted an administrative position in the athletic department. Clemson could retain Scott's wealth of knowledge while augmenting the roster with another of college football's top offensive line coaches and recruiters.

Robbie Caldwell had logged 33 years of coaching experience. He served as an assistant under Dick Sheridan for 15 seasons, from

1978 to 1985 at his alma mater, Furman University, and from 1986 to 1992 at North Carolina State. Caldwell remained in Raleigh seven more years to serve under Mike O'Cain. From 2002 to 2009, Caldwell assisted Bobby Johnson at Vanderbilt. Bobby Johnson announced his retirement in July, too late in the off-season for the school to conduct an adequate search for a permanent replacement. That provided an opportunity for his loyal friend Caldwell to be a head coach. Caldwell delighted college football fans with the most entertaining 2–10 season ever. His humble humor and colloquialisms made him a media darling. "I'm not a comedian. I'm not smart enough to be one," Caldwell said, understating his acumen.

Caldwell is the perfect balance of old-school toughness and open-minded cordiality. Caldwell grew up working farms in Pageland, South Carolina. His first job was inseminating turkeys, a fact he shared legendarily during the 2010 Southeastern Conference media days.

"The guy asked, 'Do you remember your first job?' I said, 'Salary or hourly?'" Caldwell recalled. "So when he said hourly, I told him."

Caldwell was also asked if he would continue Johnson's no-profanity policy at Vanderbilt. "You know, I'm no angel, that's for certain," Caldwell said. "We certainly do try to live by that. But, you know, it's just a sign of limited vocabulary sometimes."

Caldwell's jovial nature belies his intensity between the lines. He also denounced the notion that his inviting, conversational tone should be considered special. "I went in there and I was myself," Caldwell said. "Next thing I know, there's a guy tugging on my britches' legs saying, 'Coach, we hate to ask you to leave, but we've got to bring the next man in.' When I get done, everybody stood up. I thought everybody was going to lunch. They had to call me back in and gave me a standing ovation. It's kind of sad because, you know, I just talk to people. Life's about people, and I enjoy them."

When Caldwell figured out that Swinney valued people the same way, coming to Clemson was an easy decision. That decision was validated as he observed Swinney further in meetings, around the offices, and on the field.

"Sometimes you think you've got the market cornered on discipline, because my background with Coach Sheridan and Coach [Art] Baker, but this has just been ideal," said Caldwell, who appreciated the opportunity to leave the peripheral responsibilities of a head coach behind him and dig his knuckles back into the dirt.

"I like to think I've been a loyal assistant. I've loved every minute of it," Caldwell said. "Being a head coach was kind of sprung on me. I really appreciated the opportunity to do it, and I enjoyed my time, but I really missed the coaching aspect of it. I bet if you ask Coach Swinney that would be the one thing he misses most of actually coaching a position. There's just something about it. Of course, it's been implanted in me for years. Sometimes, if you're not careful, you get what you wish for. I really enjoyed it, who knows maybe one day I'll do it again, but I'm extremely happy to be right here coaching offensive line. I really feel like that's my calling."

Adversity poses only two options. One can either cower to it or power through it. Swinney has persistently chosen the latter, and that was no different in 2010. Disappointment and embarrassment did not distract his eyes from the vision he set, but it did force him to reassess how he would reach it and who would help him get there.

"A big part of our success is our failure," Swinney said. "People don't want to look at it that way. They let failure define them instead of develop them. We allowed 2010 to really develop us further."

Swinney had a new staff, a new season, a new opportunity, but the same defiant resolve. He took those lemons and traded them for an Orange.

# 6

## THE BUY-IN

PLAYING THE 2010 football season cost Clemson quarterback Kyle Parker. He was a two-sport athlete, who started in football but starred in baseball. The Colorado Rockies selected Parker in the first round, 26$^{th}$ overall, in the 2010 Major League Baseball Draft. The Rockies offered Parker a $2.2 million signing bonus, but he accepted $800,000 less so that he could play another year at Clemson.

However, that large monetary sacrifice was not the only cost Parker incurred. Through the tumultuous 6–7 season, Parker absorbed several intense hits. He cracked a rib in his final game, and doctors later concluded that he played with bruised ribs for an extended portion of the season. Parker relinquished his final two years of football eligibility to play professional baseball.

His departure prompted a promotion for Tajh Boyd, who was the anchor of Swinney's first recruiting class. A few prospects reneged on their commitments after Tommy Bowden's departure from the program. Dabo Swinney salvaged a small class of 12 signees. He called them his "Dandy Dozen."

Half of the dozen was baked in South Carolina:

- Quandon Christian, a linebacker from Lake View
- Malliciah Goodman, a defensive end from Florence
- J.K. Jay, an offensive lineman from Greenville
- Rod McDowell, a running back from Sumter
- Jonathan Meeks, a safety from Rock Hill

- Brandon Thomas, an offensive lineman from
  Spartanburg

Clemson also signed two from North Carolina—fullback Tyler Shatley from Icard and linebacker Spencer Shuey from Charlotte. Corico Hawkins (who later changed his last name to Wright), a linebacker from Milledgeville, Georgia; Bryce McNeal, a receiver from Minneapolis; and Darrell Smith, an end from Gadsden, Alabama, also signed.

Then there was Boyd, the lone five-star recruit in the class. He was a 6′1″, 210-pound gunslinger from Hampton, Virginia, who appeared to fit the tenor of toughness Swinney aimed to establish at Clemson. Boyd played his senior season at Phoebus High School on a torn knee ligament. He still passed for 1,455 yards and 23 touchdowns and led Phoebus to a state championship.

The previous year, Boyd had announced his commitment to West Virginia. Mountaineers coach Bill Stewart commemorated the revelation by kissing Boyd on the forehead. Seven months later, Boyd backed out of that commitment. He then committed to the University of Tennessee, with assurances that coach Phillip Fulmer would be retained despite falling to a 3–7 record. Two days later, Fulmer complied with university officials and stepped down. Boyd remained committed to Tennessee until the Volunteers hired Lane Kiffin, who favored pro-style quarterbacks and did not emphasize the quarterback run packages Boyd preferred. Boyd reopened his recruitment. Swinney tossed his orange and purple cap in the ring.

Major brands Ohio State and Oregon quickly became the favorites. Clemson was not given a shot, but Swinney was not giving up. "I didn't have really much of a résumé as a head coach," Swinney said. "It wasn't very sexy to come to Clemson. But we had a plan, a vision, a hope, and a belief."

That is all Swinney had to sell, but that was enough to get him into Boyd's lineup. He carried that with him to the plate in

Hampton. With Ohio State coach Jim Tressel and Oregon coach Mike Bellotti due up, Swinney took a swing.

"I had been the head coach for about three weeks. I sat in his house at his kitchen table, and Jim Tressel was in the backyard, and Bellotti was in the front yard waiting for me to leave," Swinney said with a laugh. "I said, 'Tajh, here's the plan. If you'll believe in me, we'll change Clemson. We'll change it. It's not going to be easy. We've got a lot of work to do, but we will change Clemson.'"

Swinney's swing connected. Boyd committed to Clemson in January. His parents committed to Clemson that following March. Two months after Tajh signed with Clemson, the Boyds moved from Virginia to the nearby town of Seneca. Carla Boyd was not accustomed to navigating rural roads. Even in a town with a population of approximately 8,000 people, she managed to get lost. On her second night in town.

She made a wrong turn down a dark road. Even if she could see the street signs well enough to read them, she still had no idea exactly where they would lead her. Suddenly, the road was lit—with flashing red and blue lights. "The policeman stopped me and said I was swerving a little bit," Carla Boyd recalled. "He then asked me to show him my license."

Boyd feared her Virginia plates and heavy New Jersey accent had stirred the officer's suspicion when he asked, "What brings you here?" Her fears were eased by the officer's follow-up question.

"Are you Tajh's mom?" he asked.

She nodded yes, and the officer's eyes lit up brighter than his headlights.

"This whole traffic stop turned into how he used to be a running back," Carla Boyd said with a laugh. "We're in front of the high school with flashing lights, and he's showing us little moves." After showing off his steps, the officer showed Carla Boyd how to reach her new home. In more ways than one, the gesture assured her she was in the right place.

Tim Boyd served in the Navy for 10 years and during that tenure, the family grew accustomed to moving to new bases. However, from 1995 to 2009, the Boyds were rooted in Hampton. After recruiting letters poured in from all corners of the country, Tim and Carla Boyd decided they would follow their son no matter where he decided to play. They were prepared to migrate to Morgantown when Tajh initially committed to West Virginia. Then they were all set for Knoxville when Tajh switched his commitment to Tennessee. When he reopened his recruitment and picked three new finalists in three different time zones, the Boyds maintained their relocation plans.

"Oregon was iffy when I found out how much the U-Haul cost," Carla Boyd said with a laugh.

Luckily, the Boyds avoided the cross-country rental fees. They moved 500 miles south along with Tajh's younger brother, T.J. They left family, friends, and careers. Carla Boyd said those voids were not filled, but their decision was affirmed when they realized the weather was not the only thing warmer around Clemson.

"The people are so friendly," Carla Boyd said. "When we got here they had Seneca High School's whole football team here with their jerseys on. They unloaded the truck. The neighbors brought food and welcomed us to the neighborhood. I was so impressed. It was a culture change, because, back in Virginia, it was city and the people were a little more aggressive up there. It was not always peaches and cream at first, but that helped us adapt."

Adaptation was the motive for the move. Tim Boyd anticipated the immense pressure that would be placed on his son as Clemson's quarterback. While he was confident in Tajh's maturity and resolve, he wanted to establish easily accessible support.

"If he would have played another position, we probably wouldn't have been as involved in it," Tim Boyd said. "We knew it's a big deal to be a quarterback on this level, the responsibility and the maturity that you have to have."

"When you're here as a freshman, it's like, 'Man, my parents are always right around the corner,'" Tajh Boyd said with a grin. "The older you get and the more mature you get, you realize how important that is and how special it is. There are only a few people who will really and truly stand behind you through anything. Last season, you're out there pretty much breaking down, and having somebody so close to touch, it was great to have them there. I could go over to the house when I needed to get away."

"We wanted to enjoy his college career but not invade his privacy. We've always been around each other and supported him," Carla Boyd said. "It was hard at first, but I kind of thought that we could do this as a family. We trusted Coach Swinney to come here."

Tajh Boyd could not quantify the emotional and financial sacrifice his parents made to support him. He aimed to repay them through hard work in every facet of his life. "It's just motivation for how I push myself for the future, for anything," Tajh Boyd said. "You definitely don't want to do anything to disappoint them, just because of the sacrifices they made. You can't be selfish in instances like that. Everything you do, you've got a reason behind it. It just puts everything into perspective that much more. I want them to know everything they did was worth it."

Boyd redshirted his first year. He played behind Parker for most of his freshman year. In 2011, his ascension to the starting spot appeared natural, but after the spring practice session, offensive coordinator Chad Morris was not convinced. He summoned Boyd for a debriefing before coaches and players separated for the summer. He looked at Boyd squarely and spoke in no uncertain terms. He called them his "seven-minute meetings." He talked. The players listened.

"He told me, basically 'You better get it together, take ownership and figure out what we're trying to do here," Boyd recalled. "Or I'll find somebody who will."

Boyd had never been coddled by a coach. Criticism was not new to him. He did not mind the directive. But hearing his commitment, effort, and focus questioned and facing the threat of losing that starting role, Boyd was agitated, but appreciative. Morris had just provided enough fuel to keep a fire burning beneath Boyd's behind for the entire off-season.

He trained more diligently in the weight room. He gathered his receivers for throwing sessions. He studied the playbook incessantly. "I went through the summer with a chip on my shoulder," Boyd said. "When fall camp rolled back around, he saw the difference."

However, by halftime of the season opener against Troy, no one outside the program could see a difference. Clemson exploded on the opening drive. On the first play from scrimmage, running back Andre Ellington rushed for a 26-yard gain. On the next snap, Boyd rocketed a pass to freshman Sammy Watkins behind the line. Watkins darted through traffic and blazed 33 yards to the end zone.

Watkins was Clemson's latest treasured recruit from Florida. He said C.J. Spiller's excursion to Clemson compelled him to consider the Tigers. Watkins arrived from Fort Myers, and shortly after he stepped on the field, Clemson's coaches knew he would not be there after three seasons.

"He's the most low-maintenance superstar I've ever dealt with," Swinney said of Watkins, who skewed expectations for highly touted recruits who followed him to Clemson. They were expected to arrive "no assembly required" as well.

Clemson followed Watkins' microwave touchdown with a field goal from Chandler Catanzaro, but that was on a drive that netted a loss of eight yards. Clemson did not gain more than 18 yards on any of its next eight drives. Catanzaro added another field goal on an eight-yard drive. Troy enjoyed a 16–13 lead at halftime. A faction of the Clemson fan base was already skeptical of Swinney's off-season moves before the game. Some felt Swinney himself should have been dismissed. They certainly were not thrilled when Swinney hired an inexperienced former receiver to coach running backs. They believed Morris was nothing more than a high school coach masquerading as a coordinator. They declared that this smash-mouth spread, sprint no-huddle was a gimmick and could not be sustainable. It would impair the defensive conditioning and lead to sloppy turnovers. They expected another tumultuous season.

And there is no such thing as a quiet Clemson fan. Some may use more polite language than others, but they do not whisper. They are sometimes right. They are sometimes wrong. But they are always loud. As the team trotted to the locker room for halftime, irate fans serenaded them with boos. The Tigers knew Death Valley could be hostile, but they very seldom heard that audible disdain being directed at them.

"They were not happy with us in the first half," Swinney said. "We definitely didn't have the first half we wanted. Tajh had a bad first half, but he settled down. That's why it's a four-quarter game. The second half was a thing of beauty."

Clemson outscored Troy 30–3 in the second half. Boyd completed 11 of 13 passes for 142 yards and two touchdowns in the third quarter. Clemson found its groove, and Morris became a record producer. Clemson rolled through its first eight opponents by an average margin of 15.6 points. The Tigers defeated three top 25 opponents—No. 21 Auburn, No. 11 Florida State, and No. 11 Virginia Tech—in consecutive weeks. They climbed to No. 5 in the Bowl Championship Series standings. They averaged 482.5 yards of total offense and 40.6 points per game. They ranked in the top 15 of the Football Bowl Subdivision in both categories, as well as passing offense, pass efficiency, and turnover margin.

Then Clemson visited Georgia Tech. Clemson compiled 132 yards on its first six drives, an average of 22 yards per possession. Those drives produced a field goal, a fumble, two punts, a missed field goal, and the end of the half. Conversely, Tech's triple-option offense mystified Kevin Steele's defense. The Tigers were flying to the ball. The problem is the triple option thrives against wild pursuit. It stalls against disciplined, sound assignment defense. Clemson surrendered 383 rushing yards. It trailed 24–3 at halftime. Clemson scored on its first possession of the second half with a 48-yard touchdown reception from Watkins. Tech retaliated with a 77-yard touchdown drive, propelled by Tevin Washington's 56-yard run. Clemson manufactured a 97-yard touchdown drive that was fittingly capped by Tajh Boyd's fumble at the 1-yard line and offensive lineman Brandon Thomas' recovery in the end zone.

Tech sapped the remaining life out of Clemson with a nine-minute, four-second crawl. Tech converted four third-down plays on the drive and did not attempt a single pass. Tech coach Paul Johnson perplexed Steele's unit and nearly converted the fourth-down play at the Clemson 27-yard line. Tech had taken possession with 10:33 remaining. It returned the ball to Clemson with 1:06 to play. Then Tech intercepted Boyd to thwart Clemson's final two possessions and seal the 31–17 victory.

"We just physically got whipped," Steele said. "We got out-executed. From a defensive standpoint, we did not play to our expectations."

Clemson recovered with a win against Wake Forest. Catanzaro kicked a 43-yard field goal as time expired to lift Clemson to a 31–28 victory. It sealed an Atlantic Coast Conference Atlantic Division championship. In celebration, Catanzaro sprinted toward the end zone with his arms stretched like the wings of an airplane, imitating the same celebration his mentor, former NFL kicker Morten Andersen, performed after a game-winner. Catanzaro spent the previous summers learning some of Andersen's other techniques.

Through his 26-year NFL career, Andersen converted 565 field goals and 849 extra points. In 2017 he became the second place-kicker to be inducted into the Pro Football Hall of Fame. He knew how to suppress the pressures of the position. He helped Catanzaro get past the disappointing miss at Auburn in 2010. He strengthened Catanzaro's leg by first strengthening his resolve.

"What we talked about at great length, not only to him but also to his family, was to be on the same page and move on together," Andersen said. "Very satisfying, very gratifying to see a young man develop from where he's been, as a walk-on to getting a scholarship, and then exorcising all his demons, and then really stepping it up another level and becoming one of the premier kickers in the NCAA."

Clemson climbed to No. 7 in the BCS standings, but the Tigers faltered on the road again at North Carolina State and at rival South Carolina. Clemson scored 13 points in each of those contests, its lowest output of the season. At Clemson's expense, South Carolina reached 10 wins in a season for only the second time in school history. It was the first time Clemson had dropped three consecutive games to Carolina since 1968–1970. After that game, South Carolina radio announcer and former quarterback Todd Ellis interjected on air an embellished quote from coach Steve Spurrier in which Spurrier distinguished the Gamecocks from the SEC powers Carolina aspires to match. "As Coach Spurrier says, we may not be LSU or Alabama," Ellis said, "but we ain't Clemson, folks!"

Ellis editorialized that last part. Spurrier never said it. Yet, by the end of the night, South Carolina football's official Twitter account had posted the quote and attributed it to Spurrier. Swinney does not have a Twitter account, but the message soon reached him. He was asked about it the following Thursday while his team prepared to face Virginia Tech for the second time that season in the ACC Championship Game.

"It's sad that I get asked a question like that on a Thursday before a championship game," Swinney said before he unleashed a rant on the imbalance of the rivalry. "I heard that. That's the kind of thing that gets back to you. And I don't know if he really said that or not, but I guess he did. There's been no rebuttal," Swinney said. "If he said that, that's disappointing, to be honest with you, because I was taught to win and lose with class. That's kind of a childish thing to put out there to be honest with you. I think that our program here speaks for itself. If I had to say anything, I'd say he's right. They're not Clemson, and they're never going to be Clemson, and no three-game winning streak is going to change that. It's not the first time they've won three in a row, and it won't be the last time. It might be 50 more years. But it'll probably happen again.

"I've gone out of my way to be complimentary to them and complimentary to Coach Spurrier. I have a lot of respect for Coach Spurrier, but I am going to defend my program. I am going to defend my players, my coaches, and I'm going to defend Clemson University, because I believe in it. There are a lot of rivalries out there. This is more of a domination, and that's a fact," Swinney added, referring to the 65–40–4 record Clemson compiled in the series from 1896 to 2011. "My kid's grandkids won't live long enough to ever see this really become a rivalry....The best era they've had in 115 years of South Carolina football is right now. And they've whipped our butt the last three years. It's my job to change that. Coach Spurrier's been there seven years, and after five years, I think he had 35 wins and a new contract and all that kind of stuff. After five years at Clemson, if I only got 35 wins, there's going to be a new coach here. And you know what, there should be because there's a different standard.

"He's exactly right. They ain't Alabama. They ain't LSU, and they're certainly not Clemson. That's why Carolina is in Chapel Hill, and USC's in California, and *the* university in this state always has been, always will be Clemson....You can print that, tweet that, whatever."

One could not decipher if Swinney was more agitated by the quote or aggravated by the timing of the question. Either way, he and Spurrier had developed a respectful relationship and they eventually clarified the misattribution. Nevertheless, video of Swinney's fiery monologue had already spread virally through the Internet. It resonated with Swinney's fan base and galvanized his players. Whether he was speaking honestly off the cuff or calculated the message, he produced a favorable effect. And it did not sully his relationship with Spurrier, who never ran from a war of words—because he rarely lost one.

Spurrier would later quip about how LSU had the *real* Death Valley and referred to Clemson as that "team from the Upstate." Swinney joked that he was from Mars and Spurrier was from Pluto. Spurrier retorted that Pluto was technically no longer a planet. The two would volley back and forth to the amusement of media members and to the enmity of the opposing fan base. The rivalry series is a few generations from being even, but the verbal rivalry was always tightly contested.

Clemson proceeded to knock off Virginia Tech 38–10 in Charlotte. Clemson claimed its first ACC championship since 1991 and secured a spot in the Orange Bowl.

"We all had dreams and aspirations, and that was definitely one of the goals coming into the season," said Boyd, who set four school records as a sophomore in 2011, compiling 298 completions, 3,828 passing yards, 4,046 yards of total offense, and 33 touchdown passes. "Coach also promised us that things would change. He's like, I promise you, I'm going to do everything in my power to make sure we win games. He went out there and went out on a limb and hired Coach Morris. Coach is like, 'This is going to work.' We believed in everything he told us, and definitely came out there and just put the plan to use."

"This was a process, and things take time," said Eric Mac Lain, a redshirt freshman on that team who recognized the seeds that were planted that season. "We just started winning and beating everybody, and I think that's the best thing, especially when you're thinking of younger kids. Theories and explanations only go so far, but directly winning and kicking somebody's tail, that pretty much sends a message really quickly to someone. I think that was the easiest way. We just had a bunch of good guys who started that. Going back all the way to Dwayne Allen and Tajh Boyd and all those guys who created that culture."

# 7

## FOURTH-AND-16

EARLIER IN THE DISCUSSION, Clemson defensive coordinator Kevin Steele suggested that *embarrassed* was not quite the correct word to describe how he felt that evening. Later, when asked for a more accurate term to depict his emotions, Steele did not need to deliberate long. He turned and uttered *ass-kicked*.

Neither Shakespeare nor Fitzgerald could have crafted a sharper exclamation. Few could match the abrasive elocution of the Pee Dee poet. Steele's tough exterior and blunt diction effectively masked his brilliance. On this night, his unit's performance achieved the same end.

West Virginia booted Clemson 70–33 in the Orange Bowl. Quarterback Geno Smith passed for 401 yards and six touchdowns, many of which were credited to him on jet sweep plays to eventual NFL speedsters Tavon Austin and Stedman Bailey. Austin amassed 123 yards and four touchdowns. Clemson trailed 24–17 early in the second quarter, and then a rapid succession of points and turnovers and missed tackles and cuss words unraveled the Tigers.

"That was like a virus," coach Dabo Swinney said, specifically referring to the 99-yard touchdown West Virginia defensive lineman Darwin Cook scored in the second quarter after ripping the ball from Andre Ellington near the goal line. West Virginia compiled 35 points in the second quarter alone.

"That was about as ugly as it gets," said Steele, who asserted that, although the result was far less than desirable, the trip to the Orange Bowl showed Clemson what was required to reach a Bowl

Championship Series game, what it took to win the Atlantic Coast Conference. Swinney recognized that, but also concluded that in order to return to a BCS Bowl and win it, he needed a different coordinator. A week after that game, Steele and Swinney parted ways.

That same night, Swinney texted Brent Venables, the coordinator at Oklahoma. Venables directed the Sooners' defense for Bob Stoops for 13 years. He helped Oklahoma capture the national championship in 2000. He was famously, fiercely loyal. Swinney was tossing a Hail Mary on the opening drive. But five minutes later, Venables responded. Swinney and Venables discussed football and family for the next three hours. Venables visited Clemson soon after that conversation.

"When I left Clemson, I knew this is what I needed to do, what I wanted to do," Venables said. "The last hurdle and obstacle was dealing with things back in Norman." His loyalty to Stoops and the idea of uprooting his family frightened him. But he felt comfortable enough with Swinney to leave the familiar.

With Venables on the staff, Clemson was building something groundbreaking. Two months later, Clemson broke ground on a new building. An indoor practice facility. After the 2009 season, Clemson scheduled a Pro Timing Day for star running back running back C.J. Spiller and other NFL Draft aspirants. Rain poured over Clemson that day, but there was no indoor option to relocate the audition. Spiller was forced to perform on the Tigers' outdoor turf field.

"Here's C.J. Spiller, the greatest player I'd been around," Swinney said. "This guy set the standard for what the Clemson athlete should look like, on and off the field. Graduated in three and a half years. A person of excellence in every area of his life. I'll never forget it. We're standing out there, and the biggest day of his life. And Pro Day is Pro Day. It's not, 'Oh, now, all y'all fly across the country and come back tomorrow.' It doesn't work that way."

Spiller lined up for each drill and every measurement with the rain cascading over him. Swinney huddled under a small umbrella with John Fox, who then was the head coach of the Carolina Panthers. C.J. completed his audition. He never complained. Swinney did. And that day, *embarrassed* was the correct word.

"I went back to the office, and I talked to the media and I said, 'I'm embarrassed. I'm embarrassed that we didn't have better for C.J. Spiller,'" said Swinney. "I told Terry Don Phillips, we need an indoor facility. This is an embarrassment. We're better than this. Best is the standard."

Phillips considered Swinney's plea and began arranging fundraising and development campaigns for the indoor facility. Plans for the 80,000-square-foot, $10 million building were soon in place. Clemson continued similar pointed progress on the field. Off the field, Swinney utilized a regrettable incident to advance his stance on discipline. Star receiver Sammy Watkins was arrested in May of 2012 in Clemson for misdemeanor possession. Swinney suspended Watkins for the first two games, which included the Chick-fil-A Kickoff against Auburn.

That placed a heavier burden on the broad shoulders of junior DeAndre Hopkins, a Clemson native and product of nearby Daniel High School who molded himself into a prolific playmaker with a combination of raw talent and dogged desire.

Hopkins notched a career-high 13 receptions for 119 yards and a touchdown in the opener against Auburn. Clemson won that game 26–19. Hopkins followed with three touchdowns on six catches in the blowout of Ball State. Hopkins was prepared for the added pressure. He was fortified through misfortune. He never knew how to accept a break. He learned how to make his own.

In 2002 Hopkins' mother, Sabrina Greenlee, found her boyfriend at the home of another woman. After a dispute, the woman doused Greenlee with a boiling concoction of lye and bleach. As the skin peeled off her body, Greenlee's boyfriend picked her up, placed her in a car, drove her to a nearby gas station, and left her there to die.

The station's attendant retrieved help. Greenlee was rushed to a local hospital and then flown to a medical center in Georgia. She healed for three weeks in a medically induced coma. She was left with only 20 percent of her vision, completely blind in her right eye. Doctors treated the damage to her face with skin grafts. She endured an arduous recovery process, but she persisted.

"All over a man I'd been dating for three months," Greenlee said. "I went through a lot of adversity and depression. Anxiety set in, but I was determined to raise my kids."

Hopkins was 10 years old when that happened. The tragic caveat is Greenlee's survival is one of the most fortunate stories of Hopkins' family history. In 1992, five months after DeAndre was born, his father was killed in an auto accident on Interstate 85. His car hydroplaned, flipped three times, and collided with a guard rail. Greenlee escaped the wreck with only a concussion. Steve Hopkins died a week later. Greenlee raised Hopkins and his three siblings primarily on her own.

"The times I struggled the most were when school started and I wasn't able to give them everything they needed," Greenlee said. "I look back and I know that there had to be some type of higher power at work. Nobody ever told me how to do this, but I think my biggest thing was I was determined to never lose control."

DeAndre inherited his mother's resilience and independence. His family legend asserts that he inherited his astounding athleticism from "Big Terry," his grandfather.

On a Wednesday afternoon, in the fall of 2012, Terry Smith sat in his living room in Easley, South Carolina, and leisurely surfed through the sports channels. He unexpectedly found a replay of Clemson's 1992 football game against Florida State. Smith's son, Terry Jr., led Clemson in receiving from 1990 to 1993. Even 20 years later, that old footage evoked mixed emotions.

"It's still tough to watch," Smith said, although he handles the replays better than he did the first time he saw "Little Terry" play at Clemson.

"I never will forget the first home game they had that I knew he was actually going to play," Smith said. "I can remember him coming out on the Hill, and I can remember almost fainting. Really, they had to catch me. My breath just left me, and I said, 'Gosh, I can't keep doing this.'"

Smith imagined that emotional tension would double that following Saturday during Clemson's game at Florida State. Smith was traveling to Tallahassee, Florida, to watch his grandsons, DeAndre and Florida State linebacker Terrance Smith—Little Terry's son—for the first time on the same field.

"My daddy is ecstatic. He's called me like 100 times, because he's so excited for this game," Greenlee said that week. "It'll be like a flashback to watching my brother. I don't know how my daddy will handle it. He'll probably have to wear a Clemson hat and a Florida State shirt."

Close.

Big Terry wore a Florida State hat and a Clemson shirt. His deep devotion to Clemson was not swayed. He wanted the Tigers to win, but he wanted both DeAndre and Terrance to perform well. Then, after that night, he wanted neither team to lose another game.

DeAndre led Clemson to that point with 26 receptions and four touchdowns. Terrance, a redshirt freshman from Southwest Dekalb High in Decatur, Georgia, started on special teams and wore his father's No. 24.

The cousins consistently communicated through the season, but Big Terry hoped they would avoid contact in that game. He shared that desire with them a few months earlier when they both were in Easley to visit their grandfather.

"Don't you hit him too hard when he catches it," Big Terry told Terrance.

"Don't worry, Granddaddy," DeAndre replied. "He won't touch me."

"It's just great to be able to watch both of them get out and compete with each other," Smith said.

When Terrance signed with Florida State, Big Terry was forced to sprinkle some Seminoles gear around his den, which could be considered the Smith Family Hall of Fame. There are countless trophies, photos, and newspaper clippings commemorating his family's athletic achievements.

It is more than a men's club. DeAndre's older sister, Kesha Smith, scored 1,000 points for Daniel before earning a college basketball scholarship. Another of Big Terry's granddaughters, Shanterria Cobb, made Daniel's varsity volleyball team that year as a freshman.

"All of his kids and grandkids are athletes," said Terry Smith's cousin, Kitty Hallums. "People ask, 'Where does this all come from?' Terry sticks his chest out and says, 'From Granddaddy.'"

"I'm not surprised," said Easley mayor Larry Bagwell. "Those are good genes."

Bagwell was Smith's coach at Easley High School when Smith established the family's athletic lineage. Smith was captain of Easley's first integrated team in 1969. He quarterbacked the Green Wave to an 11–1 record. The only loss was in the state championship game.

"Terry might be the best leader I've seen come through," Bagwell said. "If I saw a problem lurking, I could go to Terry with it and things would quiet down. People just seem to fall in behind him and have no problem following him."

"Sunday mornings before church were just full of, 'What did Terry do?'" Hallums said. "We had family in Detroit, and they would call all around to hear what Terry did on the football field. There are people who will tell you neither one of these boys is quite the athlete their granddaddy was."

Smith estimates he passed for about 30 touchdowns at Easley, but he never imagined he would pass along such strong genes. "I'm super proud of them all. They..." Smith stopped and turned his attention to the TV. Little Terry had just caught a touchdown in the fourth quarter, soaring over a defender to snag the ball like DeAndre had done several times at Clemson.

"That place went crazy," Smith said, before further explaining why those replays still stirred such emotion. Little Terry died in 1997. DeKalb County police near Atlanta responded to a disturbance call at the home of Little Terry's estranged wife, Angela Smith. Policed reported that they found Smith attacking his wife with a kitchen knife while she was holding their two-year-old daughter. According to police reports, they told Little Terry to drop the knife, and Smith responded, "Kill me! Kill me!" and raised his arm to attack the woman. Police opened fire. Little Terry was killed. Angela and the child were wounded. The family did not believe the police reports. Big Terry hired a lawyer to investigate, but eventually the attorney fees became too much of a burden.

Little Terry never got to do what Big Terry would do that weekend—watch Terrance play in a college game. "It's tough, but it's really something to be able to watch him on TV still," Smith said. "Anytime I get a little lonely for him, I can get on YouTube and pull up one of his games. I know he would be so proud of both of them, especially of Terrance."

Clemson fans may have thought the 10 receptions, 107 yards, and touchdown Hopkins recorded were impressive enough amid the 70–33 onslaught Clemson endured in the Orange Bowl. But once fans discovered what Hopkins endured days before that game, they understand how truly miraculous it was.

Hopkins was running late to catch the team bus at Memorial Stadium. He lost control of his car on a wet road and collided with a tree. Hopkins' position coach Jeff Scott noticed the accident from another road, recognized the car, and immediately feared the worst.

"I looked up in the tree and I could see the back of the car," Scott told *USA Today*. "Your stomach just drops. We turned around and got over there, and one of the police chiefs told me he was conscious."

Like his mother, DeAndre escaped that wreck with a concussion. He joined the team in Florida and served as one of the few bright spots in that game for Clemson. He served in that same capacity for the game in Tallahassee that nearly a dozen members of his family traveled to watch. DeAndre scored Clemson's first touchdown, a 60-yard pass from Tajh Boyd. He closed the game with a team-high 88 receiving yards. Clemson lost the game 49–37. As Terrance Smith logged his snaps, his family may have been the only people in Clemson's section who wished any Seminole well. But Smith said family will always trump fanhood.

"They said it all started with me, but I'm so proud of what they've done," Big Terry said. "Family is the most important thing. What I stress to DeAndre and Terrance is sports is only going to be there for a short time, but family will always be there."

The family was there as often as they could be that season as DeAndre paced Clemson with 82 receptions, 1,405, yards and 18 touchdowns. He passed his uncle on Clemson's career chart. He earned All-America honors in 2012 and contributed one of the most memorable plays in school lore.

Clemson closed the regular season with a 10–2 record after dropping the Palmetto Bowl to South Carolina 27–17. Clemson earned an invitation to the Chick-fil-A Bowl to face LSU. Clemson trailed 24–13 at the end of the third quarter but did not surrender another point. The Tigers trimmed the deficit to eight points with a field goal. Hopkins caught a 12-yard touchdown pass from Boyd on the next drive to close the gap to 24–22. Clemson capitalized on

LSU's conservative play-calling on the ensuing drive and forced a three-and-out.

Clemson reclaimed possession at its own 20-yard line with 1:39 remaining. Boyd targeted Hopkins on the first two downs, but both passes fell incomplete. Greenwood, South Carolina, native Sam Montgomery sacked Boyd on third down for a six-yard loss. Clemson called a timeout with 1:22 remaining. Facing fourth-and-16, Clemson lined up four-wide. Hopkins opened outside of the numbers on the right side of the formation. As tight end Brandon Ford cut outside, Hopkins broke inside and slipped behind LSU defensive back Eric Reid. Boyd delivered the ball over Reid's shoulder.

"I knew I had it. I knew I had to make a play," Hopkins said. "Reid was in the middle of the field, and it was a crossing route between me and Brandon Ford to kind of isolate the safety and the corner. I was supposed to break in actually, but Eric Reid played the play great, so I kind of made an adjustment to go around, and Tajh threw it off his back foot. I adjusted my route to go upfield, and he put the ball in the air, and I saw a glimpse of it. I didn't see the ball all the way through, because Eric was on top of me. I was just kind of hoping and timed my slide, and it fell right in there. Couldn't ask for a more perfect ball."

Hopkins cradled the pass at the Clemson 40-yard line for a 26-yard gain and a first down. Hopkins followed with a seven-yard reception and then drew a pass-interference penalty on Reid. Boyd completed each of his next three passes and then lined the ball up for kicker Chandler Catanzaro. In the Georgia Dome, where his mentor Morten Andersen once kicked for the Atlanta Falcons, Catanzaro nailed a 37-yard field goal as time expired, lifted Clemson to a 25–24 victory, and propelled Clemson into a new class of college football.

It was Clemson's first bowl win against a team ranked in the top 15 of the Bowl Championship Series standings. Catanzaro's kick sealed Clemson's first 11-win season since 1981.

"Fourth-and-16" became an emblem of Clemson grit. It became a slogan of perseverance. It became a tagline for T-shirts, bumper stickers, and license plates. It became the inspiration for poems, speeches, and sermons.

"Shortly after the game, it occurred to me—2 Corinthians 4:16," Swinney said, linking the play with the Bible verse that begins, "Therefore we do not lose heart."

"That fourth-and-16 play will always be a reminder to me of why you never give up," Swinney said. "It will also be a reminder to me of what can happen when a group of people come together to achieve a goal and work hard to achieve something bigger than themselves.

"We converted fourth-and-16, and we got a first down, but if you remember, we still had to make several more plays to have an opportunity to make that kick. Once they saw us overcome that obstacle, there was nobody who didn't know right then that Clemson was fixing to get it done.

"It's exactly the same in life. There are people who wake up every single day facing fourth-and-16. If we can help somebody, get a first down, then chances are they're going to go on and be successful."

DeAndre Hopkins and his family converted a series of fourth-and-16s throughout their lives. They pieced those first downs together and eventually reached the end zone. DeAndre finished that bowl game with 191 yards on 13 receptions. He proceeded to the NFL Draft and was selected by the Houston Texans in the first round, 27th overall.

DeAndre used his newfound fame and resources to assist his mother in establishing SMOOOTH (Speaking Mentally, Outwardly Opening Opportunities Toward Healing), a foundation dedicated to combating domestic violence through mentoring, counseling, and outreach.

DeAndre carried his fire and fortitude with him to the league. After everything he and his family survived, no cornerback was ever going to intimidate him.

"It all makes me so much stronger," DeAndre told *USA Today* two weeks before the draft. "I feel like I've got so many angels around me, it's like I'm going to be protected no matter what. Little obstacles, if they don't go my way, I really don't even get down. I've been through so much."

# 8

# THE ONE THAT GOT AWAY

SOUTH CAROLINA once was an overlooked page in the college football atlas. Simply a break on the scenic route between Knoxville and Athens. A pit stop between Blacksburg and Tallahassee. In 2013 South Carolina was a landmark. For the first time in the 117-year history of their rivalry, South Carolina and Clemson both entered the season as top 10 teams.

South Carolina was ranked No. 6 in the Associated Press poll and No. 7 in the Coaches Poll. Clemson was No. 8 in both polls. South Carolina was the only state represented by two teams in the top 10 of both polls. Florida, Texas, and Oklahoma are the only other states that have earned that distinction through the previous 15 seasons.

Most South Carolinians, whether orange, garnet, indecisive, or impartial, were proud that their tiny state could produce two top 10 teams when its population barely cracks the nation's top 25. Fans were eager to discover if Clemson and South Carolina could live up to the lofty rankings or if they had been living in a state of delusion.

"I have lived in South Carolina all my life, Upstate, Midlands, and the Lowcountry," said Duane Parrish, director of the South Carolina Department of Parks, Recreation, and Tourism. "Never have I seen the anticipation as high as it was."

"It's great for us and South Carolina," Dabo Swinney said. "Both of us finished in the top 10 last year, and I think that's a good thing for the state."

Clemson and South Carolina were two of 13 FBS teams that notched at least 10 wins in each of the previous two seasons. The rivals were two of only seven teams that were ranked in the AP top 25 for at least 30 consecutive weeks.

"The key thing is that, at both Clemson and South Carolina, you've got incredible commitment and really good coaches," said Dan Wolken, a *USA Today* national college football writer who visited both programs in the summer of 2013. "They're very different schools and very different programs. Yet I'm not real surprised they're both doing well. Both programs are just very stable in the coaching department, and they're both committed in terms of facilities and resources."

Before the arrival of Swinney and Steve Spurrier, both programs were in a state of disrepair. From 1985 to 2004, South Carolina averaged merely 5.2 wins per season. Spurrier was hired as head coach in 2005. He directed the Gamecocks to 66 victories through his first eight seasons, one more than the program managed through the previous 13 years.

Clemson enjoyed four consecutive 10-win seasons from 1987 to 1990 and won four Atlantic Coast Conference championships from 1986 to 1991. Yet Clemson finished higher than third in the ACC only three times through the next 17 seasons. Clemson opened the 2008 season ranked No. 9 in both polls but lost three of its first six games. Swinney was named interim head coach the following week. He lost his first game then won 40 of the next 61. That included the ACC championship in 2011.

The schools' commitment to remain nationally prominent was exhibited in the facilities sprouting at their campuses. Clemson continued its 10-year West Zone project, adding offices, locker rooms, a dining area, and fan seating to Memorial Stadium. It also opened the indoor practice facility that spring.

In February 2013 South Carolina's Board of Trustees approved construction projects that would include a new indoor practice facility and renovations to Williams-Brice Stadium. Upgrading their facilities helped Swinney and Spurrier upgrade their talent. They managed to steal standouts like Sammy Watkins and Connor Shaw from nearby states and persuade local high school All-Americans like Charone Peake and Jadaveon Clowney to stay home.

The Mr. Football Award is presented annually to the state's top high school player. Before Spurrier's arrival in Columbia, only six of the previous 13 Mr. Football honorees signed with an instate team. From 2008 to 2011, Spurrier signed four consecutive Mr. Football winners, two of whom spearheaded Carolina's emergence as a national contender.

"You get Lattimore. You get Clowney. That changed everything," said Mark Snyder of the *Detroit Free Press*, alluding to South Carolina's former star running back Marcus Lattimore and Clowney, who was a junior defensive end and Heisman Trophy dark horse in 2013.

Lattimore served as Carolina's bright ambassador, who plowed through defenders and smiled through adversity. Clowney vaulted the Gamecocks into the national spotlight with his superhuman highlights, none more compelling than the hit he dropped on Michigan running back Vincent Smith in the 2013 Outback Bowl.

Snyder covers Michigan for the *Free Press* and watched the helmet-jarring hit in person—and in awe. The play later won Clowney an ESPY award from ESPN. Yet Snyder said that day it won over a collection of skeptical Michiganders, who initially suspected the national attention around the Gamecocks was overblown.

"To see the versatility and athleticism of that team, it was very impressive," Snyder said. "You get so much attention from the [Southeastern Conference] with Alabama and LSU and Florida and Georgia, and you hear about all those other teams. But South Carolina, to see that they have players that can match all those guys, it was overwhelming."

Like Clowney, Clemson quarterback Tajh Boyd was a Heisman hopeful and potential first-round NFL Draft pick. However, Swinney's top recruit had never played a down. Swinney hired offensive coordinator Chad Morris before the 2011 season. With his inventive ingenuity and electric personality, Morris reshaped Clemson's identity and helped the Tigers earn a national reputation.

Before Morris' arrival, Clemson never gained more than 5,500 yards in consecutive seasons. The Tigers gained 6,171 yards in 2011 and finished ninth in the nation in 2012 with 6,665 yards.

Spurrier's string of Mr. Football winners was not the four-year streak over which Clemson fans agonized the most. South Carolina won five of its 20 meetings with Clemson from 1985 to 2004. Under Spurrier, South Carolina won five of the next eight meetings, including four consecutive from 2009 to 2012. The rivalry always sparked fiery banter, well before those outside of the state acknowledged it. It was heated even in 1998 when the teams met with three wins between them. Fifteen years later, legitimate national title hopes fanned that flame.

"You've got these people who live together, family members, brothers and sisters, husbands and wives, who went to the opposite schools," Snyder said. "So it gets kind of intense when it's in your family. It just kind of builds, so every time one of them does something it's like a one-up situation."

"It's fantastic for both schools," said Parrish. "Certainly, I think one makes the other stronger, at the end of the day, in terms of recruiting, in terms of attendance, in terms of excitement around it."

Clemson won its first six games of 2013. The Tigers climbed to No. 3 before being walloped 51–14 in a primetime game against eventual Heisman Trophy winner Jameis Winston and Florida State. Clemson rebounded with four consecutive wins and climbed back to No. 6.

South Carolina dropped road games to Georgia—which Clemson defeated in its season opener—and Tennessee, but the

Gamecocks were still ranked No. 10 in the final week of the regular season. Clemson and South Carolina were not undefeated, but the Palmetto Bowl yielded the top 10 matchup the state yearned.

They rested. They dieted. They lifted weights. They climbed stadium steps. They ran suicides. Yet, despite their persistent efforts, Clemson's seniors could not get rid of their *but*.

The 2013 class was justly lauded for spearheading the revival of Clemson's program. Up to the Palmetto Bowl, the seniors won 37 games, including the conference title. Still, their highest praises are tarnished slightly by their lowest letdowns. Their commendations are followed by an abrupt conjunction and a contrasting clause.

They won a school-record 24 ACC games, but…

They earned three consecutive 10-win seasons, but…

They defeated a top 10 team in three consecutive years, but…

"Throughout our careers, we definitely left a good culture here," senior linebacker Spencer Shuey said. "I feel like we definitely made an impact on this program, but there's that one thing."

This commendable class never tasted a victory against rival South Carolina. Clemson endured the four-year famine in the rivalry, and the hunger pangs had these seniors salivating for the 2013 meeting. They were reminded frequently of their rivalry whiffs—on campus, in the barbershop, and especially back home.

"The instate rivalry is crazy," tackle and Spartanburg native Brandon Thomas said. "I have some close friends I went to high school with, and actually in my family there are South Carolina fans. It's tough, but it comes with the territory of playing at Clemson."

Before 2013, there always was another chance. When taunted about the skid, these seniors could look optimistically toward the next year. This time, there would be no other chance. There was no next year. So there were no two ways about it.

"We need to beat them," Shuey said. "To not have anyone on the team that's actually beaten them is something that doesn't seem real."

Shuey, McDowell, Thomas, kicker Chandler Catanzaro, line-backer Quandon Christian, and quarterback Tajh Boyd were the six Clemson starters who redshirted during the 2009 season. Thus, they experienced each agonizing moment of the losing streak.

Clemson had never dropped five consecutive games to South Carolina. No senior wanted that dubious distinction affixed to his class. "It's bragging rights," McDowell said. "People keep saying, 'Don't get that thumb.'"

Clemson could have avoided the thumb if it had avoided the six-pack. Clemson donated six turnovers to South Carolina. Receiver Sammy Watkins underthrew a double pass on the opening drive, and it was intercepted. Adam Humphries muffed a punt. Carolina recovered and scored a touchdown four plays later. Despite that charity, Clemson managed a 17–17 tie with 3:01 remaining in the third quarter. The Tigers did not score again. South Carolina manufactured an 11-play, 75-yard, 6:14 touchdown drive. Clemson trailed 24–17 with ample time remaining, but the Tigers committed a turnover on each of their final four possessions.

In his final shot at South Carolina, Boyd tossed two interceptions and no touchdowns. He netted 16 rushing yards on 15 carries, including the five sacks he absorbed. Clowney notched the final sack of his college career in that 31–17 victory. He proceeded to the NFL with 24 sacks. He recorded 6.5 against Clemson.

Connor Shaw became the first South Carolina quarterback to log four wins against the Tigers. That evening and for the next 365 days, Shaw, his teammates, coaches, and every garnet-clad fan throughout the state posed for pictures with their fingers stretched wide, including the thumb Clemson dreaded. It became known as the five-bomb, and Swinney himself even caught it a few times after agreeing to pose for photos with undercover Gamecocks.

Clemson agonized over the one that got away...again. But its postseason draw provided an enticing distraction. The Tigers closed the regular season with a 10–2 record. They officially finished second in the ACC standings, especially significant with regards to their bowl aspirations. Because Florida State won the ACC title and earned a spot in the Bowl Championship Series National Championship Game, Clemson earned the league's automatic bid to the Orange Bowl. The Tigers were pitted against Ohio State. Clemson's defense embraced the challenge of Ohio State running back Carlos Hyde, quarterback Braxton Miller, and a Big Ten offensive line.

Defensive backs should never starve at Clemson. As long as they hang with defensive linemen, they will never need to pay for a meal. "We're really nice to our defensive backs," said Clemson defensive ends coach Marion Hobby. "I tell my guys all the time, 'You treat him nice. You buy an extra sandwich for him, because he is your lifeline.'"

However, defensive backs coach Mike Reed believes his unit should pick up the tab. "I'm always a big fan of the defensive line," said Reed, who replaced Charlie Harbison on Swinney's staff in 2013. "I'll always be in that room, talking about, 'Hey, fellas, good job,' because they make our job a lot easier. It's one of those things where, 'Hey, we need another defensive end? Take a defensive back scholarship from me and get a defensive end.'"

The debate is football's version of the "chicken or the egg." Is a secondary elevated by a dominant, disruptive defensive line, or are defensive linemen only as good as the defensive backs who cover for them? For Hobby and Reed, that is equivalent to asking an auto mechanic, "What is more important, the wheel or the axle?"

"We work together," Reed said. "If you get pressure, my guys don't have to cover long, and if they do, it's an erratic throw, and we get an interception."

"We like to get those coverage sacks too," Hobby said, "where the quarterback just has to hold it and you finally get him. Somebody is running free every play. They always say, 'The quarterback missed him!' Well, it's that pressure of someone in his face that won't allow him to see it or you taking away the strong point of the route. They go hand in hand."

Statistics seldom reflect that reciprocal relationship. Only three teams—Fresno State, Houston, and Southern Cal—finished the 2012 season ranked among the top 15 in the nation in both sacks and interceptions. Eleven teams were ranked in the top 25 in both sacks and pass-efficiency defense. Clemson finished 22nd in sacks (34), 43rd in interceptions (13) and 62nd in pass-efficiency defense (131.24).

The variance reveals that, like the wheel and axle, the collective unit will not operate effectively if one component is faulty.

Junior defensive linemen Grady Jarrett, Vic Beasley, Corey Crawford, Josh Watson, DeShawn Williams, and Tavaris Barnes were thrust into the trenches in 2012 and benefited from the pounding. In 2013 the defensive line was a proven force with depth and experience. Conversely, questions of injuries, inexperience, and inconsistency lingered in the secondary. The unit was so thin the previous year the staff switched receiver Adam Humphries to defensive back for a game. Reed said Swinney revealed his concern by signing eight defensive backs in the latest recruiting class.

"Coach made it known that we were the question mark," Reed said. "So that's what I told my kids, 'We're the question mark.'"

Reed said the defensive backs returned an encouraging response.

"'Coach, we'll take care of it,'" Reed recalled. "That's what you want. You want those guys to take ownership of it and run with it."

In 2012 Clemson allowed 41 completions of more than 20 yards, 23 of which produced touchdowns. Hobby said he has used those plays in the film room to charge his ends, because what may appear to be blown coverage can result from a blown assignment on the line.

Like the wheel and axle, when both components are working in concert, the collective unit rolls along smoothly. "You have to get them into the mentality of it," said defensive tackles coach Dan

Brooks. "At this level, it's so much about the whole unit. It's about all of us together."

In the second season under coordinator Brent Venables, Clemson closed 2013 ranked 13th in the Football Bowl Subdivision in both sacks and interceptions. Beasley was ranked third individually with 13 sacks. He earned consensus All-America honors that year and notched 23 tackles for loss. Beasley started his career at Clemson as a tight end. He even played quarterback on the scout team. He found a home on the defensive line with Hobby and blossomed into an explosive pass rusher and a first-round NFL Draft selection. Beasley left Clemson with 33 sacks, the highest career total in school history.

Beasley, Jarrett, Shaq Lawson, and Shuey each notched a sack against Ohio State. Cornerback Bashaud Breeland added one for good measure. Breeland forced a fumble to thwart Ohio State's penultimate drive. Linebacker Stephone Anthony intercepted Miller on the next drive and preserved Clemson's 40–35 victory.

Tajh Boyd saved perhaps his best performance for his last. He redeemed his South Carolina showing and torched the Buckeyes with 505 total yards and six touchdowns. Sammy Watkins excelled in his finale as well. He caught 16 passes for 227 yards and two touchdowns.

Boyd graduated holding a tie for the most wins for a starting quarterback in school history. He navigated Clemson out of mediocrity and into prominence. He did not snap the streak against South Carolina, but he notched signature wins against Ohio State, LSU, Georgia, Florida State, Virginia Tech, and Auburn.

"It was a very special night," Boyd said. "Just the significance of the game, not for me particularly, not for this team particularly, but for the university, for the fans that support us day in and day out. I couldn't pick a better way to go out as a senior."

Clemson lost Boyd, Watkins, Martavis Bryant, Breeland, Brandon Thomas, Chandler Catanzaro, Tyler Shatley, Spencer Shuey, and Darius Robinson from that 11–2 team. There was a grand haul rolling in the next recruiting class, but one of the most stirring additions was the return of defensive tackle Carlos Watkins, a native of Forest City, North Carolina.

It may be nestled in the Tar Heel State, but Forest City is Tiger territory. According to another Forest City native Daniel Bailey, the town officially turned orange in 1981. That year, brothers Chuck and Rod McSwain, former stars for Forest City's Chase High School, helped Clemson win the national championship.

"Because of football, our community is very tight-knit. That's how most people are introduced to one another," said Bailey, who served as the Chase head football coach in 2014. "But when you talked about college football, everybody talked about Chuck McSwain and his brother, Rodney. We've had some go to different schools, but it's a Clemson town."

Approximately 7,500 people live in Forest City, less than half the number of undergraduate students enrolled at Clemson. Four years earlier, Carlos Watkins, then a junior defensive lineman at Chase, worried that college coaches were overlooking his small, close-knit community. His peers at surrounding schools were receiving recruitment letters, but his mailbox was empty.

"He was kind of discouraged," Bailey said. "I told him, it doesn't matter how small your school is. If you can play, they're going to find you."

Still, Bailey wanted to assist the search. He compiled a highlight film for Watkins and mailed it to coaches. "One of the first plays was him at wide receiver running a fade route, catching it, making a move, and running for 15 yards," Bailey said. "It didn't take long at all after that got out."

Coaches began bombarding Bailey's phone, partly to ensure what they watched was real. "They said, 'There's no way that kid is doing that and weighs 275 pounds,'" Bailey said. "I said, 'You're right. He's 290 pounds now.'"

Watkins' mailbox was not large enough to hold all of the letters. He attracted scholarship offers from several major programs,
including Alabama, Auburn, Georgia, North Carolina, and Florida. To the delight of nearly all in Forest City, Watkins signed with
Clemson. He played in nine games as a freshman in 2012. He started
the season opener in 2013.

"It seemed like almost everything went his way," said Travis
Durkee, former sports editor of the Forest City newspaper, the
*Daily Courier*. "He's an All-American. He gets recruited. He goes
to the school he wants. He's getting playing time. Everyone in his
community loves him. Then, in just one night, everything went
horribly wrong."

That night was September 21, 2013. Watkins enjoyed a rare
weekend at home after notching four tackles in a Thursday night
victory at North Carolina State. He spent much of the downtime
with his best friend, Dache Gossett. "It was like as soon as we were
born, we were at his house every day," Watkins said. "He was like
a big brother. When I go home, that's the first person I'd hit up."

That Saturday, Watkins and Gossett hopped into an SUV with
their friend Tajae McMullens. Rain poured that evening, but it did
not deter their plan to attend a nearby cookout. A hazardous left
turn did. The vehicle lost traction, overturned, and collided with
a utility pole. Gossett was ejected from the rear seat. He died at
the scene. Watkins and McMullens were trapped in the car with the
pole lodged across their laps. They waited nearly two hours before
rescuers and utility workers could remove them from the wreckage
safely. What made Watkins a marvel on the fade route saved his life
that night.

"My dad talked to one of the firemen, and he said, if I was a
smaller guy, I could have most likely broken both of my legs," Watkins said. "I guess it was good that I'm 295."

Miraculously, the worst of Watkins' physical injuries were two
large hematomas, localized swelling caused by a break in the wall of

blood vessels. His promising season was cut short. He was awarded a medical redshirt but endured extensive physical therapy to regain strength and confidence in his legs.

Watkins was certain he would recover fully and return to the field. He was heartbroken that his best friend would not be able to see him do it. "It just shows me how quick things can change, how quickly your life can be taken away," he said. "So you really can't take any days for granted. It just really changed my mindset."

Watkins found solace through his teammates and coaches at Clemson. He found encouragement from his old neighbors back home.

"'Small-Town Friendly.' That's the Rutherford County motto, and the whole county embraced Carlos. There was a huge outpouring of support for him," Durkee said. "You don't want to say a tragic accident where a young man died was good for a community or good for someone else, because it never is. But he really grew from it, and it kind off brought the community together for one cause for a while."

"It's just family," Bailey said. "That's what our community is about. We've got to help each other out when somebody needs a hand."

In July 2014 Watkins broke from his intensive summer training to coach a youth football camp at Chase. He returned to Clemson ready to reclaim his tackle rotation spot.

"The wreck really affected him, mentally and physically," Swinney said. "It took us a while to get him back."

Physically, Watkins recovered from the accident, although he would never fully recover from the loss of his friend. "Sometimes the hardest thing in life is having those memories," Bailey said. "You're recalling them all the time, and then the realization hits that they're not there anymore. You never fill that void. You never forget."

Watkins did not try to forget. He wrote Gossett's name on his practice cleats. More permanent markers rest on his arm—the dark scars from the cuts he sustained during the accident. "When I look down, it reminds me of him," Watkins said. "You really don't move forward from it. It's always going to be with you. I just try to use it as a motivational thing."

Watkins channeled his heartbreak into his recovery. He channeled his gratitude into his play. That was the best way to repay all those Clemson fans nestled in that corner of the Tar Heel State—especially Gossett, who may have been the most devoted Tiger in Forest City.

"Oh, he was a big Clemson fan," Bailey said. "He was probably even more of a Carlos fan."

"I do it for him as well," Watkins said. "I'm pretty sure he's looking down, telling me to go for it."

# 9

## THE LEGEND OF DESHAUN

DESHAUN WATSON figured that the full-sized Snickers bars were the highlight of his haul that year. He returned home from a church Halloween festival with a stuffed bag. An information card protruded from beneath the load of candy. Like any eager nine-year-old, the only reading he intended to do that evening was scanning the labels to distinguish the peanut from the plain M&Ms.

"I was just in it for the candy," Deshaun admitted.

Deann Watson was a vigilant single mother. She proudly protected and provided for her four children. Before she allowed Deshaun to dig into it, she examined his bountiful bag. She discovered that the card was from Habitat for Humanity, the nonprofit organization that builds affordable houses for deserving families. The form encouraged Deann to seek more information. She attended an introductory meeting.

She figured her living conditions could only improve. She and her children resided in unit A4 in the Harrison Square apartments, a government housing development on the east side of Gainesville, Georgia.

"I was a little kid running around the neighborhood, hanging out with all kinds of people," Deshaun said. "It wasn't the best place. We were playing football in the yard, but also seeing drugs, gangs, and fighting all around us."

Deann desperately wanted to take her children out of that environment. So, when a representative from Habitat contacted her and explained that she would actually have to help build a house to receive it, Deann did not flinch. She informed her sister-in-law, Sonia Watson, that the family had been approved for a Habitat home and that she had agreed to contribute 300 work hours toward the project.

"Deann was a single parent and she wanted to have a home for her children," Sonia said. "She always worked and wanted what was best for her kids. But I said, 'You don't know nothing about building no house, girl!' And she said, 'Yes, I do.'"

Even if she exaggerated her expertise, Deann quickly sharpened her construction skills with the help of Habitat. She hammered nails, painted walls, and carried materials at the home site, after she completed her workday at her full-time job. Deshaun was still too small to do any heavy lifting, but he was able to tote some two-by-fours from one end of the worksite to the other. Observing his mother's diligence and dedication inspired Deshaun to take a "different approach to schoolwork and the game of football."

The Watsons completed the home in November 2006. They received the keys two days before Thanksgiving. They expected to walk into an empty house, but when they opened the door to their new home, they found it fully furnished. Warrick Dunn, who then was an All-Pro running back with the Atlanta Falcons, funded the furnishing through his charity Homes for the Holidays. Dunn's benevolence was a tribute to his mother, Betty Smothers, a single mother who worked ardently with the dream of securing a home for her children. While working a second job as a security guard in Baton Rouge, Louisiana, Smothers was ambushed and killed. When he entered the NFL in 1997, Dunn started the charity to assist single mothers and honor his mother's memory.

"It was so exciting," Sonia said. "Warrick, he furnished that whole house—the beds, the furniture, the spreads, all the kitchen stuff, everything. It was beautiful."

"Once I moved into that Habitat home, my life changed," Deshaun said. "I was able to go to school and come home to a happy place and not have to worry about something happening with the cops around or drug dealers walking around. Coming home safe and with a smile on my face was something special."

The Watsons moved into their new home two years after Deshaun unloaded that goody bag. It remained the family's home as Deshaun progressed to Gainesville High School. Deshaun was an outside linebacker in the eighth grade. Gainesville coach Bruce Miller recognized Deshaun's dazzling athleticism, but he was not quite sure where he would play him the next season. He let him try quarterback in the spring game before that freshman year. Deshaun completed 22 of 25 pass attempts and solved Miller's vacillation.

Deshaun started his first game as a freshman in 2010. He tossed three touchdown passes in a loss to Buford. He closed that season with 2,088 passing yards, 569 rushing yards, and 22 total touchdowns. That winter, an unexpected spectator showed up for one of Deshaun's basketball games. It was Clemson's newly hired offensive coordinator, Chad Morris.

"It took me about three clips to see him as a player," said Morris, who called Miller to inquire about Deshaun's character. The more he learned, the more he wanted to learn. He began making the 80-mile drive from Clemson to Gainesville more often after that basketball game. He and Deshaun developed a genuine relationship.

"He was the first one to offer me. He was the first coach who believed in me, who saw a bright future for me," Deshaun said. "The relationship was bigger than just football and getting me on campus, more like a father-son relationship."

The following football season, Deshaun compiled more than 4,000 yards of total offense. That same year, Deann was diagnosed with tongue cancer. She was forced to undergo major surgery, chemotherapy, and radiation. A portion of her tongue was removed. She conquered the disease, but her ability to speak was impaired. Deshaun appeared to be his same stoic, steady self during that ordeal, but it troubled him deeply to see his hero suffering.

"When his mom went through cancer, he was sad, but he was able to get through it," Sonia said. "I watched that teenager cry, but I told him that God would keep his mama here. I told him that all sickness is not death, and we will overcome it, and she did."

As his mother recovered, Deshaun contemplated his college choice. He had plenty of time to accept suitors, but whenever he prayed and pondered the decision, he always circled back to Clemson. Morris nurtured his relationship with Deshaun and offered encouragement and support during Deann's illness. He honored that connection with Morris and committed to Clemson in February 2012 while still a sophomore.

"I just started praying on my decision. My mom, she was praying about it," Deshaun said. "She knew everything was going to take care of itself, and she just wanted me to go play football and keep praying and make sure I made the right decision. I just felt like that day I committed to Clemson, God was talking to me, and I just felt like the time was perfect. That's what I wanted to do, and I stuck through it, and it was the best decision of my life. I just thank God that he was a part of it and gave me that opportunity."

In his junior season, Deshaun passed for 4,024 yards, rushed for more than 1,600, and scored 64 total touchdowns while leading Gainesville to the state championship. He closed that season with state records in career passing touchdowns and total yards. He added to those totals as a senior, with 4,431 passing yards and 1,057 rushing yards. He tossed 57 touchdowns, surrendered merely five interceptions and rushed for 14 touchdowns. He was named state player of the year in each of his final three seasons at Gainesville. He vaulted up recruiting ledgers. ESPN listed Deshaun as the No. 1 dual-threat quarterback in the nation. Despite his commitment to Clemson, colleges continued to court Deshaun. Every major program in the country extended an offer, including the hometown Georgia Bulldogs.

Gainesville High is less than 45 miles from Sanford Stadium in Athens. Gainesville honors the town's connection to UGA by utilizing the same oval G logo. Most Gainesville residents would have loved to see Deshaun in red and black. But, despite Georgia's late and desperate overtures, Deshaun held to his commitment. He signed with Clemson and enrolled early in the spring of 2014.

"He's a special person," Clemson coach Dabo Swinney said. "He's a better young man than he is a player, and that's what I'm most proud of. He's just continued to stay humble. He's a great teammate and just comes to work every day ready to go."

Through the spring practice session, Deshaun challenged senior Cole Stoudt and sophomore Chad Kelly for the starting role. He suffered a small fracture in his collarbone that disrupted his progress, but Kelly's dismissal from the team trimmed the competition to two headed into the summer. Clemson opened the 2014 season against Georgia in Sanford Stadium. Deshaun could open his career at home, Between the Hedges.

But the launch was delayed. Swinney started with Stoudt, and Morris revealed his confidence in the veteran from the opening drive. Stoudt attempted a downfield pass on three of the first four snaps. The scheme, pace, and tilt of the offense appeared to be the same as they were during the previous three seasons, when Tajh Boyd steered the Tigers. Morris trusted Stoudt with designed runs in short yardage and deep throws on first down. Stoudt justified that trust through the first half. He completed nine of 20 pass attempts for 115 yards. At least three of those incompletions were dropped passes placed directly into receivers' hands.

Stoudt was steady in the pocket and smooth through his throws. He even flashed his running ability. He rushed for 24 yards on three carries during the opening drive. Two of those runs, an 18-yard scramble and a four-yard option keeper, converted third downs. Stoudt directed Clemson to the end zone on that drive. Through those 12 plays, he hushed the raucous crowd and the critics who doubted he was equipped to secure the starting role. The assurance lasted merely three more possessions.

With 35 seconds remaining in the first quarter, Morris upheld the guarantee he reiterated through August camp that Deshaun would play against Georgia, regardless of how Stoudt performed. Although Stoudt had steered the offense sufficiently, Morris inserted Deshaun for Clemson's fifth possession. On the sixth play of the drive, Deshaun launched his legend.

All Ramik Wilson had to do was turn his head. Wilson, a senior Georgia linebacker, sprinted behind Clemson receiver Charone Peake, as Peake broke his route inside and slipped in front of strong safety Quincy Mauger. Wilson turned his back to the line of scrimmage to chase Peake, and Deshaun delivered a daring dart directly over Wilson's shoulder. Deshaun left no room for error. He did not need any. Even after a jarring hit from Mauger, Peake clutched the pass for a 30-yard touchdown. All Wilson could do was shake his head.

Like most spectators in Sanford, he did not expect such precision and nerve from a freshman quarterback. Swinney did.

"The throw was good. I've seen that in practice 100 times," Swinney said with a slight shrug.

Swinney was not as impressed by what happened after the release as he was by what happened before the snap. Deshaun recognized the defensive formation and anticipated a particular blitz. He adjusted the pass protection and signaled the appropriate audible.

"He just executed the game plan. That's the best part of it," Swinney said. "The throw, that's why we went and signed him, because he can make those throws. But him being able to make the right decision in that environment, and to be poised, that's what's going to make him really special."

According to Morris, Clemson planned Deshaun's debut for the fifth drive. The staff did not share that plan with Deshaun. "We weren't going to tell him," Morris said. "We wanted him to be ready for any given moment."

When that moment arrived, Deshaun was composed and confident. "He said, 'Coach, let me have it. I want it. I'm ready,'" Morris said. "The moment was not too big for him at all."

Deshaun conducted three drives in the 45–21 loss. He completed two of four attempts for 59 yards. He compiled a pass-efficiency rating of 256.4. He also rushed for 13 yards on a designed run and two scrambles, but he was sacked twice for a loss of 16 yards. In his brief appearance, Deshaun proved he was poised, precise, and polished enough to command the offense. The cameo prompted petitions for Deshaun to start ahead of Stoudt, or at least, for the pair to split series evenly.

Deshaun was a more agile, explosive runner. He threw deep passes more accurately, but he needed to extend his prolific play through a longer sample size before he could persuade Swinney to promote him.

Stoudt completed 16 of 29 passes against Georgia for 144 yards. He led two touchdown drives and compiled an efficiency rating of 89.99.

"We don't have a quarterback controversy. We've got a clear starter," Swinney said the following week. "Deshaun Watson is special. That's not a secret. But old '18' is pretty good, too."

Swinney expected the appeals for Deshaun. He attempted to mitigate them preemptively, during August camp, when he initially committed to playing him sparingly.

"Had he gone out and played bad, then everybody would've said, 'Why are you playing that guy? Your starter's playing good,'" Swinney said. "But, if he goes in and plays good, which we expect him to play good, it's, 'How come he ain't playing more?' You just can't win in that situation."

Thus, along with his poise and precision, Deshaun also needed to display his patience.

He signified Clemson's future. No one was certain when that future would arrive. Yet that glimpse at Georgia revealed one certainty—Wilson would not be the last defender to leave the field shaking his head after a Deshaun Watson throw.

Clemson assailed South Carolina State 73–7 the following week. Stoudt started and completed 22 of 31 attempts for 302 yards and a touchdown. Watson completed eight of nine attempts, but three of those completions were touchdowns. Stoudt's grip on the starting role loosened in Tallahassee. A terribly underthrown pass marked his demotion. Clemson faced third-and-3 from the Florida State 6-yard line with 11:24 remaining in the first quarter. Tight end Jordan Leggett broke free into the end zone. Stoudt rolled right and fired a pass, but it landed short and low. Clemson settled for a field-goal attempt, but it sailed off target.

Two series later, Deshaun seized command of the offense. He never relinquished it. He steered the offense for the remainder of the game. He completed 19 of 28 passes for 266 yards. He committed no turnovers and was sacked only once. Behind Watson, Clemson wrestled the No. 1–ranked team in the country to overtime.

"We know we've got something special in that young man," Swinney said that evening. "To actually see him go and execute like he did was fun to be a part of."

Swinney was so moved by Watson's performance that he moved Watson to the top of the depth chart. He announced immediately after the game that Deshaun would start the next one. According to Swinney, Stoudt was disappointed but not disconnected as he watched Watson seize his job. "He made some good suggestions. He was trying to be very helpful," Swinney said. "It's a tough situation, and it's really not as much as what Cole did, as it is what Deshaun did in that situation."

Deshaun's promotion did not mark the end of the dual quarterback system. An injury did.

In his first start, Deshaun torched North Carolina for 435 passing yards and six touchdowns. He followed with 267 passing yards,

62 rushing yards, and four total touchdowns against North Carolina State. However, Deshaun broke a bone in his throwing hand late in the first quarter against Louisville. Stoudt relieved him, and Clemson relied on its defense, which produced a touchdown, and its kicker, Ammon Lakip, who converted three field goals. The Tigers defeated Louisville 23–17.

Deshaun's hand required surgery. Stoudt reclaimed the starting spot, but he was nursing an injured AC joint in his non-throwing shoulder. Even with extended treatment, Stoudt practiced and played through discomfort.

Through the first six games, Deshaun completed 67 percent of his passes. He tossed 12 touchdowns and threw only two interceptions. Despite attempting merely 10 fewer passes, Stoudt produced 44.8 percent less yardage. Stoudt tossed one touchdown with two interceptions. Clemson scored 91 points in Deshaun's first two starts. It scored 90 total during the next four games. Stoudt's physical limitations, which were compounded by the persistent shoulder injury he endured, induced Morris to abridge his playbook. He wisely simplified his scheme rather than stubbornly directing his players into situations they were not equipped to handle. Clemson won all three games Deshaun spent on the sideline, although its average yardage dipped by 24.9 percent. Point production declined by 37.5 percent. Clemson improved to 7–2 and rose to No. 18 in the Coaches Poll.

Deshaun was cleared to start November 15 against Georgia Tech. He instantly restored a true threat in the zone-read option running scheme. He also was a more accurate downfield passer than Stoudt. Sophomore receiver Mike Williams, Clemson's most explosive and reliable deep target, amassed 12 receptions for 277 yards and four touchdowns against North Carolina and N.C. State. He netted 252 yards and no touchdowns during Watson's absence.

Deshaun's return was expected to answer a lot of questions. But by the day's end, another even bigger question had surfaced—namely, who would be the team's quarterback for the rest of the season? Deshaun injured his left knee with 2:03 remaining in the first quarter and did not return. An MRI revealed that he did not tear a ligament, but the prognosis on his return was not immediately clear.

Considering what transpired to that point, Stoudt would have been the natural choice, but yo-yoing in and out of the lineup disrupted his rhythm and confidence. He suffered through the worst game of his career in the Tigers' 28–6 loss in Atlanta. Redshirt sophomore Nick Schuessler, a former walk-on, relieved Stoudt in the fourth quarter and completed all four of his attempts, albeit for 19 yards. Swinney and Morris bet on Stoudt the following week against Georgia State. He completed 19 of 29 attempts for 132 yards, a touchdown, and an interception. The defense blanked Georgia State, and the Tigers rode running back Tyshon Dye, who rushed for 124 yards and two touchdowns in the 28–0 drubbing.

Early upon his arrival at Clemson, Deshaun declared he would snap and reverse the five-game losing streak Clemson endured against rival South Carolina. He proclaimed that he would not lose to the Gamecocks. He did not want an injury to derail his volunteer duty. The initial MRI on his knee revealed no torn ligaments, but there was damage that cautioned team doctors and trainers. It was classified as a sprain, and Deshaun could delay an operation on it. He returned to practice ahead of the Georgia State game. He went through all the drills, but on one pocket pressure simulation, Deshaun shifted to avoid the rush and went straight to the ground. Another MRI revealed that this time the ligament was torn. Surgery was necessary, but Deshaun still wanted to delay it.

"You can imagine how we all felt at the time," Swinney said, "but Deshaun is like, 'I still think I can go.'"

Swinney repeatedly stated his stance on injuries. He declared that he invariably concedes to the assessments and recommendations of the medical staff. He asserted that team doctors assured him that Deshaun could not injure the ligament further. Thus, if

Deshaun was willing to endure the discomfort, Swinney was willing to allow him.

Deshaun stood behind center, wobbly, somewhere between undeniably gutsy and unnecessarily risky. He attempted to maintain his balance on his left knee, somewhere between inspiring and imprudent. Equipped with a bulky knee brace and resolute grit, Deshaun commanded Clemson to a 35–17 victory against the Gamecocks. He was relegated back to the sideline when the brace locked up. At one point, he motioned right in the Wildcat formation but struggled to hold his wide-receiver stance. His performance was much steadier.

Deshaun completed 14 of 19 pass attempts for 269 yards and two touchdowns. He also rushed five times for 13 yards. He boldly churned into the line of scrimmage for a pair of one-yard touchdowns. Deshaun contended that he merely felt the discomfort of adjusting to the brace, but he never felt any severe pain. However, with his resilient effort, he remedied the nagging pain Clemson endured for five years.

Deshaun only observed Clemson's five-game losing streak. He did not experience the anguish in the locker room after each defeat. He did not endure the torment of wasted opportunities. He did not share the agony his senior teammates had felt three consecutive times. Yet he accepted an obligation to ensure that they never felt it again.

"I knew I wasn't 100 percent," Deshaun said, "but I was going to help the team out."

Every time he limped, every time he fell awkwardly, every time he stood tall in the pocket and absorbed a hit, every time he tucked the ball and pushed for extra yardage, Deshaun crafted his legend.

"Basically, that brace was his ACL," Swinney said. "The only issue he had was his brace was so tight that it made his calf go to sleep. It was losing its circulation. His will to win, his preparation, his mental capacity, his toughness, his leadership, it is off the charts."

Considering the magnitude of the victory and the avoidance of further damage, one could justify the risk in hindsight. However, no one envied Swinney's position. On one side of the scale, he was forced to weigh the threat of a sixth consecutive loss to South Carolina. The desperation to end that streak was evident in the swell of clamoring fans the staff passed during the pregame walk to the stadium. It was evident in the onside kick Clemson attempted in the first half. It was evident in the nail-biting that persisted in Memorial Stadium even when Clemson held an 18-point lead in the fourth quarter.

On the other side of the scale, Swinney balanced Deshaun's future, his health, and his livelihood. The decision is easier when a medical staff recommends that a player should sit. The decision is easier when the opponent is Georgia State. The decision is easier when there is a reliable alternative. Clemson caught a glimpse of what the game would have been like without Deshaun. Stoudt attempted two passes Saturday. He completed both. One to running back Wayne Gallman for a three-yard loss. The other to South Carolina linebacker Skai Moore. One could presume that, without Deshaun, the alternative was a sixth consecutive loss to the Gamecocks.

Assuming he adheres steadfastly to his own stance, one could conclude that Swinney would not risk the long-term health of a player simply to sooth short-term suffering. Swinney felt 100 percent comfortable as Deshaun stood behind center, even though Deshaun was far from 100 percent.

"He is a mental and genetic freak," Swinney said. "I don't know how else to say it."

At the end of the night, Swinney stood assured in his decision, somewhere between jubilantly relieved and emotionally exhausted. And Deshaun stood somewhere between the satisfaction of a snapped streak and the exuberance of a reassured fan base. And in the glory of his budding legend.

Restoring Clemson's crown in the rivalry endeared him to Tigers fans. From that moment forward, he had a permanent home in Clemson. But Deshaun never forgot the one he, his mother, and his siblings built with their own hands. He emblazoned his arms with tattoos of symbols that reminded him of that journey. Playing cards that remind him to play the hand he is dealt. A Gainesville championship ring with the inscription *815*, the address of the Harrison Street Apartments, to remind him of the pinnacles he reached from those humble origins. He will never forget Dunn's generosity, and he vowed to pay it forward.

As his celebrity rose at Clemson, he developed a relationship with the local Habitat organization. He and his teammates volunteered on worksites to build that same joy and hope in other families.

"That place was a blessing," Deshaun said. "It's very special when you have a foundation and a home that you can go to. Ever since we moved into that house, my life has been at a peak, and each year seems to get better and better and better. It took a long time for me to put a smile on my face. It's great to be able to give back and share my story about what I went through. I want it to be an inspiration for young kids and show them that anything is possible."

# 10

## THE AUDITION

TWO DAYS AFTER he helped return the Palmetto Bowl bragging rights to Clemson, Chad Morris agreed to return home to Texas. He agreed to become the new head coach at Southern Methodist University. Under Morris, Clemson amassed 24,357 yards, or 13.84 miles, of total offense. Clemson averaged at least 30 points per game in each of those four seasons. He helped the Tigers climb back to the top of the Atlantic Coast Conference and drafted the blueprint for its explosive hurry-up, no-huddle offense. During those four years, he pulled the other offensive assistants into his game planning. Tony Elliott mastered the intricacies of the system and could develop rhythm as a playcaller. Swinney recognized that he could maintain the staff continuity and grant an opportunity to one of his young coaches.

Immediately after his plane took off for Dallas, Clemson missed Morris' quick-draw wit and candor. But surprisingly, Clemson did not miss him while developing a game plan for Oklahoma in the Russell Athletic Bowl. Swinney promoted Elliott and Jeff Scott as co–offensive coordinators. Elliott would remain in the booth to oversee the play-calling. Scott would spearhead adjustments on the field. They had nearly a month to devise their first game plan, and they already had the luxury of a reconnaissance man down the hall.

Defensive coordinator Brent Venables was not thrilled about facing his old friends and colleagues at Oklahoma. He had not been incredibly thrilled about leaving them. Folks examined the circumstances and assumed Venables left snarling and fuming.

Venables steered Oklahoma's defense for eight years, but after the 2011 season, Oklahoma head coach Bob Stoops hired his brother Mike Stoops and named him and Venables co-coordinators. Venables repeatedly asserted that he was delighted to work with Mike Stoops again and that the personnel shift had nothing to do with his departure. Venables agonized over the decision. Oklahoma was the only home his children had ever known. He also had a family in the office. He was not certain that uprooting from a powerhouse and joining an upstart halfway across the country was wise. But ultimately, the family atmosphere Swinney nurtured reminded Venables of what he would be leaving. That eased his heart. He took a chance, and he took the job. But he was not eager to take a shot at his old friends.

"Definitely my last choice. You're facing people that you care deeply for," Venables said. "At the end of the day, when you're coaching your guys on the field, your whole goal is to beat somebody's brains in. That's from an alpha male football coach standpoint. You really want to dislike your opponent. It's hard to dislike them. But for a few hours, trust me, I'll find a way.

"It's just a game. It's a big game, and we want to win the game. But our friendships won't change, won't be affected one bit. I'm totally indebted to Bob Stoops for where I am today. The coach that I am is a reflection of the things that he's taught me through the years. He stood on the table for me to get my first job [at Kansas State] when Bill Snyder was interviewing other people. He's been there for me and my family in the best days in both my professional and personal lives, and he's been there for me and my family in the most difficult days."

Like Venables, senior quarterback Cole Stoudt was tormented by a mix of emotions leading up to the bowl game. He endured a twisty, convoluted route, but he could close the season where he opened it. Atop the depth chart. Deshaun Watson, who unseated Stoudt for the starting role, elected to undergo surgery on the torn ligament in his left knee. The estimated range for recovery from ACL surgery is between six to eight months. Expediting the surgery allowed Watson to participate in Clemson's summer training program. It also reduced the risk of Watson missing any portion of August camp. But he did miss the bowl game.

Stoudt battled through his own ailment. During consolation time in the fourth quarter of Clemson's 41–0 rout of North Carolina State on October 4, Stoudt sprained his left shoulder and was forced to leave the game. He did not have time to rest it. He was thrust back into the lineup a game later when Watson broke the bone in his hand.

Before each of the next three games, Stoudt was administered a painkilling shot in the shoulder. Players typically do not resort to those desperate measures for minor aches and bruises. Despite the nagging injury, Stoudt steered Clemson to four consecutive victories, while completing 100 of 155 pass attempts, a rate of 64.5 percent, with four touchdowns and four interceptions.

He was relegated to the backup role again when Watson returned for Georgia Tech. That lasted less than a quarter. Stoudt was thrust back into the lineup again. He completed 23 of 42 attempts, a rate of 54.8 percent, for one touchdown and five interceptions. Each of those errant throws pierced through the ragged threads holding the remnants of the reputation Stoudt constructed through the previous three seasons. In his brief appearances behind starter Tajh Boyd, Stoudt portrayed a reliable, poised, and accurate conductor. He could deliver precise intermediate passes, read schemes, and adjust calls. He could even dupe a defense for a first-down rush. Somewhere along that twisty, convoluted route, Stoudt lost that confident, composed demeanor. Consequently, many Clemson followers had lost confidence in him.

Stoudt could not be shielded from the criticism. The steady stream of Internet insults revealed the low expectations his own fan base collectively held for his potential performance. Yet Stoudt arrived in Orlando feeling refreshed and relieved. The bowl game granted him a final opportunity to silence his detractors and prove that he could command an offense. That he still could deliver the post route. That he could deliver the quick slant. That he could deliver a victory.

Clemson pursued its fourth consecutive 10-win season. The program had not achieved that feat since 1987–1990. It also would be another victory against one of college football's elite brands, joining previous bowl wins against LSU and Ohio State.

The additional bowl preparation period provided ample time for a sprained shoulder to heal and for Stoudt to restore his confidence. He no longer needed a shot in that shoulder, but that final chance at redemption did give him a shot in the arm.

Playmakers can make play-callers look brilliant. Elliott and Scott intended to start simple and stay simple. On their first play-call, they ordered a simple screen to freshman wide receiver Artavis Scott. The result was not simple. However, Elliott knew the touchdown resulted from Artavis Scott's natural agility and acceleration, not from the staff's scheming.

"I'm going to give that to Artavis Scott," Elliott said with a laugh. "He's the one that made the play."

Nevertheless, the opening call revealed the unpretentious, yet promising policy Elliott and Scott adopted for their new role: get the ball to the playmakers, early and frequently. That should be the priority of every playcaller. Yet, as simple as that objective is, it often gets lost in the playbook behind pages and pages of overcomplicated strategy. Evidently, Elliott and Scott already knew better.

They committed to feeding Artavis and sophomore receiver Mike Williams on quick flips and deep passes, down the field, across the middle, along the sideline, and even on pre-snap motion sweeps. By halftime, Artavis had gained 95 yards. Oklahoma's offense had gained 90. Artavis closed the game with eight receptions for 114 yards. Williams amassed nine catches for 112 yards. With 7:34

remaining in the second quarter, Williams slipped a tackle on a quick outside route and converted what should have been an eight-yard gain into a 26-yard touchdown.

"A lot of that is DNA," Jeff Scott said. "That's why we spend as much time as we do in recruiting, going out and getting some of the premier playmakers to play in our offense. It's really nothing magical in the plays. It's really having guys out there who can make guys miss."

The explosive playmakers made Elliott and Scott look brilliant. The manner in which they managed Stoudt actually was brilliant. Stoudt's lineup shuffle disrupted his rhythm. He tossed five interceptions in his final 31 attempts of the regular season. Elliott and Scott trusted that Stoudt had not forgotten how to throw a pass, that he could still zip a quick perimeter route. They trusted that he still could spin a deep fade. They formatted the game plan around Stoudt's strengths and allowed him to operate comfortably. They dialed a series of short outs, screens, and crossing routes. The deep passes he attempted mostly were positioned outside the hash marks. That limited the risk while enhancing the reward.

"We tried to simplify it to where there were not so many checks, not so many reads," Elliott said. "He could go out and know exactly what he was doing, know where the ball was going to go, and be confident getting it there."

The strategy helped Clemson sustain drives and appeared to ignite Stoudt's confidence. He completed 26 of 36 attempts for 319 yards, three touchdowns, and no interceptions. He rushed for another touchdown, a three-yard plunge after a nifty option fake.

"Lean toward the things that he does well," Elliott explained. "There's a lot of things that Cole does well. The whole season may not be a testament to that, but he found his magic."

Elliott and Scott may never duplicate the series of fortunes that facilitated their dynamic debut. They could not expect so many missed tackles, so many wide-open receivers on plain out routes or the defense to generate so many turnovers. Thus, they could not expect to tally 22 first downs, average 4.9 yards per play, score four touchdowns, and kick two field goals in every game. However, if they adhered to their simple strategy to facilitate their playmakers, Elliott and Scott could expect success.

"Go back to what we did when we were very successful," Elliott said, referring to the previous two seasons in which Clemson averaged at least 500 yards and 40 points. "We played fast. We played with tempo. We kept it pretty simple. We wanted to kind of get back to that and put the kids in position to be successful."

# 11

## 15-FOR-15

SEVERAL COLLEGE FOOTBALL coaches mingled throughout the ballroom at Pinehurst Resort on a Monday night in July during the Atlantic Coast Conference Kickoff. Anticipation was steadily building for the 2015 season, and the league's coaches accepted the fact that the only one among them who could sit comfortably was Mack Brown.

No level of bowl victories, rivalry wins, or graduation rates can grant the luxury of such contentment. It is only enjoyed in retirement. Brown stepped down from the University of Texas in 2013. He transitioned to a career as television studio analyst. He no longer encountered the scrutiny of each season. He no longer was a captive of his success. He no longer was a casualty of his failures.

Swinney contended that every active coach, regardless of his record, is on the hot seat. Every coach faces the demands of his fans, both the rational and the impractical. Every coach must manage the operating costs of winning. Some seats are warmer than others. Some of the heat is superficial. Some of it is self-inflicted. Yet Swinney asserted that no coach has been padded well enough to sit on his accomplishments.

When Swinney attended his first ACC Kickoff in 2009, he shared the room with coaching legends Bobby Bowden, Butch Davis, and Al Groh. In four years, Swinney transitioned from the rookie to the fifth-most-tenured coach in the league. Only Virginia Tech's Frank Beamer, Duke's David Cutcliffe, Georgia Tech's Paul Johnson, and Wake Forest's Jim Grobe had coached at their schools longer than Swinney.

Johnson alerted Swinney to all the new faces in the room.

"He said, 'There's only two guys in here who were even here when I got the job. I hardly know anybody here anymore,'" Swinney recalled. "It's a scary, humbling thing when you look at it from that perspective. It's a volatile business."

Social media outlets are microphones for malcontents. They amplify their gripes and magnify their conceived crises. If those same outlets were available in 1992, Beamer may not have coached a seventh season at Virginia Tech. Through his first six seasons in Blacksburg, Beamer compiled a record of 24–40–2. Through his next 19 seasons, Beamer went 185–58.

"Frank Beamer never would have survived at Virginia Tech if he had been hired in 2000 or 2005," said David Teel, a sports columnist for the *Daily Press* in Newport News, Virginia, who has covered college athletics for more than 30 years. "It just never would have happened, just because nobody has any patience anymore with coaches and allowing them to develop a program."

Clemson offensive line coach Robbie Caldwell said, amid faceless, unfounded Internet gossip and widespread fixation on winning, the true purpose of college football has been diminished. "What we do is entertainment. Let's face it," Caldwell said. "To us, it's not. It's coaching, because we're trying to build young men and make productive citizens. But people don't want that crap anymore. That doesn't mean anything to them. That's what this game is supposed to be about, but now it's just about winning. They pay more money, so the risk is greater. You can get fired in a heartbeat. Loyalty now, it's hard to find it running both ways anymore."

"When there's more money involved, people expect results quicker," Beamer said. "This is a business sometimes where you're depending on kids maturing, and it may not happen right now. The administrations that understand that are probably the ones that are ahead of the game."

Job security is a luxury few coaches enjoy. Yet, after 26 years, 216 wins, and six Coastal division titles, if fans can heat the seat under Beamer, who is beyond reproach?

"Every season, you have the same type of pressure and expectations," Swinney said. "I know how quick you can go from being in the so-called penthouse to being in the so-called outhouse."

Swinney cited the drastic decline he and Clemson experienced from the ACC Atlantic Division championship in 2009 to the disappointing losing season in 2010. Swinney reconfigured his staff, reinforced his vision, and reaffirmed the trust of then–athletic director Terry Don Phillips. Clemson won 10 games in each of the next four seasons.

"You've got to be patient. A lot of times, people aren't patient anymore. It's two years, three years, and you're gone," Swinney said. "That is really a shame. There's a lot of potentially great coaches who don't get to come into fruition. There are a lot of past great coaches who would have never happened if that had been the mentality."

Tolerant observers can forgive a stumble. Yet even Swinney could not deny the fires blazing under the seats of some of his conference colleagues that day. The flames burning under Beamer's chair spread to the other side of the state where Mike London's reputation as a national championship coach on the FCS level was being incinerated by criticism of his 23–38 record at the University of Virginia. The flames spread to Dave Clawson, who earned a 3–9 record in his first season at Wake Forest. The flames spread to Al Golden, who, after four seasons, was still struggling to pull Miami out of its disciplinary ditch.

According to Mark Richt, who compiled 132 wins in his first 14 seasons at Georgia, the burners remain lit for even the most successful and seasoned coaches. "It's just the nature of the beast in the profession. If you can't take criticism, then you shouldn't coach," Richt said. "Anybody who's in a leadership role is going to get critiqued. Even as a parent, if you say, 'You've got to be in at 11:00,' and everybody else gets to stay out until midnight, you might get criticized for that."

Most coaches can handle the heat as long as it is not ignited inside their own building. A supportive athletic director who will dedicate time and resources to the program can insulate coaches.

"As someone who is making the decision on the coach, you have to have some football knowledge realistically," Swinney said. "'Where is this program? What can I do to equip this person and help him?'"

Athletic directors face their own pressures, though, with rising costs of scholarships, facilities, and operations. Exorbitant ticket prices and booster club donations are pitched to fans as investments for their favorite programs. Thus, some investors feel entitled to a competitive team. When a coach's record dismays the fan base, ticket sales and donations decline. Patience becomes more expensive. Administrators may not be able to afford grace periods.

"They're just going to look at the bottom line year in, year out. What we have to do as coaches is peel off those layers and look at those things that mean the most in creating a program we can be proud of," said Scott Shafer, who then was the head coach at Syracuse. Shafer faced heat before graduating his first recruiting class. He led Syracuse to a 7–6 record in 2013, his first season at the helm. It was the Orange's third winning season since 2002, but it did not alleviate the anguish of the 3–9 record Syracuse endured in 2014.

"At the end of the day, as coaches, we are judged on wins and losses," Swinney said, "and you know that."

An unfavorable record can overpower an exceptional graduation rate, a flawless disciplinary record, or even consideration for the condition of the program when the coach arrived.

"The goal as a leader is to do what you think is in the best interest of the people that you're in charge of," Richt said, "the people that you're blessed to be in authority over, and focus on that."

The process to build a solid program, at least one with integrity, has not changed since Beamer arrived at Virginia Tech in 1987. It cannot be microwaved to meet the demands of impatient, conditional devotees.

"Some places out there, their expectations are unrealistic. It takes time to get your culture built. It takes time to figure the landscape out," Swinney said. "All of a sudden, now you look up and it's been three years and you feel like, 'Man, I'm making progress.' But other people are like, 'We're not where we need to be.' That's a shame that it's the way it is, but that's the world we live in."

Swinney was blessed to start his head coaching career with an athletic director as strong and sharp as Phillips. He played football at Arkansas and served as an assistant coach at Virginia Tech from 1971 to 1978 before venturing into administration. He understood the importance of patience, and he had the fortitude to withstand criticism and cover his coaches. Swinney was blessed again when, upon Phillips' retirement, Clemson searched for a replacement who was equally strong and sharp.

Dan Radakovich played tight end at the Indiana University of Pennsylvania. He served as an associate athletic director at Long Beach State University, the University of South Carolina, and Louisiana State University before becoming Georgia Tech's athletic director in 2006. Radakovich guided Georgia Tech to stability. He supported his beleaguered coach Paul Johnson after lean years. He spearheaded the transformation of Tech's facilities.

He arrived at Clemson in 2012 with that same focus on optimizing revenue, upgrading facilities, and enhancing the fan experience. He took the torch from Phillips and then built a new sconce to hang it on. Sustaining a competitive athletic department requires money, and Radakovich devised methods to direct new revenue streams to Clemson. And he did not mind spending those funds. Prudently.

In 2014 Radakovich, his staff, and the Clemson Board of Trustees agreed to make Swinney the Tigers' longest tenured head coach since Frank Howard. Swinney signed an eight-year, $27.15 million contract. Swinney earned $3.15 million the first year of the contract and was set to earn $3.3 million in 2015, excluding specified performance increases and incentives. That made Swinney the second-highest paid coach at an ACC public school, behind Florida State's Jimbo Fisher, who signed a contract extension that promised $4.02 million per year five days before leading the Seminoles to the 2013 national championship.

Swinney believed Clemson could affirm his contract the same way that season. He had already developed the mantra for that season, while on vacation. He was sitting on a beach and was suddenly reminded of the ESPN documentary series *30 for 30*. Its logo is an old admission ticket, the kind now used commonly for raffles. The wheels of wit began to churn in Swinney's mind. He drew a parallel. It was 2015. Clemson could win its 15th ACC title. And it could be the first team to notch a 15–0 record and win the national championship. Swinney had shirts printed up for the team. On the front, they read, "Dream the Dream." On the back, they read, "15 for 15."

"You've got to lay the vision out there," Swinney said. "August 3rd, I came in and I kind of put a bunch of numbers on the board, and I kind of talked about what each one of them represented. 'It's 2015. Right now, we've sold every ticket, but there's only 12, and we want to make them print 15 tickets. You know, there's nothing wrong with winning them all, guys.'

"We started talking about the mentality of what it was going to take and just kind of laying the roadmap out there. These guys embraced that. It wasn't necessarily about being 15–0, it was about being the best that we could be. Ohio State wasn't 15–0, but they won the national championship. But you can't win 12 until you win six, you can't win 12 until you win seven, and just kind of that weekly focus that we went about our business with. You have to be able to articulate it and lay a plan out there."

The possibility of being the first 15–0 team emerged from the advent of the College Football Playoff. Florida State's title was the final installment of the Bowl Championship Series. The NCAA adopted a four-team bracket to crown the national champion. The 13-member committee selects the four teams at the end of the conference championship weekend. There were no stipulations on conference representation or any rigid criteria for qualification. And with five major conferences and four slots, one league will be left forlorn each year. It was an intense game of musical chairs, and some ACC coaches worried that the unfavorable perception of the league would leave it standing without a seat when the music stopped.

Swinney, now a senior member among ACC coaches, rejected that trepidation. During the league spring meetings before the 2014 season, Swinney challenged his conference colleagues to change that public perception, by changing their own attitudes.

"Any of you who don't think this league is going to be a prominent part of the playoff, you need to take a look in the mirror," Swinney told them. "If you play the right people and you develop your program enough to win enough of the right games, there's no reason we shouldn't be in the playoff every year."

"We were always complaining about this, and I was like, 'Let's shut our mouths and go play,'" Swinney said. "We're good enough to win, but we've got to change our mindset a little bit. If we don't like it, let's do something about it."

Swinney did not run from expectations. He did not mind that Clemson was selected as the favorite to win the 2015 ACC championship. Swinney wanted his team to embrace that goal and enjoy that journey. He wanted them to dream even bigger and relish that ride. Clemson had the fuel to reach that destination. Quarterback

Deshaun Watson was healthy. So was fifth-year receiver Char-one Peake. Receiver Mike Williams and tight end Jordan Leggett were positioned to emerge in their junior seasons. Artavis Scott augmented that receiver corps along with highly touted freshmen and Tampa natives Deon Cain and Ray-Ray McCloud. Newly promoted offensive coordinators Tony Elliott and Jeff Scott were comfortable in their new roles. The offensive line added five-star freshman Mitch Hyatt and returned its anchor, their fierce, fun-loving, bearded leader, Eric Mac Lain.

He eventually became known as "Mr. Clemson," but Mac Lain grew up loving a very different shade of orange. Mac Lain's mother graduated from the University of Tennessee. The family lived in Knoxville for 10 years. Mac Lain also grew up rooting for a different set of Tigers. Mac Lain's father earned a master's degree from Auburn. His grandmother and several other relatives were alumni of Alabama. He inherited a Southeastern Conference bias.

"I was in SEC country. Growing up I was going to one of those three schools. That's the only football I thought existed for so long," Mac Lain said. "The first time I met Dabo, I didn't know what Clemson was, where it was, who he was."

Mac Lain met Swinney when he and his family visited during a spring practice session. The Mac Lains were on the tail end of a tour of SEC schools. They stopped by Clemson to see defensive line coach Dan Brooks, whom the family befriended during Brooks' 15-year tenure at Tennessee.

"We were just really coming to see him. Had no interest in the school at all," said Mac Lain, whose interest and bias completely changed once he arrived on campus and was introduced to Swinney. "I fell in love, man, the first time I heard him speak and the amount of passion and power in his voice," Mac Lain said. "I knew that he was a guy I wanted to play for and honestly a guy I'd do anything for. Then just to learn about his faith and his beliefs and how much he loves his family and all that stuff. I went to all those

SEC schools, up to Penn State, and over to Ohio State. I saw all these great things, but, man, when we made that pit stop in Clemson, it was so different on the feeling, the players, the culture. I think I'm a pretty good judge of character, and I know when people are bullshitting and when they are being real. I knew this wasn't fake. It was so real and passionate. I knew this was it."

Mac Lain had no trouble breaking his parents' SEC bias either. They witnessed the same things he witnessed and felt the same things he felt.

"Being a military guy, my dad knew right away that this place was super special," Mac Lain said, referring to his father's service in the Air Force. "And that's before we even knew much about Clemson. As we learned more, it was confirmed every single day of my attending Clemson. There's just something different about this place."

Mac Lain also recognized there was something different about that 2015 Clemson squad. He arrived at Clemson in 2011 from Jack Britt High School in Fayetteville, North Carolina—as a tight end. Mac Lain slid down the line to guard in 2012. He ascended to the starting position and to the chair of the Beard Gang, the nickname the offensive linemen earned for the Grizzly Adams–level facial hair they sported.

Mac Lain experienced Clemson's progression through the previous four seasons. He recognized the maturation of a program on the brink of greatness.

"It was just knowing that we could be special, if we came together as a team and really believed in it," Mac Lain said. "We had the talent. We had dudes who bought in, who knew something was different. We just needed to take that final step of believing in ourselves and not getting caught up in a name that was right across from us."

While confidence swelled inside the locker room, outside of the program, a cloud of doubt hovered over the defense. From where junior safety Jayron Kearse stood and from what he understood, the questions he fielded during August camp were outlandish. Kearse was one of three starters returning to the defense. The unit closed the previous season ranked first in the FBS in total defense. Then it lost its entire starting front line and six of its top eight tacklers. Nevertheless, Kearse asserted that no one should have doubted Clemson's ability to remain the nation's top stoppers.

"They ain't ask nobody else these questions," Kearse, a Fort Myers, Florida native, said. "They lose great players, they don't get asked these types of questions. It's just the territory, I guess. We're in the [Atlantic Coast Conference]. We're Clemson. I guess we can't be as good as those guys."

Kearse contended that the doubt revealed the fallacy of citing returning starters as the only measurement of proven prowess. For instance, after the departure of All-American Vic Beasley, junior Shaq Lawson was promoted to a defensive end starting slot. Lawson logged 295 snaps the previous season, 262 fewer than Beasley. Yet Lawson tallied 44 total tackles, seven more than Beasley.

"[Lawson] had got one career start, and you know what's great about that?" coach Dabo Swinney asked. "Nobody cares."

Swinney suggested that starts simply are a formality in Clemson's system. They are not always a distinction of vast superiority. Swinney encouraged his staff to develop experience through its substitution strategy. Coaches rotated qualified players to generate reliable depth at each position.

"I've always had the philosophy of, 'Play everybody who deserves to play,'" Swinney said. "We have to do a great job early on in getting some experience for some guys. You're only going to get any experience if you go play. You have to be able to see yourself on tape in practice reps, and certainly game reps."

Clemson's substitutions would be less frequent and more noticeable in 2015. There was more separation between starters and backups. Thus, there was less equity in playing time. Swinney said, in the previous season, Clemson "had a bunch of 50-50 guys. You just rolled. We were very fortunate with that."

Swinney said that, in 2015, Clemson had "some 90-10, some 80-20, some 70-30. But it's very important for the morale of our team, for the development of our program, for the development of that player, that they get those reps."

Talent was not Clemson's problem. Clemson perennially reloads speed and size on defense through its recruiting classes. That was clearly evident from observing the blurs sprinting downfield at their first camp practice. Clemson simply needed to grow those guys up.

At that time, the doubt lingered. It perplexed Kearse in August, but it did not bother him. From where he stood and from what he understood, that doubt would be answered once the season kicked off.

Clemson opened 2015 ranked No. 12 in the Coaches Poll. It opened the season against Football Championship Subdivision foe Wofford. Watson conducted an 11-play, 75-yard drive on Clemson's opening possession. He tossed a four-yard touchdown to Mike Williams, who clutched the ball as he collided with the large padding around the base of the goal posts. Williams writhed in pain and rolled to his back. He eventually was carted off the field. After tests, Williams learned that he fractured the C6 vertebrae in his neck. He would miss the remainder of the season. It was a scary moment, then a debilitating blow for Williams, who was projected as a top NFL Draft prospect. He was also positioned to be Watson's top target, as evidenced on the two receptions Williams snagged on the opening drive. Clemson regrouped and closed the game with 533 yards of total offense and a 49–10 victory.

Clemson's defense stymied Wofford's triple-option. Critics considered the caliber of the competition and were not yet convinced, but speed is speed, and strength is strength. No one could discredit the performance of senior linebacker B.J. Goodson, who was the latest product of a tiny football factory in the South Carolina Pee Dee region.

Levon Kirkland knew he would not be the last, because he is certain he should not have been the first. As a 6'1", 205-pound wide receiver, tight end, linebacker, and kick returner, Kirkland impressed spectators through his high school career in Lamar, South Carolina. Unfortunately, the crowds rarely included college scouts.

In 1987 Lamar's population was estimated at less than 1,400. There were no national football recruiting services to uncover talent in tiny towns. There were no summer combines and exposure camps that allowed players to audition for college coaches. There were no video websites to document every game highlight. Kirkland could do little to intensify interest. He simply continued to impress. Finally, during one of Lamar's playoff games, a college scout joined the crowd. Kirkland earned a scholarship from Clemson and opened a new road from Lamar to the National Football League.

Nearly three decades later, Goodson was driven to follow that same road—guided by the standards set before him and fueled by the dignity, respect, and support of his small town. Always proud of where he comes from, Goodson is never content with where he is.

Like Kirkland, Goodson was lightly recruited out of Lamar High. Like Kirkland, Goodson seized an opportunity to become one of Clemson's most reliable linebackers and most dependable leaders. And like Kirkland, Goodson aimed to represent Lamar in the NFL.

Kirkland garnered All-America honors in his final two seasons at Clemson. The Pittsburgh Steelers selected Kirkland in the second round of the 1992 NFL Draft. He played nine seasons in Pittsburgh and earned All-Pro recognition in 1996 and 1997. In 2015 he served as an assistant coach with the Arizona Cardinals.

"I might have been three years old, but Levon Kirkland was the first football player I had ever heard of by name. To have him represent our town was big," said Goodson, who seeks advice from Kirkland whenever their busy schedules allow them to communicate.

Goodson would be the fourth Lamar native to follow Kirkland to the NFL. John Abraham starred on the defensive line at the University of South Carolina before the New York Jets drafted him 13th overall in 2000. He played 15 seasons, including seven with the Atlanta Falcons. He was named to five Pro Bowls.

Michael Hamlin was an All-ACC safety in his final two seasons at Clemson. He was selected in the fifth round by the Dallas Cowboys in 2009. He played three NFL seasons. He returned to Clemson to serve briefly on Swinney's staff. In 2015 he was a special-teams quality control coach with the Buffalo Bills.

Former South Carolina State linebacker Marshall McFadden earned a free-agent contract with the Steelers in 2012. Through the previous 25 years, Lamar produced more NFL players than traditional state power Gaffney High, whose enrollment is more than twice Lamar's entire population.

"That was one of my goals and dreams to see our small town become somewhat known for football players," Kirkland said. "Sometimes once one person does it, other people follow."

Kirkland contended that several other Lamar natives could have preceded him on this path. Many of them had the talent but never had the chance to showcase it. "I have brothers who should've went to college and played ball. I had cousins that probably should've went to college," Kirkland said. "Maybe it was just from a lack of things to do in Lamar, so most kids just played sports from a young age. We just had a lot of good athletes then, but just not a whole lot of opportunity."

Twenty-five years ago, opportunity often bypassed small towns like Lamar. Business owners, tourists, and coaches rarely took that exit off Interstate 20. According to B.J.'s mother, Deirdre Goodson, Lamar still is easy to bypass. "We have one traffic light, one grocery store, one bank," she said with a laugh. "It's such a small town. Everybody knows everybody, but everybody just looks out for everybody. It definitely reminds me of a little village."

In 2010, Goodson's senior year at Lamar High, the town's population was estimated at less than 1,000. There were national football recruiting services that rated Goodson against linebackers from larger schools. There were summer combines and exposure camps through which Goodson could audition. There were video websites available to document the 156 tackles he amassed. Nevertheless, recruiters did not speed to Darlington County. Scholarship offers trickled in from Clemson, Tennessee, and LSU.

"There were some that doubted him, doubted his ability to play and compete at a Division I school," Deirdre Goodson said. "I just felt like if he was given the opportunity and the chance to show his ability, his talent, his gifts from God, everybody would see the real B.J."

Goodson needed four years to climb Clemson's depth chart. He redshirted his first season on campus. He battled nagging injuries through his next two years and played infrequently behind standout starters Tig Willard and Stephone Anthony. Goodson started six games in 2014 but split the outside linebacker–nickelback role with Korrin Wiggins.

"Through all that adversity, he just kept his faith," Deirdre Goodson said. "He was determined to keep working hard and keep plugging in there, because his time was coming."

In Lamar, Goodson grew accustomed to toiling tirelessly in obscurity. He was conditioned to accept hard work but never to accept defeat. He would not be diverted off that road. "Most guys who come up in that area have worked hard at some point in time. They're doing either farming work or they're doing some kind of manual labor just to earn some bucks," Kirkland said. "We're not afraid of that. I've been to some high schools where football is probably the hardest thing kids have ever done. Whereas in Lamar, football is not hard at all. Because you work hard, when you actually get on the field, it's more of a release."

Teammates observed Goodson's cathartic transformations on gameday. "All through the week, he's quiet, just an old country dude," fellow linebacker Ben Boulware said. "He's a totally different animal on the field. He's a completely different person, outspoken, just a leader. He just flips a switch. You need that to play at a high level."

Through persistence and diligence, Goodson claimed the starting role at middle linebacker in 2015. He led Clemson with 29 tackles through the first three games, including 12 in the opener against Wofford and 12 in the Week 3 win at Louisville.

"A big part of college is just figuring life out," Swinney said of Goodson. "He is a grown man. He's ready for whatever he wants to do in life. He is just mature and focused and driven and committed."

Goodson asserted that those adjectives could describe most folks in Lamar. It is a culture of encouragement, a haven for hard work. It is a village that does not need many stoplights, because its people are too driven to slow down.

"I remember asking B.J., 'When you're out there on the field, what are you feeling? What gets you fired up?'" Deirdre Goodson recalled. "He said, 'Ma, I think about this little town where I come from. I think about my family here.' That just pushes him to go all out."

Goodson helped Clemson survive a slugfest with Louisville on September 17. With boxing legend Muhammad Ali back in attendance in his hometown, Clemson and Louisville exchanged blows in a scoreless first quarter. Clemson broke the tussle with a five-play, 61-yard drive. Watson tossed a 32-yard touchdown to freshman Hunter Renfrow. Louisville captured the lead at 10–7 on its first possession of the second half, a 58-yard scoring drive capped by Jeremy Smith's one-yard touchdown plunge. Clemson responded with Greg Huegel's 36-yard field goal. The Tigers reclaimed the lead with 2:37 remaining in the third quarter, as Watson delivered a 25-yard touchdown pass to Leggett. Clemson added an insurance field goal and withstood the ensuing 100-yard kickoff return touchdown Louisville produced.

Running back Wayne Gallman helped Clemson grind out the fourth quarter and seal the 20–17 victory. He ran violently, relentlessly, and effectively. He amassed 139 yards on 24 carries. He landed punches with the stunning power of an Ali cross. He slipped through tight holes with the speed of the Ali shuffle. He emerged as the lone heavyweight in Clemson's crowded backfield. He had the tools to become Clemson's first 1,000-yard rusher since 2013. As long as Clemson let the young man rumble.

# 12

## BYOG

EVEN DABO SWINNEY struggled to secure additional tickets for Clemson's game against Notre Dame. Regardless of who asked for them.

"I couldn't get Jesus tickets," Swinney said with a grin.

Yet that did not stop those on this side of Heaven from inquiring.

"I've got people calling me I hadn't talked to in 20 years," Swinney said. "'Hey, man, got some tickets? I really want to come up this weekend. Just need...five.'"

As of noon Wednesday, September 30, 2015, three days before the game, 1,747 tickets remained available on StubHub.com, the official secondary marketplace for Clemson athletics. They ranged from $189 to $1,450 each. According to another secondary ticket marketplace, SeatGeek.com, the average resale price for a Clemson–Notre Dame ticket was $320. That was $41 more than the previous record average resale price for a Clemson home game, set in the 2013 season opener against Georgia.

Unlike many other college programs, Clemson does not cap prices for tickets sold through its StubHub partnership. South Carolina state law permits reselling tickets above face value online. The open market produced exorbitant hikes for Notre Dame's visit to Death Valley. Face value for top-deck tickets was $85. Thus, the lowest StubHub markup for the top deck was 223 percent. The highest was 489 percent for a pair of tickets in the adjacent section offered at $416 each. Four seats on the lower level near the 50-yard line behind the Clemson sideline were offered at $1,200 each. Tickets in the same section for the next game against Georgia Tech were listed at $236 each.

According to SeatGeek, the Clemson–Notre Dame game would become the most expensive event held in South Carolina since 2010, topping performances from The Eagles and Jimmy Buffet. Even in the nosebleed sections, the five tickets Swinney's prodigal phone buddies sought would cost more than a grand.

Notre Dame had not visited Clemson since 1977, when Dan Devine was the coach and Joe Montana was the quarterback. Notre Dame won that game 21–17 and proceeded to the national championship. Clemson avenged that loss in South Bend two years later. Considering Notre Dame's national scheduling conventions already included annual clashes with major conference foes USC, Stanford, Michigan State, and Purdue, there was no impetus to renew the series with Clemson. Until 2013, when Notre Dame joined the ACC, in every sport except football. Notre Dame retained its football independence, to retain its individual media rights, but it agreed to play five games each season against ACC teams. Clemson's first turn on that roulette hit in 2015. Clemson and Notre Dame are scheduled to meet again in 2020, 2022, and 2023.

The rare matchup drew national acclaim. Notre Dame was ranked No. 6 in the Coaches Poll. Clemson was No. 12. ESPN's popular pregame analysis show *College GameDay* selected this game as its featured broadcast destination. Clemson had an opportunity to showcase its championship mettle to the entire country. The torrential downpour in the forecast could not dull the electricity.

"They're Notre Dame. Are you kidding me? This is the winningest program in the history of college football," Swinney said. "Hopefully, 50 years from now some other old boy will be standing here, and hopefully, they'll be asking that other coach what's it like to play a storied program like Clemson University. That's what I hope. But it's pretty obvious in this case. They've won 11 national championships, and they're Notre Dame."

To materialize that 50-year dream, Clemson had to start with this opportunity to peel a little shine off the Irish. The Tigers were counting on another intimidating crowd in Death Valley. But the steady rain that drenched the campus stirred uncertainty about the anticipated attendance. By kickoff time, the field was a soggy bog. And the stadium was overflowing with fans. Clemson is not a fair-weather fan base. Faithful Tigers stuffed the stands in slickers, ponchos, and hoodies. The rain continued to pour over their heads, but it never dampened their spirits. A well-timed image captured Notre Dame coach Brian Kelly just before his team entered the field. As he looked out over the crowd, his eyes stretched to the size of baseballs. That was not the most startling thing he saw that night.

Watson was not bothered by the rain. He tossed two touchdowns in the first half, and Clemson led 14–3 at halftime. On the opening kickoff of the second half, Clemson place-kicker Ammon Lakip, who was suspended for the first three games of the season, drilled Notre Dame returner C.J. Sanders and jarred the ball loose. Clemson backup running back C.J. Fuller recovered the ball at the Notre Dame 29-yard line. Three plays later, Watson lifted Clemson to a 21–3 lead with a 21-yard touchdown scamper.

Clemson's defense surrendered 212 yards through the first three quarters. Notre Dame advanced past the Clemson 40-yard line only once. Fighting Irish cornerback Cole Luke intercepted Watson in the end zone late in the quarter. Notre Dame capitalized on the turnover with a 56-yard touchdown sprint from running back C.J. Prosise. Clemson responded with a 35-yard field goal from Greg Huegel, but Notre Dame trimmed the margin to 24–16 on the next possession. Quarterback Deshone Kizer completed a 33-yard pass to Chris Brown that advanced the ball to the 12-yard line. Kizer rushed twice to reach the end zone.

Clemson did not record another first down. Notre Dame outgained the Tigers 225–64 in the fourth quarter. The defense salvaged the lead by refusing to concede. Goodson intercepted Kizer on the opening play of Notre Dame's next possession. On their next drive, the Irish marched 68 yards to the 12. Two plays later, Kizer connected again with Chris Brown, who darted inside the 5-yard line. As Brown was entangled by three Clemson defenders, safety Jayron Kearse slapped the ball from Brown's hands. Goodson recovered the fumble. Clemson's offensive futility granted Notre Dame one more chance. Defensive end Kevin Dodd sacked Kizer on the first snap and recovered his own fumble. Kizer settled and completed three of his next four passes, including a one-yard touchdown to Torii Hunter Jr. with seven seconds remaining.

Trailing 24–22, Notre Dame lined up to attempt a two-point conversion. Kizer collected the snap from the shotgun and darted immediately to his right with Prosise as his lead blocker. Linebacker Ben Boulware crashed into Prosise and pushed him back into Kizer. Defensive tackle Carlos Watkins kept the center and the guard off his chest and escorted them down the line of scrimmage like they were on water skis gliding across the rain-drenched turf. The rushing lane quickly clogged. Notre Dame linemen dropped as Boulware attacked, and Watkins corralled Kizer at the 2.

Death Valley erupted. Clemson incurred a 15-yard unsportsmanlike conduct penalty for the celebration, but it was irrelevant. Zac Brooks recovered the ensuing onside kick. Watson took a knee and exhausted the clock. The Tigers celebrated a signature win in a defining moment for the team and the fan base.

"Rain, sleet, or snow, Tiger Nation, they show," an exuberant Dabo Swinney said on the field.

A throng of ecstatic fans crowded Swinney as he attempted to conduct the postgame interview with ESPN reporter Heather Cox. Swinney shouted through the congested commotion. "Man I'm so proud of our team," Swinney said. "It ain't always perfect. But what I told them tonight was, 'Listen, we give you scholarships. We give you stipends, meals, and a place to live. We give you nice uniforms.'" Swinney's voice continued to rise as the litany continued.

"'I can't give you guts. I can't give you heart.' Tonight, hey, it was BYOG—Bring Your Own Guts! And they brought some guts and some heart, and they never quit."

At the time, Swinney had no idea what he had done. He was simply speaking passionately from the moment, from his heart, as he has always done. He proceeded to thank "the Good Lord" and his father, Ervil, whom Swinney believed were both watching over him that night. He then proceeded into the locker room to celebrate with his team. Before he reached the podium for his meeting with the media, both videos of his postgame speech and his locker room dance session were circulating social media. But Swinney was not done producing viral content for the evening.

"I don't know who Aaron Taylor is, but I guess he's an analyst or a commentator," Swinney said. "The comment was that Clemson wouldn't be ready and the word was our crowd was going to be *lugubrious* when the game was over."

Swinney referred to Taylor, a former Notre Dame lineman, who served as an analyst for CBS Sports Network. On the *Inside College Football* show prior to the game, after the rest of his fellow panelists picked Notre Dame to win, Taylor offered his projection. "I think this is going to be the game that elevates the Irish to the national championship that they're going to go on, I believe," Taylor said, "and is going to make Clemson fans very lugubrious."

Swinney did not watch the show, but the word got back to him.

"Jayron Kearse sent me a text message. He was hot," Swinney recalled. "We do a 'Video of the Day' every day, and it can be anything from prison rodeo to crazy people at Walmart to something inspirational to motivational to the best dunks in the NBA. I mean it can be anything. It doesn't really matter. Then I tried to figure out some way to pull something that I can use to set the tempo for the day. He sent me a text saying 'Coach, I want this to be the Video of the Day. I want the guys to see this.' I clicked on it, and I got a good laugh out of it, because it was all the experts with all their opinions. I just laugh at that stuff. The team got a kick out of it, but the funniest part to me was the guy who said we'd be *lugubrious*. I had never heard that in my life, no clue what that meant. I promised the guys that if I had the opportunity that I'd somehow find a way to use that in my postgame vocabulary."

Swinney emphatically kept his promise.

"I'm hooked on phonics. I just sound it out, *lugubrious*, but I did look it up!" Swinney said. "And *lugubrious* means to look sad and disappointed. And so I want to wish Notre Dame and their lugubrious crowd safe travels to South Bend. I appreciate the vocab lesson."

Swinney optimizes opportunities to develop solidarity in his players. Crafting the "Clemson versus Everybody" narrative promotes pride. Clemson plays best when their efforts are seasoned with a little saltiness.

"I used to always say that we didn't listen to the media, but I was so locked in on everything," lineman Eric Mac Lain said. "To a healthy standpoint, to just know what people are saying, what the narrative is on Clemson. Absolutely, I was very knowledgeable about what was said about us as players and used it as fuel to the fire. Complacency is the biggest killer of programs. There were sometimes when he had to get creative, that 2015 season, when we were ranked No. 1. But I think we had a lot of good leadership and a lot of good seniors, guys who had been in for four to five years. We kind of naturally handled it, but there were definitely some weeks when we were playing Wake Forest or some mid-major school where Coach had to kind of pull some stuff out of his tail."

Through the previous two seasons, Clemson faced five teams ranked in the top 10 of the Coaches Poll. Clemson lost those games by a combined score of 178–75. Clemson's encounters with the elite seemed to stir nothing but disappointment, delusion, and doubt. But after stuffing that two-point conversion, Clemson began to turn those disappointments into dominance, the delusion into definition and the doubt into defiance. The Tigers did not simply impede.

They attacked. They did not simply cover. They smothered. They did not simply regroup. They responded.

Behind the leadership of Goodson, Watkins, Boulware, Kearse, and cornerback Mackensie Alexander, Clemson adopted the attitude of a team that is no longer content with staring through the window of the elite clubhouse. They were ready to kick the door in.

The next morning, Chris Bandy's phone would not stop buzzing. He knew then that BYOG was not just another Dabo Swinney catchphrase. It was a slogan. Bandy is co-owner of Tigertown Graphics, a design and printing company with a storefront in downtown Clemson. After Swinney's postgame speech went viral, fans bombarded the company's phone lines, inbox, and social media feeds asking about BYOG apparel.

"You get the reaction from the fan base on whether something is worth printing," Bandy said. "By Sunday morning, the demand was through the roof."

Tigertown Graphics has longstanding licensing agreements with Clemson and Swinney that permit them to sell merchandise featuring the university's trademarked paw logo. Before Tigertown Graphics offered BYOG shirts to the public, Bandy contacted Swinney to ensure he approved the use of the slogan. Once consent was granted, Tigertown Graphics added the design to the website.

Bandy estimated that through the first six weeks it was offered, Tigertown Graphics sold nearly 15,000 BYOG T-shirts. Six days after Swinney's remarks, upon the suggestion of his agent, Swinney's company, Katbo, LLC, submitted applications to register trademarks for "BYOG" and "Bring Your Own Guts."

"It was just one of those things that kind of took off," Swinney said.

The Clemson football brand was enhanced in 2015 as the Tigers climbed up the national polls and appeared more frequently on prime-time television broadcasts, magazines covers, and nationally syndicated radio shows.

"I try to represent Clemson and build our brand, that's been a goal from day one. I think we have built our paw, that brand, nationwide," said Swinney, who recognized that his personal brand was a lot more valuable in 2015 than it was five years earlier. No one was interested in printing his phrases when Clemson had a 6–7 record. "I guess we've got a good team, so it's like E.F. Hutton, when you say something, all of a sudden it's a bigger deal," Swinney said. "I had a lot of good things in 2010, and nobody would listen. Y'all missed some good stuff in 2010."

Like many Clemson fans, Allison Van't Hof watched the Notre Dame game from the comfort of her couch. She jumped off that couch after the Tigers' sealed the victory, and she jumped even higher when she heard Swinney's BYOG speech. Van't Hof knew the phrase would catch.

"I said, 'Oh, my gosh, I bring my own guts every day,'" recalled Van't Hof, who lives in California. "BYOG, it kind of became my mantra the rest of the night. I was just like, 'I hope somebody is doing something with this.'"

Van't Hof did not know then that she would be that somebody. She owns and operates Out of the Box Promotional Marketing. Through a chance encounter with Swinney's agent, Mike Brown, and an impromptu business proposal, Van't Hof partnered with Swinney and developed BYOG into more than a catchphrase, more than a trademark. She developed BYOG into a full-fledged brand and clothing line. The four-letter mantra is emblazoned on hats, shirts, sweaters, and other items.

A portion of the proceeds from sales are allocated to Dabo's All In Team Foundation, which supports breast cancer awareness and educational initiatives. "BYOG, it's a way of life. That's the brand messaging Clemson has taken on through Coach Swinney's impassioned directive," said Van't Hof, who grew up in Belmont, North Carolina, before venturing west to attend Pepperdine University. "I work with clients all over the world," she said, "but this has reignited my southern roots. Working with everybody around Clemson, I feel like the luckiest girl in the world.

"I have met so many people and have heard so many stories about their trials, tribulations, and triumphs. It's inspiring," she said. "Whether it's blocking the offense in an impassioned game or doing what you have to do tomorrow to pay your bills, you 'Bring Your Own Guts' in every move you make."

# 13

## PIZZA PARTY

GAMEDAYS IN DEATH VALLEY are spectacles of fanfare under-scored by tradition. Fans in deep philosophical conversation will halt mid-sentence to join the cadence count chant. The band blares its lively fight song with the final notes accompanied by a choir of 82,000. There is cannon fire. A sky full of balloons. Reverence to a rock. A run down a hill. An array of smartphone flashlights that give those gray stands a charming glow. Clemson's devotion to vigor can transform something peculiar into something remarkable.

Its latest gameday tradition aimed to augment that energy and enhance the entertainment value of each ticket. With attendance figures declining and the television experience improving, Clemson sought to entice fans with features a camera cannot capture. So it put the needle to the groove. After working a few shows in downtown Clemson two years earlier, Donsha Butler earned an invitation from Swinney to attend a recruiting event. As D.J. Sha.

"He loved it. He said he was going to get me out at some of the practices," Butler recalled. "At that time, I thought it was just him caught up in the moment, enjoying himself. But a few weeks later, he kept his word."

Butler began appearing at Clemson's practice fields, and a few months later he was in Memorial Stadium for the 2015 season opener. As Clemson's house disc jockey, he steers the stadium sounds during warmups, breaks in action, and halftime.

He plays popular music, from legends like Run-DMC and Outkast to current chart-toppers like Kendrick Lamar, Justin

Timberlake, and Drake. He even works in original songs he produced solely for Clemson.

"My first vision was that I just wanted my songs played in Death Valley at games," said Butler, a Ninety Six, South Carolina, native who also mixes for an Upstate radio station.

Clemson cleared space for Butler in its game operations booth. He could not be seen from the stands, but a camera transmitted his introductory performance on the screens around the field. "The feedback I received most was from people wondering if he was actually in the stadium," said Mike Money, Clemson's assistant athletic director for marketing and game management. "It was a roaring success. A lot of what he's playing was music that players were requesting to hear in pregame, so it wasn't a sweeping change from what was already being played. He's just the centerpiece now."

Clemson later moved Butler from the suite to a custom booth near the west stands outside the Tigers' locker room. "Right now, we're in an era of trying to do anything to improve the fan experience. Not just at Clemson. That's anywhere across the country," Money said. "Anytime you do something different, there's always going to be some comments to the negative, but overall, it's been a pretty overwhelmingly positive reaction."

Butler was instrumental in getting the Clemson crowd all spun up, especially on third down. And not just in the student section. Gray-haired grandmothers would enthusiastically turn toward the open-air press box to ask the existential question, "Turn down for what?"

Even the most tone-deaf fans would have a tough time arguing with the results...or at least the coincidences. Clemson won its first five games with Butler on the ones and twos. And when something is working, Clemson usually does not mess with it. That is how novelty becomes tradition, how something peculiar becomes something remarkable.

D.J. Sha had Death Valley charged on October 10, as Clemson hosted Georgia Tech. Running back Wayne Gallman netted 115 rushing yards, 44 more than Tech collected as a team. Clemson tallied 11 tackles for loss and sealed a 43–24 victory. Clemson marched on to No. 5 in the poll and appeared to be stepping too highly to be snagged by the notion of a trap game. The program had matured. Its vocabulary should be adjusted accordingly.

*Clemsoning* was a term initially used during Tommy Bowden's tenure as head coach to describe inexplicable losses suffered to presumably inferior opponents, especially following an impressive victory. It fit the 16–13 loss at Duke in 2004 the week after knocking off No. 11 Miami. It fit the 12–7 loss at Wake Forest that prompted Dabo Swinney's appointment as Bowden's replacement. The term stuck with the program through its loss to South Carolina in 2009 after clinching a divisional title. It fit the 31–26 loss to South Florida in 2010. It fit the 37–13 loss at North Carolina State in 2011.

The term eventually was used to pronounce any unfavorable Clemson moment, from typical turnovers and midgame miscues to unflattering fan photos and corny postgame quotes. After Swinney's transformation of the program, critics were forced to create alternate meanings, because the original definition no longer fit. After that embarrassing blunder at N.C. State, Clemson won 31 consecutive games against opponents who were not ranked in the AP or Coaches Polls. That included the drubbing of Georgia Tech.

"I'm sick of it. I don't even know why even bring up the daggum word," Swinney said after the game when asked how Clemson players feel about the term. Swinney's disdain for *Clemsoning* swelled as he continued his three-minute response. "That's all media bullcrap. I'll tell you how [the players] feel about it. They don't like it. It's a lack of respect. It's not doing your homework and paying attention to what reality is."

At that point, Clemson held the second longest active winning streak against unranked FBS teams. Clemson trailed only Alabama, who had defeated 56 consecutive unranked teams since 2007. Each of Clemson's 31 victories in the streak were decided by at least three points. From 2012 to 2015, when facing an unranked team one week after defeating a ranked foe, Clemson defeated the unranked opponent by an average margin of 28 points. The residue of past letdowns still stained Clemson's victory over No. 6 Notre Dame the previous week. Clemson's past disposition provoked concern of a disappointing, relaxed effort against Georgia Tech. Clemson had grown out of that character flaw.

*Clemsoning* is sluggish starts. Against Georgia Tech, Clemson scored on its first two drives and amassed 318 yards through the first half. *Clemsoning* is lazy lapses on defense. Clemson limited Georgia Tech to 10 yards through the first quarter while stalling the Yellow Jackets on four third-down attempts. *Clemsoning* is squandering leads. Even while shuffling in backups, Clemson outgained Georgia Tech 130–88 in the fourth quarter. *Clemsoning* was, from that point on, an archaic term.

Clemson cruised through its next three games against Boston College, Miami, and North Carolina State. Offensive coordinators Tony Elliott and Jeff Scott continued to dispel doubt as the Tigers averaged 49.3 points and 574 yards during that three-game stretch. Conversely, Clemson's defense surrendered an average of 19.3 points and 260 yards. Clemson improved to 8–0 and earned the top spot in the first College Football Playoff rankings.

Swinney was indifferent. He did not host a campus-wide viewing party for the rankings show. He did not lobby for a parade through downtown. Clemson was never ranked higher than No. 17 the previous year. Although Clemson was positioned perfectly to secure one of the four playoff spots by the end of the season, Swinney understood this early distinction assured nothing.

"I don't care, not unless they gone give me an exemption," Swinney said with a laugh. "Maybe that would be a good addition. 'When the first poll comes out, if you're in the top four, you get two mulligans or something.'"

The College Football Playoff selection committee, which included Clemson athletic director Dan Radakovich and former Clemson player Bobby Johnson, could not pardon losses. That initial ranking did not entitle Clemson to a spot in the final bracket. It was simply a deposit. Clemson could pay off the remaining balance with a clean sweep through the remainder of its schedule. The initial designation was not cause for a grand celebration. Yet Swinney revealed plans for one, when the appropriate time arrived.

"The only poll we're excited about is December 6," Swinney said, referring to the release date of the final CFP rankings. "I promise you, we'll have the biggest poll party you've ever seen. We'll open up Death Valley and serve pizza to everybody."

Once again, Swinney spoke passionately and colorfully off the cuff, before he assessed the aftermath. Luckily, Radakovich supported Swinney's impromptu planning. Administrators confidently began coordinating the event with local distributors.

Swinney may have tried to temper the reaction to the No. 1 ranking, but fans certainly savored it. The ovation was even louder than normal when the players appeared at the top of the Hill for the next game against Florida State. The canon fired. The stadium erupted. The Tigers rubbed Howard's Rock and rushed down toward the field. They had upheld that tradition at Memorial Stadium since 1967, but they had never done it like they did that day.

For the first time in its history, Clemson hurried down that hill as the No. 1 team in the nation. As Swinney warned, that honor did not come with a deed. Ownership of that ranking was not guaranteed. It was almost repossessed.

On Florida State's second play from scrimmage, running back Dalvin Cook sprinted for a 75-yard touchdown and sapped the emotion that had poured over Death Valley. All the pregame exuberance was hushed to cautious groans after the Tigers' opening drive ended on the Clemson equivalent of Haley's Comet—a rare overthrown pass from quarterback Deshaun Watson.

That aberration became commonplace through the first half. The offense sputtered. The defense faltered. The distinction Clemson chased since 1981 appeared in jeopardy.

Yet Clemson diluted its faults with grit. The Tigers shook off their mistakes and tightened the lapses in their run defense. They limited Cook to 44 yards in the second half. Florida State did not return to the end zone.

Watson opened the game flawed. He sailed balls over the stretched arms and surprised eyes of wide-open receivers. He squandered a potential touchdown drive with 42 seconds remaining in the half by spiking a ball on third down.

"He didn't play very well in the first half," Swinney said. "It's one thing when you miss three pointers. It's another thing when you miss layups."

Watson closed the game flawlessly. He completed each of his last eight pass attempts. The seventh in that series exhibited his prudence. Two of Watson's passes were batted down at the line of scrimmage in the first half. On third-and-6 in the fourth quarter, Watson loaded for a quick screen, but a Florida State defender jumped in the passing lane. Watson pumped the ball then delivered a delayed strike to Charone Peake, who darted 21 yards for a first down.

Watson surpassed the 100-yard rushing mark for the first time in his career. He reached the milestone on his final attempt, a designed run through the heart of Florida State's defense. It resulted in a nine-yard gain.

"He showed why he's the best quarterback in the country," Swinney said, "with his guts."

Watson took the next snap and kneeled to the ground. Time expired. Clemson ousted Florida State 23–13, sealed the ACC

Atlantic Division championship and preserved their place among playoff contenders. The stadium erupted. Fans jumped over the walls and congregated on the field. Gatorade was poured over Swinney's head. The No. 1 ranking Clemson affirmed and celebrated that day came with no guarantees or special privileges. It certainly did not persuade Florida State to renounce its ACC throne contently.

Clemson was challenged. Past Clemson teams reached such crossroads and either raced toward ruin or idled irresolutely at the intersection. These Tigers disregarded those familiar forks and sped straight ahead down a new road. Paved with resolve. Pointed toward a championship.

While addressing his team in the locker room after the game, Swinney congratulated and thanked Florida State. "They didn't give it up easily," Swinney said. "They've been a great champion. They've represented this league very well. They've represented this league well. They've won the national championship. They've been to the College Football Playoff. They weren't going to give it up easy. But it was our night, and it was our freaking time. You either make it happen or you watch it happen."

Clemson wrapped the ACC regular season schedule with wins against Syracuse and Wake Forest. At 11–0 the Tigers remained No. 1 as they traveled to Columbia to face rival South Carolina. While Clemson soared steadily at maximum altitude, South Carolina neared the end of a rapid nosedive. Swinney certainly could relate to the undesirable ordeal. It was eerily similar to what Clemson endured in 2008.

Steve Spurrier was in his 11th season as Carolina's head coach. He contemplated retirement after the Gamecocks opened the season with a 2–2 record. Carolina struggled to secure those two victories against North Carolina and Central Florida. Spurrier shared his concerns with athletic director Ray Tanner. "I called him up and I said, 'Coach, I'm going to try to get through this season,'" Spurrier said, "but I sensed that this is about it for me."

Spurrier finalized the decision two games later after the Gamecocks suffered a 45–24 loss to LSU on October 10. He called Tanner again. Tanner and USC president Harris Pastides attempted to persuade Spurrier to stay through the end of the season, but Spurrier felt it more prudent to step away immediately. "When something is inevitable, I believe you do it right then," Spurrier said. "You don't wait a week. You don't wait two weeks. 'This has to happen. Let's do it.'"

The timing seemed odd. The announcement seemed abrupt. But the unraveling started long before Spurrier stepped down, when Spurrier sparked a firestorm with six simple words. "Give me two or three more," Spurrier said two days after South Carolina closed the 2014 regular season with a 6–6 record and a loss at Clemson.

Spurrier suffered more than five losses in a season for the first time since 2009. He offered an honest assessment of the remaining shelf-life of his tenure in Columbia. Competitors immediately turned Spurrier's honesty against him on the recruiting trail. Prospects were cautioned against committing to a coach who could depart before their junior year. Defections ensued. Spurrier attempted to quell the damage with desperate recruiting visits. He extended his initial assessment to a "four- or five-year plan."

Yet the firestorm had already burned holes through the Gamecocks' pipelines. The previous November, ESPN had ranked South Carolina's recruiting class No. 8 in the country. By signing day in February, that ranking dropped to No. 21. By July continued concerns and criticisms about his age and investment in the program inflamed Spurrier. He called an impromptu news conference to assert his health and long-term commitment to South Carolina. His defiant rant was merely a temporary remedy. The sluggish start to the season only expedited the inevitable.

"I was sort of a recruiting liability," Spurrier said. "It's hard to recruit when your coach has done it a long time and at a certain age. Recruits want to know that guy is going to be there five or 10 years."

Spurrier was certain that he was the best coach for the job in 2005. He was equally certain that he was not the best coach for the job in 2015. South Carolina named Spurrier's offensive line coach and co–offensive coordinator Shawn Elliott as the interim head coach. Like Swinney in 2008, Elliott had no previous head coaching experience. Elliott may have had the same shot at retaining the job as Swinney had, but he did not inherit the same caliber of talent. Elliott won his first game, an emotional 19–10 victory at home against Vanderbilt. Elliott ran onto the field before the game with his arm stretched above his head, waving one of Spurrier's signature visors in honor of the departed coach.

Despite the way Spurrier left the program and the condition he left it in, Gamecock fans still revered Spurrier for spearheading the most successful period of South Carolina football. He helped an underrated rivalry stretch its reach outside of the state's borders. He galvanized administrators and fundraisers and kickstarted facilities campaigns. He challenged Swinney. The coaches' fiery exchanges among media members belied their respectful relationship, and their classic battles gave Swinney even more incentive to improve.

Under Elliott, Carolina did not win another game that season, which included a 23–22 loss to FCS foe The Citadel. That was the week before Carolina hosted Clemson at Williams-Brice Stadium in Columbia. With a 3–8 record, the Gamecocks had nothing to lose. They threw everything they had left at their rival.

Swinney remembers the previous years when he walked off that worn field at Williams-Brice Stadium and plodded somberly through that dark tunnel to visitor's quarters. Disheartened. Disappointed. Dissatisfied. "I've walked in that locker room sick to my stomach a couple of times," said Swinney, who lost each of the previous three visits to South Carolina—by an average margin of 17.3 points. "A couple of years, I thought we had the better team. A lot of people played their best game of the year, and we lost the game. But that's football."

Swinney could recall a pattern of mistakes that negated those exceptional performances. Clemson did not avoid those same miscues in 2015, but it managed to avoid those familiar sunken feelings.

The Tigers claimed a 37–32 victory in the Palmetto Bowl. Clemson improved its record to 12–0 and completed its first undefeated regular season since 1981. The Tigers preserved their plans for the College Football Playoff and made their trip through that tunnel a lot more enjoyable.

No longer disheartened. No longer disappointed. But still dissatisfied.

The Tigers appeared appreciative of the victory, but they did not spend an hour after the game posing with the new Palmetto Bowl trophy. They did not saunter around Williams-Brice for a victory lap. Their race was not done.

A one-year renewal of bragging rights might have been gratifying. It might have been worth treasuring. However, the Tigers could not truly enjoy it, at least not until perhaps February. Clemson needed to turn its attention immediately to its next stage—the ACC Championship Game in Charlotte against North Carolina.

Zero has never carried more weight. The zero in Clemson's loss column magnified each contest. The pressure of perfection mounted, but the margin for error did not shrink. It disappeared. From that point forward, Clemson could not afford to give away possessions, miss extra points, or blow coverages. It could not afford to flinch.

"When you're undefeated, the next game is a little bit bigger and a little bit bigger and a little bit bigger," co–offensive coordinator Jeff Scott said. "You're sitting there 10–0, and you've got everything on the line. So it's difficult on the guys. They know what's at stake. They're human. They've got phones. They read all the stuff, even though we don't want them to."

Somehow, a team with a sophomore quarterback and new starters at every position on the offensive and defensive lines did not succumb to the pressure. Somehow, an offense that was missing a top receiver to injury could compile more than 500 yards of total offense in eight consecutive games. Somehow, a defense that lost 10 players to the NFL could reload and remain in the top 15 in yards and points allowed. Somehow, the Tigers found a way to win. And if they could take the next three steps without stumbling, they finally could enjoy a satisfied walk back to the locker room.

On the Thursday before the ACC Championship Game, Clemson University released a résumé for Watson. Not a simple stat sheet. Not a box score. An actual résumé. Under education, it listed his communication studies major and 3.01 grade-point average. Under experience, it listed his undefeated record as a starter. Under skills, it listed character, clutch, and winning. Under references, it listed each of the defenses he had thrashed that season. He added another in Charlotte on December 5. Watson padded his résumé as he propelled Clemson to victory against North Carolina in the ACC Championship Game.

Clemson sent hundreds of those résumés across the country. Watson expected a callback the following week from New York City. While helping Clemson seal a spot in the College Football Playoff, Watson secured a seat at that Heisman Trophy presentation ceremony.

The pressure swelled each week through Clemson's enchanted undefeated season. Execution did not match the program's standard sharpness. Mistakes mounted. The Tigers did not play perfect games, yet they maintained a perfect record. Because the Tigers had Deshaun Watson, and their 13 opponents did not.

Those 13 teams did not have a player who could turn a broken play into a pivotal first-down rush with a simple, smooth stride. They did not have a player who could pirouette out of a collapsed pocket with fluid grace and then fire a bullet downfield with ferocious power. He was not troubled by the errant snaps fired at his ankles. He was not flustered by the passes he sailed over wide-open receivers or bounced in front of his targets. He was not daunted by the three-and-outs. He was not deterred by the tackles for loss. He was not dismayed by the pass that was tipped at the line and snagged for an interception.

He was his usual, steady, spectacular self.

"He's like Secretariat. If you open him up, he's got an oversized heart," Swinney said of Watson, referring to the legendary Triple Crown thoroughbred. Through the final four weeks of the regular season, Watson sprinted a few lengths behind University of Alabama running back Derrick Henry in the Heisman race. The ACC championship performance should have closed the gap.

Watson passed for 191 yards and two touchdowns. He also rushed for 99 yards and another score. That was all in the first half.

In Alabama's SEC Championship victory against Florida, Henry rushed for 189 yards and a touchdown on 44 carries. He raised his rushing totals to 1,986 yards and 23 touchdowns. He averaged 5.9 yards per rush and a touchdown on every 16 touches.

Watson finished his game with 420 yards of total offense, an ACC Championship Game record. He averaged 6.4 yards per play. He amassed 4,399 yards of total offense and 41 total touchdowns through 13 games. He averaged a touchdown on every 14 snaps in which he either passed or rushed.

Between Watson, Henry, and Stanford running back Christian McCaffrey, opening the Heisman Trophy ballot was like opening a fresh carton of Neapolitan ice cream. Three neatly distributed flavors. Three alluring options. Each presented its own wonderful qualities. Each deserved palatable prestige. Yet, instead of scooping out of each stripe, each voter was forced to choose only one.

Henry won the award. He was remarkably durable. He broke the SEC record for rushing yards in a season. Herschel Walker set the previous benchmark at Georgia in 1981. Henry surpassed him with 71 fewer carries.

McCaffrey also broke a longstanding record held by a Heisman legend. McCaffrey amassed 3,496 all-purpose yards and surpassed former Oklahoma State star Barry Sanders for the NCAA record. He rushed for 1,847 yards and eight touchdowns, and added 540 yards and four touchdowns on 41 receptions. He gained 1,109 yards and a touchdown on kick returns. He even passed for two touchdowns.

Henry was the steady workhorse who kept the Crimson Tide rolling. McCaffrey was the versatile entertainer who enticed us to stay up late for West Coast kickoffs. Watson was just as reliable as Henry. He was just as dazzling as McCaffrey. And he was slightly more influential.

Watson impacted more victories for Clemson University. His influence was not simply a byproduct of his position. Several quarterbacks handled the ball on every play. Few delivered that ball to end zone as frequently and efficiently.

Watson averaged 338.4 yards of total offense through 13 games. Between his 163 rushes and 413 passes, Watson averaged 7.64 yards per play. Between 339 rushes and 10 receptions, Henry averaged 5.97 yards per touch. Between 319 rushes, 41 receptions, and three passes, McCaffrey averaged 6.68 yards per play.

Watson accounted for 41 touchdowns, three more than Henry and McCaffrey combined.

Henry had been touted for his strong finish. Through his last six games against FBS opponents, Henry averaged 214.8 yards and 35 carries. He produced 6.14 yards per rush and scored 11 touchdowns.

Through his last six games, Watson averaged 362.5 passing yards and completed 69.2 percent of his passes. He averaged 93.2 yards per game on designed runs and scrambles. He amassed 23 touchdowns, the same amount Henry scored through the entire season.

Henry was the beneficiary of a defiantly one-dimensional offense. Henry left. Henry right. Henry middle. Alabama did not complicate its strategy, because it was never forced to. Henry rushed 90 times through his last two games—46 for 271 against Auburn and 44 for 189 against Florida. Commend Henry for his power, speed, and endurance. Those attributes allowed him to punish defenses even when everyone in the stadium knew Henry would get the football.

However, nothing on film or in any statistical analysis suggests that McCaffrey, Florida State's Dalvin Cook, or LSU's Leonard Fournette would not have produced similar figures if they were plugged into Alabama's backfield. Henry averaged 5.86 yards per carry through all 13 games, an admirable rate but 34th in the Football Bowl Subdivision. Cook averaged 7.86 per carry. Fournette averaged 6.42. McCaffrey, 5.79.

Excluding sacks, Watson averaged 6.3 yards per carry.

Watson's contributions could not be replaced as easily. That elevates him above the other finalists, but the margin was thinner than the scouting report for Alabama's offense. As extraordinary as these three Heisman finalists were that season, none separated himself as the undeniably superior player. Like that carton of ice cream, between those three players, there was no wrong choice. If only we could have had them all in the same bowl.

# 14

## RATHER LATER THAN SOONER

A MONTH EARLIER, it was a casual, conditional declaration during one of Dabo Swinney's weekly dismissals of the College Football Playoff standings. Even then, the idea of celebrating the final poll with a pizza party seemed...well...cheesy.

Yet there Swinney was on Sunday, December 6, in Memorial Stadium, hosting an outdoor reception for 30,000 friends and family members. Instead of champagne or cigars, they toasted Clemson's charmed season with a slice of pepperoni.

Clemson procured its 15th ACC championship the previous night. Less than 12 hours later, Clemson was confirmed as the No. 1 team in the College Football Playoff. Clemson was slated to face No. 4 Oklahoma in the Orange Bowl CFP Semifinal on December 31. That left Clemson 24 days to prepare for the Sooners and at least one day to celebrate, to commemorate the journey toward Clemson's first No. 1 ranking and first undefeated regular season since 1981. To commend the players who propelled that pursuit of perfection. To applaud the fans who stuffed orange into every stadium the Tigers visited from Pickens County to South Florida. At least one day to revel in that milestone, even if it was just a checkpoint.

A pizza party was a stark contrast to the tempered, stoic reaction many hardened college football coaches would have had, considering the most arduous portion of the journey was still ahead. However, prioritizing the prize over the process saps the satisfaction out of success. Coaches and players benefit from approaching each game with a business-like attitude. But every businessman should mix in a little pleasure.

Swinney's postgame dance moves can be goofy. His clichéd quotes and impromptu acronyms can be corny. His fabricated underdog narrative can be hackneyed. But his perspective is refreshing. As he repeatedly declares, "The fun *is* in the winning."

Those players grinded tirelessly for months. They battled injuries. They fought fatigue. They overcame adversity. They won 13 consecutive games and a conference title. They had not reached the end of that taxing road, but they still could enjoy a moment to look at the tracks behind them with pride and gratitude.

That playoff spot signified Swinney's elevation of the program. It was not a celebration of this season alone. It was a commemoration of six years of painstaking reprogramming. Swinney established a culture of diligence, consistent winning, academic excellence, and perhaps above all, unbridled enthusiasm. A conference championship and a playoff berth are accomplishments always worth celebrating. Most coaches commemorate those achievements with hefty performance bonuses in their contracts.

According to figures compiled by *USA Today*, the four coaches whose teams qualified for the playoff—Swinney, Alabama's Nick Saban, Oklahoma's Bob Stoops, and Michigan State's Mark Dantonio—combined to earn $425,000 in bonuses for winning conference titles. Swinney earned another $375,000 for appearing in the CFP semifinal. Saban received $110,000; Stoops, $250,000; and Dantonio, $150,000.

If coaches can put all that on the table without hassle, no one should consider a slice of pizza as overkill. It was a quirky way to celebrate, but a celebration was justified. Savoring that accomplishment, if only for an afternoon, did not signify that Clemson was content. It did not suggest that the Tigers were distracted from the ultimate prize. Enjoying a small cut of the paycheck on the weekend does not mean Clemson would not be ready for work again Monday.

Swinney, his staff, his players, their fans, and anyone fortunate enough to possess any level of personality and discernment understood that the expedition was not complete. The same focus, resilience, and diligence that carried them to that point was required to finish the climb. But one does not need to reach the peak of the mountain to enjoy the view. Clemson took a second. Took a breath. Took in the moment. Then took off again toward the top.

The euphoric jubilation could not last forever. Not even on South Beach. Amid Clemson's joyous bowl trip, Swinney was faced with a small, but sobering situation.

Indiscretion is always poorly timed.

A day before directing his team in the Orange Bowl, Dabo Swinney confirmed that he had suspended senior kicker Ammon Lakip, junior tight end Jay Jay McCullough, and freshman receiver Deon Cain. The players were sent home after failing drug tests.

"They ain't gone out and robbed a bank or anything like that," Swinney said that morning. "They're not bad guys, but they forfeited their opportunity."

Lakip and McCullough's playing careers at Clemson were over. Swinney said Cain could rejoin the team after the season "at some point if he grows up and does what he needs to do."

Lakip had been arrested for possession of cocaine and driving under the influence that previous spring, and McCullough had been suspended in 2014 for a separate violation of unspecified team rules. Swinney had sat Cain out of Clemson's regular season trip to Miami in October. Considering the timing of the transgression, the opportunity it cost them, the opportunity it could have cost their teammates, their indiscretions seemed dumbfounding, selfish, and simply stupid.

They relinquished a privilege they once worked tirelessly to earn. They cast their futures even out of the reach of the man obligated to guide them. No amount of Swinney's urging, admonishment, or protection could completely eliminate immaturity. There is no such thing as a perfect program, because there is no such thing as a perfect person.

"It doesn't matter who they are or how big the game is. If you don't do what's right, you ain't playing," Swinney said. "I don't make all the rules, but I'm going to enforce them. When you break them, you put me in a situation where we're going to do what's right. That I know."

Competing for a national championship is a prize few are talented or lucky enough to obtain. Many can assume they would do more to cherish and protect it. They can assert that they would sacrifice their urges. They can declare that they would resist temptation. Those proclamations are protected in hypothetical hindsight. They are muffled by the muted memories of our own mistakes.

Most of us are fortunate that our worst indiscretions were not documented in social media posts. Recaps of our most egregious errors did not scroll across the bottom of a national television broadcast. We could grow from our setbacks in obscurity. We could mature without instant and intense indictments from a digital jury.

Good people ignore their own good sense every day. Whether it is a sharp word in anger, a distracting guilty pleasure, or sneaking an extra snack, many of us occasionally surrender to impulse. We dismiss those lapses in comparison to Cain, Lakip, and McCullough because our slips rarely cost us our relationships, our livelihood, or our freedom. However, the concept is the same. Each potentially regrettable decision hinges on fear of the consequences. If the temptation is more enticing than the consequence is intimidating, impulse prevails.

Their decision was dumbfounding. It was selfish. It was simply stupid. Yet attempting to understand the priorities of another person, especially one who has not yet managed the duties and sacrifices required of adulthood, is equally stupid. Everyone weighs risks by their own value system. Some do not respect a rule until they feel the sting of its repercussions.

Competing for a national championship is a unique privilege. Still, it is insignificant compared to the anguish Cain, Lakip, and McCullough felt after squandering it. It could turn out to be the best bad decision they ever made, if that anguish motivates them to avoid repeating that decision. Those of us who have endured similar setbacks are also fortunate that humiliation and punishment are temporary. The lessons they teach endure forever.

Win or lose, the College Football Playoff would not define Cain, Lakip, and McCullough. This setback would not either. They had the rest of their lives, their entire adulthoods, ahead of them. They could do nothing to erase that imprudent decision. They could do nothing to change some cynics' opinions. However, they could utilize that experience to improve, grow, and mature. Indiscretion is always poorly timed. Redemption never is.

Swinney asserted that the suspensions would not disrupt Clemson's preparation or performance. "Why would it be a distraction?" Swinney asked. "It's not a very complicated matter at all, just got 115 guys, and 112 of them did what's right and three of them didn't. So they don't have the opportunity. They forfeit the opportunity and the privilege to be a part of the game. It doesn't have anything to do with the rest of those guys. It's not a distraction at all. It's a distraction for me because I have to answer questions about three guys that break our rules, and I have to deal with it, but that comes with my job. Those guys, they're focused on doing what they do. Has nothing to do with them."

The rest of the team was focused on the vengeful Sooners. Oklahoma stewed over its loss to Clemson the previous year in the Russell Athletic Bowl. Yet the Sooners appeared to be less offended by the 40–6 score than the way Clemson commemorated it. A ceremonial graveyard rests outside the entrance to Clemson's indoor practice facility. Several tombstones are aligned in neat rows. The inscriptions detail victories Clemson notched against ranked opponents on the road. When photos and video circulated social media, revealing the tombstone Clemson added for its victory against Oklahoma, irate Sooners fans and players erroneously assumed it was a special targeted slight. It was the 28th game memorialized there. But the explanation for the tradition was too late. Oklahoma already had already stowed its motivation.

Baker Mayfield was forced to bear that game like most Oklahoma fans. All he could do was watch while the Sooners suffered through its second 34-point loss of the season. Mayfield transferred from Texas Tech and walked on at Oklahoma prior to the season. Big 12 Conference rules stipulate that players who transfer within the league automatically lose a year of eligibility, even if they are walkons. In compliance with that mandate, Mayfield sat out all of Oklahoma's disappointing 8–5 season. He was forced to watch as the Sooners culminated the campaign with an embarrassing bowl rout.

He watched as Oklahoma quarterback Trevor Knight tossed three interceptions and Clemson's defense held star receiver Sterling Shepard to a single catch. The Sooners struggled to score until Swinney mercifully pulled his defensive starters early in the fourth quarter. However, unlike those Oklahoma fans who watched in 2015, Mayfield had the opportunity to reconcile it.

After that bowl calamity, Oklahoma coach Bob Stoops hired offensive coordinator Lincoln Riley to install the Air Raid spread offense. He promoted Mayfield to conduct the aerial attack. Mayfield spearheaded a 76.8 percent increase in point production. The Sooners were ranked 55th in the FBS in 2014 with an average of 25.9 points per game. With Mayfield, the Sooners rose to third with a rate of 45.8 per game. Oklahoma averaged 104 more passing yards while throwing 10 fewer interceptions. In less than a year, Oklahoma climbed from 93rd to third in pass efficiency. Mayfield completed 68.6 percent of 354 pass attempts through 12 games, the seventh highest rate in the bowl subdivision. Notre Dame's Deshone Kizer was the only quarterback Clemson faced in 2015 who ranked in the top 45 in that category. Among those top 20 passers, Mayfield was the only one whose attempts-to-interception ratio was higher than 70 and attempts-to-touchdown ratio was lower than 11.

Mayfield was generously listed at 6'1", 209 pounds. Yet his compact frame was equipped for frequent fire. And he spread his ammunition to several targets. Six Sooners had caught at least three touchdowns. Clemson had not faced an offensive operation like Oklahoma's. Clemson had not faced a quarterback like Mayfield. However, Mayfield had not faced a defense like Clemson's.

Mayfield was limited to an efficiency rating below 130 once prior to the Orange Bowl—104.12 against Tennessee. That was the only defense Mayfield encountered that was ranked in the top 60 in total defense, passing yards allowed, and pass-efficiency defense. Five of Oklahoma's other 11 opponents were ranked lower than 90th in each of those categories. Three of those foes—Tulsa, Kansas, and Iowa State—were ranked 125th, 126th, and 127th in total defense, respectively. Out of 127 teams.

Clemson was ranked seventh or higher in total defense, passing yards allowed, pass-efficiency defense, and tackles for loss. Through its previous 13 games, Clemson faced five quarterbacks ranked in the top 60 in pass efficiency—Appalachian State's Taylor Lamb (7th, 166.1), Kizer (22nd, 151.7), North Carolina's Marquise Williams (24th, 151.4), Miami's Brad Kaaya (34th, 144.2), and North Carolina State's Jacoby Brissett (59th, 132.2). Against Clemson, those quarterbacks compiled 69 completions on 146 attempts for 945 yards, nine touchdowns, and six interceptions. That yielded a pass-efficiency defense rating of 113.75, which still would rank Clemson 28th.

The "Baker" had a recipe for revenge, but the Clemson defense had an appetite for domination.

Oklahoma arrived in South Florida with all the momentum and allegedly all the motivation. Several Sooners talked about appreciating the chance to avenge that lopsided loss to Clemson. They talked about how agitated they were seeing the tombstone Clemson added to its graveyard. They talked freely about containing Clemson's offense. They talked frankly about solving Clemson's defense. They talked. Clemson retorted.

The Tigers could trade blunt barbs with the most bombastic. They did not hesitate to taunt, tease, heckle, and hound. They swapped soundbites through the week and even engaged Oklahoma in a heated exchange after a joint luncheon. The chatter was extensive. Energetic. Entertaining. But it was empty.

When the time for talking was over, only one team was prepared to put some punch behind its punchlines. Clemson silenced the Sooners in a stifling 37–17 victory and then turned its dialogue toward the national championship game in Glendale, Arizona. Clemson dominated the line of scrimmage in the second half. The offensive line was more physical. The defensive front was more emphatic. By the midpoint of the fourth quarter, everything on Oklahoma's side was quiet, including the scoreboard.

"We could tell that they were done," linebacker Ben Boulware said, "physically and maybe a little bit mentally."

All-America defensive end Shaq Lawson spearheaded Clemson's trash-talking efforts that week. Lawson never masked his confidence. He also never cowered from a physical challenge. Lawson backed up his words on his first snap. He collaborated with tackle Carlos Watkins to close the pocket on Mayfield. Lawson sacked Mayfield again on the next drive. It yielded a 14-yard loss and another animated celebration. Lawson did not play another snap.

He left the game with a knee injury and did not return. Even with Lawson relegated to the sideline, using his words to encourage his teammates, Clemson notched seven tackles for loss and forced two turnovers. Oklahoma heralded the 45.8 points and 542.9 yards per game averages it logged through its previous 12 games. Clemson limited the Sooners to 378 yards, including merely 88 in the second half. Oklahoma did not score in the second half. Boulware thwarted its most promising drive with an impressive tip and interception near the goal line.

The victory was another resounding response. To those who deemed the previous blowout against Oklahoma a fluky concession from an uninspired foe, to those who considered Clemson's No. 1 ranking a hollow crown. Play after play, win after win, Clemson continued to defy its detractors. There were still flaws. Clemson needed a New Year's resolution to execute more effectively in the red zone and tackle more cleanly in the open field. Yet even a series of stutters could not reduce the impact of Clemson's forceful statement.

# 15

## ROLL TIGERS

AS IT CELEBRATED another victory against over Oklahoma and its progress to the College Football Playoff National Championship Game, Clemson watched as Alabama demolished Michigan State 38–0 in the Cotton Bowl. That surging Crimson Tide would meet Clemson in University of Phoenix Stadium in Glendale, Arizona.

Clemson's quest for a national championship played out like a 1980s video game: Poll Position. Nick Saban's Punch-Out!! Super Dabo Brothers.

Under Swinney, the Tigers slid down hidden pipelines to discover new recruiting areas. They knocked under rocks to uncover stars. They jumped on the heads of their most daunting foes. Clemson excelled through lower levels of prestige by defeating exalted underbosses Auburn, Georgia, Florida State, LSU, Ohio State, Oklahoma, and Notre Dame. To complete its mission, Clemson had to face the Crimson King Koopa.

Alabama, with its storied heritage and recent dominance, was college football's biggest boss. It is the only Football Bowl Subdivision program that claims more than 11 national championships since 1900. It is the only FBS program with four undisputed national titles since 2000.

Forget the matchups. Forget the staff ties. For the culmination of the College Football Playoff National Championship pursuit, Alabama was Clemson's optimal opponent. Not because of Alabama's documented struggles with containing mobile quarterbacks or Clemson's history of pressuring pocket passers.

Clemson could eagerly embrace this opportunity because it was the best way to silence disparagers. It was the best way to earn recognition as a national power. Alabama epitomizes everything Clemson claimed it already was:

Consistent—Clemson and Alabama were the only programs with active streaks of at least five 10-win seasons.

Dominant—Clemson won 37 consecutive games against teams that were not ranked in the AP or Coaches Polls. Only Alabama had a longer streak at 60 games.

Balanced—Clemson and Alabama were the only FBS programs that averaged at least 420 yards per game on offense while allowing fewer than 305 per game on defense.

Nevertheless, compared to Alabama, Clemson's consistency, dominance, and balance were not as widely acknowledged, accepted, or appreciated. Clemson's success was softened by skepticism. Programs are appraised through the prism of their past. Alabama earned its esteem with 15 national titles and 25 SEC crowns. Clemson, with one national title, was still characterized by its history of inexplicable blunders.

Clemson forged its reputation for underachievement from 2000 to 2007. Clemson and Alabama each played 99 games during that span. Clemson compiled a 63–36 overall record, a winning percentage of .628, with losses to Duke and Kentucky and multiple setbacks to unranked Wake Forest. Alabama compiled a 53–46 overall record, a winning percentage of .535, with losses to Central Florida, Southern Miss, and Louisiana-Monroe. That was painted as Alabama's valley. The same underachieving stretch was painted as Clemson's personality.

Those characterizations are only modified by victories. Those unfavorable stretches are only forgiven by championships. Through the previous eight seasons, coach Nick Saban directed Alabama to a 97–12 record, a winning percentage of .890. Alabama won three national championships from 2009 to 2012.

Since Swinney hit the reset button on the program in 2009, Clemson enjoyed a 71–23 record, a winning percentage of .755, two ACC titles, and 14 victories against teams ranked in the top 20 in the history of the FBS in winning percentage. Swinney elevated the Clemson brand, but it still was not yet above widespread mistrust and discounted acclaim. There was only one way to get past the final level—through Alabama. A national championship would carry its own powers of persuasion, but earning it against the Crimson Tide would sway Clemson's doubters and end the cycle of disregard.

A champion welcomes such a challenge and seizes the chance. A champion plugs in, grips the controller, and presses start.

"If I could just script it, if you could say, 'Hey, you're going to get a chance to play the national championship game at some point, who do you want it to be against?'" Swinney said. "I would pick Alabama, because they're the best. They've been the best. They've earned that."

Swinney never believed in coincidence. He was certain that the matchup was no accident. He cherished the connection. He could reach one of his dreams, coaching the program he rebuilt against the program he revered.

"God has got a sense of humor," Swinney said. "Again, you're looking at a guy who grew up in the state of Alabama, and I mean, my dream was to play there, to go to school there. I was the first one in my family to get a college degree, and to be able to get it from the University of Alabama was a dream come true for me and for my family. I went down there as an 18-year-old kid. I left when I was 31. I grew up in Tuscaloosa, basically. Going there, walking on, earning a scholarship. My last game as a player, we win the national championship. Just a lot of great memories for me, obviously. But you go on with your life. You know, to have the opportunity to be in my first national championship game as a coach, and it comes against Alabama, I just have to smile at God on that one."

There is the Snyder Sequoia, stoic, yet majestic, a symbol of strength and longevity. There is the Saban Redwood, a marvel of stature, stretched to unparalleled heights. Then there is the Swinney sapling.

His counterparts in the College Football Playoff—Bob Stoops, Nick Saban, and Mark Dantonio—stem from the most fruitful coaching trees. Yet Swinney is still planting his own. It is a colorful hybrid of exploration and experimentation. It shares roots with the Bear Bryant Oak and the Bobby Bowden Birch. It blends branches with Texas transplants. It blossoms with refined precepts and resourceful optimism.

Swinney's tree does not follow the conventional growth pattern. Among the 12 head coaches in the 2015 New Year's Six bowls, Swinney and Ohio State's Urban Meyer were the only two who had never served as coordinators. Before arriving at Oklahoma, Stoops served as defensive coordinator under Bill Snyder at Kansas State and Steve Spurrier at Florida. Saban was Bill Belichick's defensive coordinator with the Cleveland Browns for four seasons. Dantonio coordinated the defense for Jim Tressel at Youngstown State and Ohio State.

Swinney's tree has not spread its leaves across the country. On average, the other 11 New Year's Six coaches shuffled through eight programs before landing at their current position. Swinney has coached on two campuses. One not far from where he first sprouted.

"I'm from the green plum tree in Pelham, Alabama," Swinney said with a laugh, alluding to his hometown. There, Swinney crafted his competitive spirit and forged the fortitude to walk on to the football team, earn a scholarship, then win a national title ring.

Swinney's head coach at Alabama, Gene Stallings, played for Bryant at Texas A&M. He helped Swinney open his coaching career and cultivate his commitment to a forceful running game, disciplined defense, and detailed organization. As he served five years under Tommy Bowden, Swinney fashioned his fondness for a speedy smashmouth spread offense. He developed his belief in a family atmosphere and his passion for brand advancement.

A combination of old-school values, new-school technique, and after-school amusement helped Swinney earn the head coaching position after Bowden departed. Through seven years, Swinney deepened his roots at Clemson with the counsel of experience. He hired his former position coach and mentor Woody McCorvey to serve as his staff's chief administrator. He contracted Chad Morris to construct the Clemson offense. He plucked defensive coordinator Brent Venables off the Snyder-Stoops tree. He picked the brains of countless college colleagues, NFL savants, pastors, and parents.

"I was a walk-on player, and I'm a walk-on coach," Swinney said. "I just work hard. I'm not afraid to fail. I don't know everything, but I'm always trying to learn and get better."

Utilizing the fortitude he forged in Alabama, the lessons of his failures, and the advice of his mentors, Swinney fertilized his vision and produced the most fruitful period of Clemson football.

In addition to the two conference titles, from 2011 to 2015, Swinney compiled 50 victories, two Bowl Championship Series appearances and a College Football Playoff berth. His winning percentage through that span (.820) was second among CFP coaches, trailing only Saban (.896).

Swinney's trunk does not reveal as many rings as Stoops' tree. Swinney cannot match Saban's forest of former assistants in head coaching positions—Dantonio, Kirby Smart, Will Muschamp, Jim McElwain, and Jimbo Fisher.

Swinney's tree withstood the whipping winds of heartbreaking losses. It withstood the thrust of his critics' axe. It swayed but it stood firmly, with a tire swinging from its strongest branch, with its fruit nearly ripe with the nectar of a national title.

Swinney's tree is small but strong. It is slender but sturdy. It is evergreen. As the seasons change, it never loses its color.

"I'm just a mutt. I've been able to really draw from a lot of great coaches, at two different places, and enjoyed every second of it," Swinney said. "At the end of the day, though, you've just got to be who you are. I learned that early on. You can't be somebody else. You can learn from others, but you can't be somebody else."

As the national title game neared, Tom Causey recalled that day in December 2014. He was just hired as the head football coach at Pelham High School. He answered countless phone calls that day, but there is one that he will never forget. It was from an eager Pelham High alumnus: Dabo Swinney. "He congratulated me on the job," Causey said, "and he told me if there was ever anything he could do for us to let him know."

Causey quickly redeemed Swinney's offer. He asked Swinney to send an autograph, not for his personal collection but to display in the Pelham High athletic offices. Merely three days later, a package arrived from Clemson. Inside, Causey found a white football stamped with a bright orange Clemson Tiger paw and Swinney's signature. Causey displays it proudly, to honor Swinney's journey from Pelham to the pinnacle.

"Pelham's had a lot of really big-time graduates come out of here, but that guy has made it," Causey said. "We need to celebrate that. We need to wrap our arms around that."

According to Causey, the city of Pelham embraced Swinney through his rapid rise as a college coach. Yet its arms loosened slightly that January, when Swinney led Clemson against Alabama. It is Swinney's alma mater. It is Pelham's priority.

"It is mixed emotions," said Jim Latham, a 1961 Alabama graduate who has lived in Pelham since 1978 and rooted for the Crimson Tide his entire life. "If Dabo wins, that's good, because he's one of the city's sons. But if it's just a one-point difference with Alabama on top, I'll probably be more happy than if it's one point less."

In Pelham, a suburb of Birmingham approximately 60 miles from Alabama's campus in Tuscaloosa, "Roll Tide" can be used as a substitute phone greeting. "Alabama's always been the team of the state," Latham said, "except for very few people who know of a place called Auburn."

Football fandom is not a hobby in Alabama. Rooting for Alabama or rival Auburn is not a Saturday diversion. It is a mandate. "When you come out of the hospital, they've got to stamp your birth certificate. You're either Alabama or Auburn," Swinney said. "You've got to choose. That's just the way it is."

Kim Kiel was not aware of the mandate before she moved to Alabama in 1989. She spent the previous nine years in Greenville, South Carolina. She attended several Clemson football games with her father and celebrated the national championship Clemson won in 1981. When she moved to Alabama to start high school, her affinity for Clemson was challenged as abstention. "Everybody asked if I was an Alabama or Auburn fan," Kiel said. "Nobody accepted that I didn't have an allegiance either way. I understand now. It is die-hard. It is like a religion here."

Kiel was converted.

"I am now a Roll Tide Alabama fan," said Kiel, who is the athletic director for Pelham city schools and one of many Pelham residents who were conflicted during that week between their devotion to Alabama and their support of Swinney. "It leaves them torn, because they want to pull for Dabo, but they have to pull for Alabama," she said. "When Dabo's back in the community, people always know he's around. He spends time with friends and family and gives back to the community. He's a role model for our student athletes. I think that's what brings the community to pull for him."

However, even considering Swinney's contributions to his hometown, even considering Alabama has enjoyed 15 national championships, including three since 2009, some Pelham residents were not willing to concede the game to one of the city's favorite sons. "Dabo's a good guy," said Jason Little, a service manager at a Pelham auto repair shop. "I just like him as a person, but he's one guy, and we're rooting for a team."

Under coach Nick Saban, Alabama compiled a 97–12 record from 2008 to 2015. According to Latham, losses were so rare in Tuscaloosa, they could dampen the mood of the city. "Two years ago, we lost two games, and it liked to kill us," teased Latham, who has a solution for conflicted fans who are not willing to backslide from their devout Crimson faith. It may be more difficult for Clemson fans to endure than an Alabama win.

"Maybe someday when Saban decides to hang up his cleats, we can get Dabo to come back over here," Latham said. "I would imagine that if something were to happen, Dabo would be at the top of the list."

Clemson fans would prefer it if Swinney simply continued to make Pelham proud from afar. He could bloom where he was planted, and conflicted fans could root for a tightly contested, flawlessly coached Alabama victory. "For us here in Pelham, nobody really loses," Causey said. "This has been good for Pelham and definitely for the state of Alabama. So, I'm saying, 'Roll Dabo.'"

Dabo Swinney started the 2008 season as Clemson's wide receivers coach under Tommy Bowden (top right), was named interim head coach on October 13 (lower right), and was hired permanently by athletic director Terry Don Phillips on December 1 (left).

C.J. Spiller, whom Swinney recruited to Clemson in 2006, would become one of the great running backs in school history, as well as the first member of his family to earn a bachelor's degree.

*Tigers quarterback Tajh Boyd drops back to pass against the Gamecocks on November 24, 2012. An All-American and the ACC Player of the Year, he led Clemson to an 11–2 record and a victory in the Chick-fil-A Bowl that season but could not overcome rival South Carolina.*

*Clemson offensive lineman Maverick Morris (69) leads his Tigers teammates down the Hill at Memorial Stadium before a game in September 2017, in one of the greatest and most-beloved traditions in all of college football.*

Pursued by a South Carolina defender, Tigers quarterback Deshaun Watson (4) runs around the left end while leading Clemson to a 35–17 win on November 29, 2014, the team's first victory over the Gamecocks after suffering through five straight losses in the Palmetto Bowl.

Watson (4) looks for an open receiver in a heavy rain when Clemson hosted Notre Dame on October 3, 2015. He gets blocking help from Tyrone Crowder (55) and Eric Mac Lain (78) during the Tigers' 24–22 victory over the Fighting Irish.

*Tigers defensive end Shaq Lawson (90) celebrates a sack during Clemson's 37–17 defeat of Oklahoma in the College Football Playoff semifinal game on December 31, 2015, in the Orange Bowl.*

*Clemson running back Wayne Gallman runs with the ball in the open field against Oklahoma in the 2015 Orange Bowl CFP semifinal. Gallman ran for 150 yards and two touchdowns against the Sooners in the Tigers' victory.*

Alabama running back Derrick Henry runs for a touchdown in the first half of the CFP National Championship Game on January 11, 2016. Clemson lost a heartbreaker, 45–40, setting up an eventual rematch in 2017.

Deshaun Watson scores in the second half of the Fiesta Bowl CFP semifinal versus Ohio State on December 31, 2016. Clemson won the game 31–0 and earned a second straight trip to the National Championship Game versus Alabama.

Clemson wide receiver Hunter Renfrow (13) celebrates his game-winning touchdown catch with 0:01 remaining in the CFP National Championship Game against the Crimson Tide on January 10, 2017. The Tigers won the rematch 35–31 and earned Clemson its second-ever national championship.

Clemson wide receiver Mike Williams (7) celebrates his fourth-quarter touchdown reception in the CFP National Championship Game with tight end Jordan Leggett (16). The score trimmed Alabama's lead to 24–21.

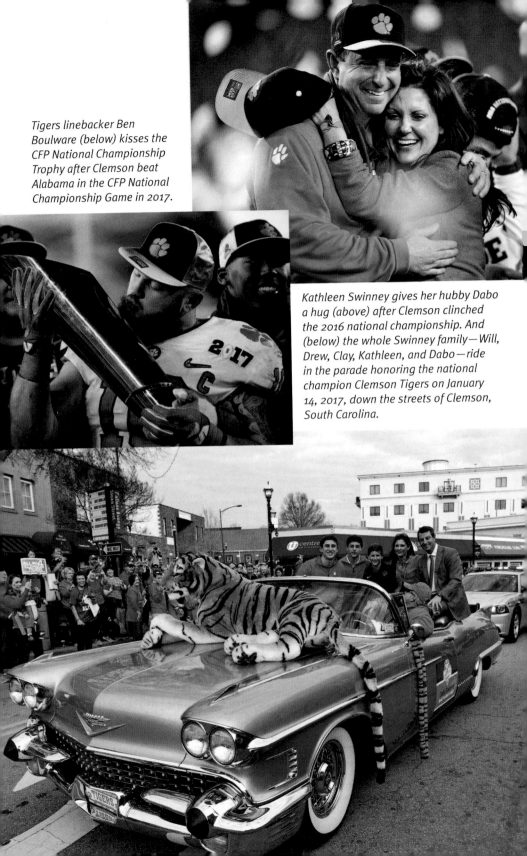

Tigers linebacker Ben Boulware (below) kisses the CFP National Championship Trophy after Clemson beat Alabama in the CFP National Championship Game in 2017.

Kathleen Swinney gives her hubby Dabo a hug (above) after Clemson clinched the 2016 national championship. And (below) the whole Swinney family—Will, Drew, Clay, Kathleen, and Dabo—ride in the parade honoring the national champion Clemson Tigers on January 14, 2017, down the streets of Clemson, South Carolina.

# 16

# DESERT DISAPPOINTMENT

ALABAMA COACH Nick Saban could not have devised a better way to slow down Clemson quarterback Deshaun Watson. Watson deciphered the coverages. He sidestepped the blitzes. He shook out of tackles. He was nearly unstoppable with the ball in his hand.

So Saban took the ball out of his hand.

Alabama converted a field goal to tie the College Football Playoff National Championship Game 24–24 with 10:34 remaining in the fourth quarter. The Crimson Tide lined up for the subsequent kick-off. Alabama kicker Adam Griffith placed the ball a few steps inside the left hash. Clemson shifted the front line of its return tightly as well. Alabama scrunched the right side of its coverage team inside the opposite hash. Griffith approached the ball in normal rhythm, but he twisted his torso to the right sideline as he loaded his kick. He popped the ball up and toward the numbers. Alabama cornerback Marlon Humphrey strolled under the ball, caught it near the 50-yard line, and shuffled out of bounds into rows of shocked Tigers.

Alabama seized an extra possession. Watson could do nothing but watch. Two plays later, Alabama tight end O.J. Howard slipped free down the seam. Quarterback Jake Coker delivered an easy pass for a 51-yard touchdown. Alabama reclaimed the advantage at 31–24 with 9:45 remaining, and despite a valiant effort when the ball returned to Watson's hand, Clemson never erased the deficit.

"Deshaun Watson is a fantastic player, probably had as big an impact on the game as any single player in the game," Saban said. "To get ahead, when you're playing against a player like that, is really, really important. It helped us change the momentum of the game. It's a calculated risk when you do something like that, but I think it's calculated based on your ability to execute relative to what the other team is sort of giving you. The way we line up on kickoffs with squeeze formation and try to corner-kick the ball when a team squeezes the formation like that, we call it pop-kick. I thought we had it in the game any time we wanted to do it. I made the decision to do it because the score, and we were tired on defense and weren't doing a great job of getting them stopped, and I felt like if we didn't do something or take a chance to change the momentum of the game that we wouldn't have a chance to win."

Swinney commended Saban's calculated risk, but he acknowledged that its damage was exacerbated by the defensive lapse that granted open passage to Howard. "First of all, he put it right in a good spot, and their kid did a great job of going and getting it. It was a huge play," Swinney said of the onside kick. "But then we followed it up with a bust for a touchdown. So it was a combination of mistakes. It was one thing to give up that play, but that doesn't mean you don't go out and do your job on another play."

After that pivotal sequence, Watson completed 11 of 15 attempts for 174 yards and two touchdowns. Clemson rendered an honorable response, but it spent too much of that evening responding. Alabama opened with a 7–0 lead after Heisman Trophy winner Derrick Henry sprinted free for a 50-yard touchdown. Clemson answered on the next drive with a 31-yard touchdown pass from Watson to Hunter Renfrow. The Watson-Renfrow connection claimed the lead for Clemson on the next possession with an 11-yard touchdown.

Alabama safety Eddie Jackson intercepted Watson on the first possession of the second quarter. The Crimson Tide converted that turnover into a touchdown. Alabama reclaimed the lead in the third quarter, when Howard broke free for a 53-yard touchdown reception. Clemson answered again, with a field goal from Greg Huegel and a 60-yard drive capped by Wayne Gallman's one-yard touchdown plunge.

Clemson outgained Alabama 550 to 473 in total offense. Clemson netted more rushing yards and more passing yards. And on plays from scrimmage, Clemson netted more points. However, special teams thrust the Crimson Tide ahead. After Howard's second touchdown, Clemson composed a 61-yard field-goal drive. The Tigers had drained some of Alabama's momentum, but only for a moment. Kenyan Drake returned the ensuing kickoff 95 yards for a touchdown. The teams then traded touchdown drives, and Alabama led 45–33 with 1:07 remaining. Watson directed a desperate six-play, 68-yard, 50-second touchdown drive, but Clemson's onside-kick attempt meandered out of bounds. Alabama took a knee, sealed a 45–40 victory, and celebrated another national championship.

As the gameday operations team positioned the stage on the University of Phoenix Stadium field for the trophy presentation, the Tigers sauntered slowly back to their locker rooms. Senior offensive lineman Eric Mac Lain spotted his family leaning over the front row rail. He raced to their arms.

"I went straight over there, and I was crying and holding them," Mac Lain recalled. "I really just embraced the moment. That was my last time wearing that paw and being a part of something so special."

Confetti fell. Cameras flashed. Horns blared. The celebration erupted. A new king was crowned. It was not Clemson. At least not this time. Clemson's perfect season ended that Monday night. Clemson could not hold off Alabama's fourth-quarter comeback. Clemson could not hold back Heisman Trophy winner Derrick Henry. Clemson could not hold on to its national championship dream.

At that moment, there was no consolation for the loss, no comfort for the disappointment, no relief from the regret. In those first moments after time expired, the agony felt like it would never leave.

The memories of their miscues felt like they would linger forever. But at some point, beams of pride would crack through the cloud of their disenchantment. At some point, the Tigers would recognize that the loss was not the end of the run. Clemson was just getting started.

"You can't let one game define you. We really wanted, obviously, to win and to be 15–0," Swinney said. "We had a great season, and it was kind of the next step for us. We needed to win our league again, and we did that. We wanted to get into the College Football Playoff, and we did that. We won our playoff game, earned ourselves an opportunity to compete for the national championship against the best team in the country in Alabama, and had a chance to win it, just came up short."

According to Mac Lain, perspective began to break through the pain before the Tigers even left the locker room. Returning underclassmen could see the promise of the following season. Departing seniors could recognize their lasting impact on the program.

"I really think 2015 was probably one of the best teams we ever had. We just ran out of time," Mac Lain said. "But there was definitely encouragement, because we had so many guys coming back. And 2016 was when we were supposed to win it, anyway. When Deshaun and all those guys came in, they were saying, 'When these guys are juniors, it is going to be crazy.' We were a year early, but just ran out of time."

Regardless of what analysts, Las Vegas odds-makers, and tradition declared, Clemson was not an underdog. Clemson belonged in that bout with Alabama. Clemson earned its spot on that stage. The Tigers did not stumble into success. They need not apologize for their breaks. They need no excuse for their schedule.

They ran through 14 opponents. Regardless of the conditions, locations, or stakes. They restored confidence in a fan base. They attracted rare positive national attention for a state struggling through political and natural disasters.

Through that enchanting run, Swinney validated his "work-hard, play-hard" approach. His corny acronyms and goofy dance moves showed that one could enjoy every step of the journey without losing focus on the ultimate destination. The outcome of that championship game was not sufficient ammunition for any detractor aiming to shoot holes through Clemson's achievement. Alabama is a formidable foe. The Crimson Tide made more big plays and fewer bad ones. Losing is never an honor, but the setback did not discredit anything Clemson accomplished that season. Clemson was outplayed but not outclassed.

"We stand toe to toe with everybody in the country," Swinney said. "This program doesn't take a backseat to anybody. We can play with anybody. We can beat anybody, and that's a fact."

Clemson completed its initiation process into the elite club of college football. The program could rub elbows with Alabama, Florida State, LSU, Ohio State, Notre Dame, and Oklahoma—the more celebrated and decorated programs against whom Swinney had notched victories.

Swinney poured the foundation in 2008. He constructed a program on top of it. Success was the new standard. A new level of recruit would fill the roster annually. A new level of support would fill the donation buckets. A new level of success would ensue.

Since its lone national championship in 1981, Clemson endured several downturns. The program plodded through losing seasons and perplexing letdowns. It took Clemson 34 years to climb out of that monotonous mediocrity, 34 years to reach that grand stage. But everyone in attendance that night knew it would not take them another 34 years to return.

"Where is this thing next year? Is it in Tampa?" Swinney asked that night. "We'll see if we can reload and go do it again."

They knew the route. They knew the hazards. They knew the requirements.

The Tigers earned invaluable experience during that playoff run. They discovered the difficulty of preserving a perfect record through 14 games. They discovered the pressure of maintaining the No. 1 ranking for six consecutive weeks. They were prepared to discover the adversity of a repeat performance.

They could ask Ohio State. Florida State. Oregon. Alabama. The climb is never easier the second time. Regardless of how often one has reached the peak previously, the hazards and the requirements never lighten. There are no alternative routes. There are no shortcuts. And this time, everyone would know Clemson was coming.

"At least the nation saw why we've been so successful," Swinney said. "They saw the heart of our team."

Swinney referred to his team's resolve. He could use the same statement to refer to his team's quarterback. Watson passed for 405 yards and four touchdowns against Alabama, who had allowed an average of merely 186 passing yards through its previous 14 games. Alabama allowed 70.8 rushing yards per game against its previous 14 opponents. Watson netted 73 alone. He was poised and decisive. He was electric and explosive. And after the loss, he was dissatisfied and motivated. "At the end of the day, I wanted the *W*," Watson said. "All the stats, that doesn't really matter to me. I just wanted to get the win and do something that we haven't done in 34 years."

Watson exhibited the same captivating skills that helped him steer Clemson to wins against Louisville, Notre Dame, Miami, and Florida State. It was why he was the ACC Player of the Year and a finalist for the Heisman Trophy. It was why his return to the 2016 roster propelled Clemson to a No. 2 preseason ranking. The underdog narrative that persisted in 2015 was replaced with the expectations of dominance.

Despite the defensive starters it lost from graduation and early departures, including NFL draftees Shaq Lawson, Jayron Kearse, and Mackensie Alexander, Clemson remained one of most talented teams in college football.

Watson welcomed back all his weapons. Running back Wayne Gallman returned after breaking the Clemson school rushing record with 1,527 yards and 13 touchdowns. Tight end Jordan Leggett returned after developing into a reliable midfield third-down target. Receivers Artavis Scott, Ray-Ray McCloud, and Hunter Renfrow returned, along with first-round talent Mike Williams, who recovered from the season-ending neck injury he suffered in the first game. Coupling the reloaded offense with a replenished defense and rebooted specialists, Clemson was positioned for another playoff push.

"Guys were so encouraged," Mac Lain said. "We knew what was coming back. Those guys loved football. It was just important to them. They were so good and so focused."

Clemson would need the same breaks it enjoyed in 2015. It would need to win at Auburn and Florida State. It would need to defend Death Valley against Louisville and Pittsburgh. It would need to hold off rivals Georgia Tech and South Carolina. It would need to sustain its health and maintain its focus. A trip to Tampa was manageable, especially with Watson as the travel agent, but it would cost the Tigers more than the journey to Arizona.

A little extra time in the weight room. A little extra fight in the fourth quarter. A little more sacrifice. A little more resilience. The question was…what were the Tigers willing to pay?

# 17

## CHASING GREATNESS

THE TEAM FORMED a circle in the middle of the practice field. Two players lined up on opposite ends. They exchanged glares. It had the intensity of an Oklahoma drill, with slightly less contact.

It was a game of cornhole.

The popular beanbag variant of horseshoes is a staple of tailgates and backyard barbecues. It normally does not generate the passion it produced during Clemson's 2016 August camp. Dabo Swinney turned cornhole from a lighthearted pastime into a motivational tool. He simply raised the stakes.

Clemson's sprawling practice facilities require players to traverse across fields between periods. In Swinney's cornhole tournament, players competed for the privilege to remain on one field throughout the entire practice. It may seem like a small wager, but under the pressure of an unrelenting practice regimen and the remorseless August sun, any amount of relief was welcome. The option to shed approximately 200 yards of jogging off the workload is worth a toss.

Pulling out those wooden boards was a delightful diversion amid the monotonous drudge of August camp. Especially considering the grand expectations already heaped on Clemson's team. The loss in the national championship game in January did not sit well with a group of leaders who believed they were talented enough and committed enough to seize that throne. But the loss convinced Clemson's leadership that the Tigers had not grinded enough or sacrificed enough. Their first team meeting for the 2016 season was solemn. There were no misgivings about the objective. There was no tolerance for anything less than complete focus.

"I walked in, and I looked at these guys in the front row, and I knew this is 'game on,'" Swinney said. "They had a look in their eye that was determined."

Swinney hoped cornhole would loosen some of the tension while also reinforcing that competitive edge. Clemson's lofty goal demanded both. The tactic fit Swinney, who admittedly is as charged for family game night as he is for the College Football Playoff. His competitive juices are always flowing, but through camp, his players may require an occasional squeeze. Of course, cornhole is not a definitive indicator of intensity or effectiveness. That arm motion is not going to help a quarterback's touch on third down. It certainly will not assist any tackles. During one Monday practice, the defense won the cornhole challenge after the stretch period. Yet, on the first play of an ensuing intra-squad scrimmage, it allowed a 99-yard touchdown run.

Swinney was less playful in his critique of that effort. Nevertheless, Swinney's strategy was shrewd. Through the next six months, the diversions could not be distractions. The otherwise innocent details required sharp focus to preserve the team's goal and protect against complacency. For a program in Clemson's position, mental clarity was just as important as muscle dexterity.

Junior quarterback Deshaun Watson was a Heisman Trophy favorite who graced the cover of *Sports Illustrated* and *ESPN The Magazine*. Clemson was ranked No. 2 in the preseason Coaches Poll. The Tigers were expected to end their 13-year drought in Atlanta against Georgia Tech and their 10-year losing streak in Tallahassee against Florida State. They were expected to repeat as ACC champions and return to the College Football Playoff.

Clemson never entered a season with such expectations. The preseason chatter was tempting because it had never been that flattering. Let widespread conjecture tell it, the Tigers already had reached Tampa, the site of the CFP National Championship Game. Swinney, his staff, and most of his players understood that they had not even reached September. They realized that most of the people supplying all of the noise then knew very little about what was required to back it up.

Whether it was a toss of a beanbag or an extra period of first-team scrimmages, Clemson poured all of its competitive juice into its preparation. Understanding that demand was draining. Swinney continuously crafted methods to replenish the supply and ensure the Tigers had enough flowing when the real competition began.

Clemson opened the season on the road at Auburn, without the expected offensive fireworks. Auburn's defense was physical and athletic and directed by former Clemson coordinator Kevin Steele. Clemson gained 399 yards, averaged 5.1 yards per play, and did not allow a sack. Running back Wayne Gallman grinded for 123 yards and a touchdown on 30 carries. Hunter Renfrow stretched into the end zone to snag a pass from Watson with 9:59 remaining in the game. Clemson may not have been as explosive as expected, but it made enough plays to beat Auburn 19–13. Yet, when every victory is judged by its margin and not by its merit, Clemson's offense drew criticism for a lack of "style points."

"There's not a real understanding of how hard it is to win, to be honest with you," Swinney said of that faulty reasoning. "If we win every game by one point and we're 13–0, I think we'll be just fine. At the end of the day, that's what it's all about."

Regardless of the score, defeating Auburn in Jordan-Hare Stadium in the season opener will always be a gorgeous win. Besides, Clemson's offense did not need a stream of points and yards. Its defense limited Auburn to a trickle. Auburn scored three points and netted 33 yards of total offense, including a single rushing yard, through the first half. Senior linebacker Ben Boulware thwarted two promising drives in the second half. On a fourth-down play at the Clemson 4-yard line, Boulware smashed running back Jeremy

Johnson and forced a fumble. Defensive tackle Christian Wilkins recovered. In the fourth quarter, Boulware intercepted a pass at the Clemson 1-yard line. Auburn did not reach the end zone until its penultimate possession.

The Clemson defense had a new face—and a peculiar mustache. Boulware stood as the Tigers' most seasoned leader. He started all 15 games in 2015 at weak-side linebacker. He finished the season with 135 total tackles, the second highest sum among Clemson defenders. An energetic run plugger and candid talker, Boulware slid to middle linebacker in 2016 to serve as Clemson's vocal conductor. Defensive coordinator Brent Venables never needed to worry about Boulware's volume, in tackles or on calls.

"My freshman year it was very tough. I think he probably chewed me out more than any player he's ever coached just because he knew I could take it," Boulware said of Venables. "At the end of the day, sooner or later, I'd be able to take it, maybe not my freshman year because he wore me down a lot. It was very tough on me. I think after that we've grown ever since. He's honest, like a father to me.

"He's helped me out in so many areas besides football. I love him like a dad. I think he obviously made me the player I am. He's made an impact in my life as a man. I don't think he knows that. But I think, equally as much impact as he's had on football, it's definitely on my life, too. We honestly butt heads a lot, two alpha males wanting the best out of each other definitely causes some problems sometimes. But I love him. I appreciate him more than anything. But I'm very glad that the freshman year happened. I think it made me who I am today. I honestly wouldn't want to go back and do it again because it sucked. It was very difficult. But I'm very appreciative of all the stuff we went through."

Boulware's brash demeanor matches his brash play. Anyone bold enough to wear a bushy vintage 1980s mustache while chewing a breakfast muffin during a national championship media day would never cower from an opponent or the challenge of added responsibility. In 2016 Boulware also added his signature beard. It fit his burly attitude but also his wisdom. It was a fitting alteration for Clemson's brawny, bruising captain.

In addition to the veteran defensive leaders, Clemson also enjoyed a *huge* debut from a true freshman. During the preseason, the advertisements were frequent but brief, intriguing but indefinite, more teasers than trailers. Clemson coaches hurled hints of praise. Players offered intimations of marvel. The ads did not do the story justice.

Dexter Lawrence was far better than advertised.

One could simply look on the roster and infer that a 6'5", 340-pound freshman defensive tackle would be imposing. One could watch him strolling through stretches before his first practice and observe that he was uniquely nimble. One could assume he would contribute early and disrupt often.

However, until spectators could see him swat away blockers like mosquitoes at a cookout, until they could see him chase down a quarterback with the agility of an outside linebacker, until they could see him for themselves, they could not know that the praise and marvel were never exaggerated.

Lawrence's premiere at Auburn was pure spectacle. He commanded attention at what is normally a thankless position. Clemson lost its starting defensive ends from the previous season, Shaq Lawson and Kevin Dodd, to the NFL. Projected replacement Austin Bryant suffered a foot injury in preseason camp and missed the opener. To compensate, Clemson shifted Wilkins from tackle to end. Yet Clemson still had enough depth in the interior, with senior Carlos Watkins and junior Scott Pagano, that Lawrence was not even in the starting lineup. Nevertheless, on his first snap, Lawrence's power was captivating. He penetrated the line so easily, he surprised himself.

"When the offensive lineman came down on me, I kind of stood him up. I was like, 'Okay, I've been blocked harder than this,'"

Lawrence said. "I just tried to embrace the moment as much as I could."

Lawrence recorded five tackles and a sack in the first half alone.

"I'm a little upset, because he got the first sack of the season. I really wanted that," teased Wilkins, who notched a sack on the next down.

Lawrence and Wilkins finished the game with 13 total tackles. They even lined up together in the jumbo package on offense and cleared a four-lane highway to the end zone for Wayne Gallman. "They kind of hopped out of the way," Wilkins said of the prudent defenders. "We didn't have to do much, but I'm glad we got the score."

Auburn running back Kerryon Johnson exploited a few cracks in the defense and rushed for 94 yards on 23 carries, including a nine-yard touchdown. Yet no other Auburn rusher averaged more than 1.8 yards per carry.

Behind the defensive line, Clemson revealed a reinforced line-backer corps, anchored by Boulware and Kendall Joseph, who filled the void left by leading tackler B.J. Goodson. Auburn notched two third-down conversions during a field goal drive in the first half. Clemson spoiled Auburn's next 11 third-down plays. Clemson recorded two interceptions and five pass breakups, including safety Jadar Johnson's victory-sealing swat on the final play of the game.

"We were confident all along," Wilkins said. "We knew it didn't matter who we put out there. We were going to go as hard as we can."

Clemson's offense encountered more resistance in its home opener against Troy. The Trojans outgained Clemson 242–200 in the first half, and Clemson held a modest 13–10 lead at the break. Troy limited Clemson to 25 rushing yards and benefited from a special-teams blunder. Clemson receiver Ray-Ray McCloud carved through the Troy coverage team and sprinted away for what should have been a 75-yard punt return touchdown. However, just before he reached the end zone, McCloud casually flicked the ball behind him. Officials ruled that it did not cross the goal line with him. Troy recovered the ball in the end zone with 1:38 remaining in the half.

Neither team scored in the third quarter. Early in the fourth, Clemson inserted Wilkins into the offense. This time, it was not to block in the jumbo package but to catch a one-yard touchdown toss from Watson. The entertaining play removed the governor from Clemson's offense. The Tigers forced a three-and-out on the ensuing possession, and then marched 75 yards to the end zone on 11 plays. Watson delivered a 23-yard touchdown pass to Deon Cain. Clemson led 27–10. Troy did not trim the deficit to fewer than 10 points until 44 seconds remained. Clemson was relieved to hold off the Trojans for the 30–24 victory. And once again, the Tigers were not concerned about style points.

"It's very hard to win, especially to win consistently when you get everybody's best, and for the past several years that's exactly what we've gotten from our opponents," Swinney said. "It takes great habits and great culture, and we have all those things in place here. That's why we've been able to be so consistent, and obviously we've got good players, but it can't just be good players. You've got to have teamwork and intelligence, and you've got to have great commitment."

Swinney demands that his players maximize their effort in preparation for powerhouse teams like Auburn and overlooked teams like Troy. And that is why, regardless of the opponent or the margin, Swinney urges players to maximize their celebration of every victory.

"We work too hard to be miserable. This ain't life or death," Swinney said. "Nobody's going to outwork us. Nobody's going to be tougher than us. Nobody's going to be more driven that us. But we're going to enjoy doing it. The way to do that is to create a great environment. Then, oh, by the way, we're winning."

Clemson satisfied its detractors the next week with a stylish 59–0 win against South Carolina State. They followed with a 26–7 win at Georgia Tech. Clemson had not defeated the Yellow Jackets in Atlanta since 2003, Swinney's first season on Tommy Bowden's staff. Clemson did not allow Tech to score until the fourth quarter. Tech closed the game with 124 yards of total offense, its lowest total under coach Paul Johnson.

Watson passed for 304 yards. Clemson opened its offensive onslaught with a four-yard touchdown pass. It was star receiver Mike Williams' first touchdown catch of the season and a stirring sign of his heartening return from a scary injury. If it had never happened, Williams does not know exactly where he would have been in 2016. He is almost certain that he would not have been in a Clemson uniform. He most likely would have been playing in his rookie season in the NFL.

He was projected as one of the top NFL prospects before the previous season and was expected to declare for the draft at the conclusion of his junior campaign. "Through fall camp, I told everybody in our room, 'Y'all enjoy Mike Williams this year, because he's going to be gone,'" Clemson co–offensive coordinator and receivers coach Jeff Scott recalled.

Scott expected Williams to follow former Clemson receivers Deandre Hopkins, Sammy Watkins, and Martavis Bryant, who all departed as juniors. "I thought Mike was going to be the next guy," Scott said, "because he really put himself in that position to have a great year."

Williams' plans were diverted on the first series of the season. He stretched daringly to catch a pass in the end zone, but he collided with the base of the goal post. He fractured a vertebra in his neck and was forced to redshirt the remainder of the year. Williams missed Clemson's run to the national title game. He agonized with compassion as his teammates suffered a five-point loss to Alabama.

"That is the part that I missed the most," Williams said. "I wanted to be out there helping my teammates. We lost the national championship, and I feel like I could have contributed. The goal was to get back—and to win it."

With intense resolve and a resilient sense of humor, Williams recovered swiftly. He aimed to restore his dominance, reclaim his spot atop draft boards, and retrieve the experience the injury denied him.

"A couple of weeks after he hurt his neck, he was in the locker room running around, playing with everybody. I thought he was ready to play," Gallman said. "Mike's focus is always to have fun. In every game, you never see him get rattled. You never see him nervous. Mike's just different."

"He has an appreciation of being healthy," Swinney said. "I've never seen a guy so happy to go and run and dive for a pass and roll on the ground. God never says, 'Oops.' He would have been a first-rounder. But it wasn't God's timing for him. He had to sit and watch, and I think he's a lot better player. He has a deeper level of appreciation for his opportunity to play, for the privilege to play."

Williams' humor and cheerful spirit helped him not only endure the injury but discover an opportunity within it. "I gained some knowledge of the game. I started to study defenses," Williams said. "That was the main part of my game I had to improve in, and that's what I did."

Williams also utilized the redshirt year to add 15 pounds of muscle. "Early in his career, like a lot of receivers, he wanted to run around a lot of those [defensive backs]," Scott said. "Now, he realizes you got to run through them."

Williams caught 25 passes for 373 yards and two touchdowns through the first five games. That included five receptions for 50 yards against Louisville on October 1.

Clemson was ranked No. 3 in the Coaches Poll. Louisville was No. 4. ESPN selected the ACC matchup for its featured prime-time national telecast. Its popular touring *College GameDay* analysis show broadcast from Bowman Field on Clemson's campus that morning. Swinney made an appearance on the show and then hopped in the car with a state trooper to return to the team hotel in nearby Anderson.

As Swinney rode along Perimeter Road outside the stadium, he asked the trooper to stop the car. "Man, pull over right here," said Swinney, who wanted to visit a few of the dedicated fans who had set up their tailgates more than 12 hours before the scheduled kickoff. "This one group had a big orange van," Swinney recalled. "Had their chairs kicked back, the doors open, and a big-screen TV."

When the patrol car pulled up, the tailgaters thought their early fun was over. "They're like, 'What's going on?'" Swinney said. "They're all drinking beer, and I roll the window down and say, 'Hey, boys, we ready to go? Y'all are drinking beer already? It's gone be rockin' in the Valley tonight!'"

The gentlemen were relieved and simultaneously stunned. Season ticket holder Eddie Hickman of Inman, his son Chris, and friend Aaron Roef were watching Swinney's appearance on ESPN two minutes earlier. Now he was at their tailgate. "I was totally shocked," Eddie Hickman said. "I could hardly speak, and I'm rarely at a loss for words. It's just amazing that he took the time on that day to stop and talk to us. It made our day, that's for sure."

Swinney continued to tour tailgates along Perimeter. He shook hands, posed for photos, and even kicked back for a spell in some fans' zero-gravity recliners. He relayed the interactions when he rejoined the team.

"I told them when I got back that it was unbelievable, that there was no telling how early those people were there," Swinney said. "And it's just amazing just to be a part of it. That's what makes Clemson special. I don't know how many people were here that weren't even in the stadium. There might have been 15,000-plus just tailgating who didn't come into the stadium."

Many of those fans lined the parking lot outside the locker room for Tiger Walk.

"It was just incredible. You could feel the intensity in the crowd," Swinney said. "It was a big doggone game, and the emotion that was in the crowd, the energy, was powerful. It was a special environment to be a part of."

A sense of urgency snapped through the air above Death Valley that night. It fused into a concoction of cautious optimism and anxious apprehension. As the uncomfortably close contest drew to a close and Louisville eyed one last chance to steal the game, deep in Tigers territory and down by six, Clemson fans knew what was at stake. It was more than fourth-and-7. It was more than a conference game. It was more than prime-time television.

It was the fleeting opportunity for a return trip to the College Football Playoff. It was the promise of prominence. It was the dream of a national championship. Louisville quarterback Lamar Jackson was one more dazzling play away from turning the remainder of Clemson's season into a series of exhibition games. Clemson fans channeled their urgency, their optimism, and their apprehension through a defiant roar that no quarterback's cadence could counter.

They understood it was more than fourth-and-7. They helped turn it into fourth-and-12.

With 40 seconds remaining, the ball resting at the Clemson 9-yard line, and the Clemson crowd singing a deafening serenade, Louisville committed its fifth false start of the game. On the ensuing play, after backing up five yards, Jackson completed a pass to James Quick. He sped toward the end zone, but Clemson defensive back Marcus Edmond forced him out of bounds at the 3-yard line.

One yard short of the first-down marker.

Death Valley erupted with unbridled relief. Just like Jackson repeatedly slipped the grasp of his defenders, Clemson slipped the clutch of impending disappointment. A loss would not have ended the season, but Clemson fans appeared to recognize the opportunity at hand.

They recognized the reasonable presumption that Watson would proceed to the NFL after this season and that he would take many of his offensive weapons to the draft with him. They recognized the heart of the defense, Ben Boulware, would graduate and the random reach of the coaching carousel that was already spinning. They recognized that the fortune of the future is always curbed by uncertainty. They recognized the promise of the present.

Clemson established the foundation of a perennial contender, like Alabama and Ohio State, who can lose first-round draft picks but not lose a beat. Clemson elevated to the echelon of expectation. The stakes were higher. The goal is singular. It was playoff or punt.

That is the reward for progress, but it can be coupled with immense pressure. Clemson acknowledged it as they struggled but survived the first four weeks of the season.

Clemson had played five games but had not yet played a perfect one. But Clemson had won each of those five games, and a perfect record is always more important than a perfect performance.

Now the urgency, optimism, and apprehension needed to be channeled into the effort to maintain that unblemished record. The sluggish start that induced doubt through the previous four weeks was forgiven. No one would remember the five turnovers the Tigers committed against Louisville, recount Watson's interceptions, or recall the missed tackles.

Those fans who witnessed—and contributed to—Clemson's victory would not forget the thrill of that fourth-down stop. They would not forget the elation of that eruption or the roar that echoed to Boston, Winston-Salem, Tallahassee, and even Orlando.

They would not forget what was at stake.

# 18

## FLIRTING WITH DISASTER

APPARENTLY, in 2016 Clemson was not content with a leisurely drive to the College Football Playoff. The Tigers did not want the sensible, fuel-efficient minivan. They wanted to wrap their legs around a speeding motorcycle and pop wheelies in the rain. Without a helmet.

They advanced through the season like daredevils. They rode closer and closer to the edge.

After doing doughnuts around Boston College, 56–10, Clemson narrowly avoided certain disaster against North Carolina State. Most of the danger was self-inflicted. At one point in a series of inexplicable blunders, the Tigers appeared to be checking dares off a bucket list, in a devious effort to make its victory more adventurous.

They turned the ball over three times inside the 25-yard line. They rushed out of the pistol formation on fourth-and-goal. They committed a pass-interference penalty on fourth down. They snapped the ball over the quarterback's head in overtime. They muffed a punt. They tossed a perplexing interception that was returned for a touchdown. They allowed what should have been a game-winning scoring drive. What should have been a layup field goal.

What should have been the end of their playoff ride and the end of Clemson's 42-game winning streak against unranked opponents. A loss would have left more than a scratch on that stunt bike. Perhaps it was the wind that pushed Kyle Bambard's 33-yard field-goal attempt on the final play of regulation. Or perhaps it was the collective gasp from the Clemson sideline that drew it right of the goalpost. Then again, perhaps it was pure providence.

Regardless of what should be credited, Clemson players, coaches, fans, and cardiologists were grateful. Their ride continued.

Dabo Swinney rested his headset on his neck, took a few steps off the sideline and crouched to watch Bambard's kick. As it sailed right and landed in front of the student section, Swinney dropped to his knees, planted the brim of his cap on the turf, spread his hands, and slapped the grass. He rose to his feet, exchanged a few high fives, and then regrouped his team.

Clemson took the ball first in overtime and advanced to the 1-yard line in seven plays. Center Jay Guillermo launched the next snap over Deshaun Watson's head. Watson recovered the ball after a nine-yard loss. On the next play, Watson faked a handoff and fired a dart low into the end zone. Artavis Scott slid to cradle the pass. Clemson took a 24–17 lead.

North Carolina State attempted to respond quickly. Quarterback Ryan Finley collected the snap and quickly spotted receiver Bra'Lon Cherry sprinting half a step ahead of Clemson defensive back Marcus Edmond. Finley launched the ball, but it sailed slightly short of his intended target. Cherry contorted to adjust to the pass, but Edmond had closed the gap near the goal line. Edmond undercut the route, snagged the ball, and clutched it as he and Cherry rolled into the end zone. Edmond sealed Clemson's seventh victory.

Clemson has a tradition of coaches, players, and fans gathering at the midfield paw after every game. After the game-winning interception, they relocated that tradition to the east end zone and on top of Edmond.

"I almost died," Edmond said. "Everybody kept piling on me, and I couldn't breathe."

Thankfully, after the wild celebration waned, Edmond managed to catch his breath. And Clemson collectively took a deep one after another narrow victory.

"Just another day in the office. We wanted to be sure ABC's coast-to-coast ratings went up," Swinney said after the game. "We've beat everybody but Clemson. We're trying to beat Clemson, but we haven't quite achieved that yet."

As daring as their escape appeared, the Tigers did not aim to make the game more adventurous. They did make it unnecessarily arduous. N.C. State was a more formidable foe than their recent history portrayed. The Wolfpack arrived with a finite game plan and capable playmakers to execute it. However, the discrepancy in talent and depth was distinct. The Tigers were not chauffeured toward an upset. Their miscues gripped the throttle. They accelerated toward destruction.

That was not their first encounter with self-induced endangerment, not the first time their execution appeared faulty. The brushes with calamity should have encouraged Clemson to straighten its course, operate more carefully, and refrain from procrastinating with productivity.

They would not get away with popping wheelies through the rest of the Atlantic Coast Conference. Eventually, the tricks would end painfully.

Clemson almost skidded out again in Tallahassee the next week against Florida State. It was another harrowing episode in Clemson's stuntman series. Promotional considerations for the program were paid for by Dabo Swinney Blood-Pressure Monitors, when your heart can barely stand the excitement; and by Brent Venables' All-Out Blitz Energy Drinks, when you need a defensive boost on fourth down.

Clemson led 17–7 with 1:44 remaining in the first half, but then the Tigers allowed Florida State quarterback Deondre Francois to steer a 78-yard touchdown drive to cut the margin to three before halftime. Clemson produced a field goal on its opening drive of the third quarter but would not score again until its first drive of the fourth quarter. Watson tossed an interception with 6:26 remaining in the third. On the ensuing snap, Florida State running back Dalvin Cook sprinted 43 yards for a touchdown. Cook produced another one-play drive later in the quarter, a 70-yard touchdown run that lifted Florida State to a 28–20 lead.

Watson led a masterful drive on the next possession. He completed all three of his pass attempts on third downs, the last of which was a 13-yard strike to Scott that advanced the ball to the 2-yard line. Running back Wayne Gallman plunged into the end zone. Clemson missed on the two-point-conversion attempt and trailed 28–26. Clemson reclaimed the lead with a field goal, but Florida State answered with another touchdown from Cook. Florida State's two-point attempt failed.

Clemson opened its next drive at its own 25-yard line, trailing 34–29 with 3:23 remaining. Watson connected with tight end Jordan Leggett on three passes for 70 yards. On that third completion, Leggett lined up to the right as the inside receiver in a trips package. He ran a simple out pattern. Two defenders trailed receiver Hunter Renfrow, leaving Leggett wide open. Watson delivered the pass, and Leggett grabbed the ball at the 16-yard line. As he sprinted down the sideline, a Florida State defender attempted to tackle him low. Leggett leaped from the 6-yard line, planted his off-hand down on the 1 and propelled himself across the goal line. Watson tossed a pass to Mike Williams for the two-point conversion.

On the next possession, Florida State progressed to the Clemson 44-yard line in seven plays. An aggressive call on third down led to a shared sack between Dexter Lawrence and Christian Wilkins and backed up Florida State 10 yards. After that, most defensive coordinators would have opted to play it safe, rush three, and drop eight cautiously in coverage. For Venables, caution was too risky.

With Florida State needing a Hail Mary, a rabbit's foot, a four-leaf clover, and a presidential pardon on fourth-and-32, Venables blitzed both inside linebackers. Ben Boulware corralled Francois for an 11-yard sack. Clemson's aggressive call helped the Tigers outlast another flirty evening with disaster. With edgy swagger and steely resolve, Clemson advanced in spite of its miscues. In Tallahassee, the Tigers faltered on both sides of the ball, but at the crest of crisis, they thrived.

Clemson allowed Cook to rush for 120 yards and two touchdowns in the third quarter alone, but in the fourth, Cook mustered merely 16. Clemson continued to roll with the creed that there is no such thing as an ugly win. It may never be pretty. It may never be easy. It may never be predictable. But no one could say it was not entertaining.

Coaches, fans, writers, analysts, and the players themselves were waiting for the Tigers to snap out of their funk, waiting for them to dominate perceived inferior foes, waiting for them to establish their rhythm and waltz back to the playoff. But eight games into the season, everyone needed to realize that the dazzling dance that carried Clemson to prominence the previous year did not carry over. It simply set a standard by which Clemson was assessed, beyond wins and losses and perhaps beyond reason.

Nothing was going to magically click. The team was not suddenly going to reach some grand awakening. Clemson was winning. That was enough. That did not mean Swinney and his staff would neglect the necessary corrections, but it also did not diminish any part of the Tigers' 8–0 start.

For the sake of their own mental well-being, fans needed to embrace the Tigers for the complex characters they were, even if that required them to watch nervously through their fingers. Clemson exhibited tenacity, poise, and resilience that its opponents had not shown. If North Carolina State had more of it, the Wolfpack may not have needed to settle for that failed field goal. If Florida State had more of it, the Seminoles may not have committed consecutive false-start penalties on their final drive.

It may not have happened in the optimal manner Swinney envisioned or desired. But folks began to accept that Clemson could wager its fate on the aggressive attitude that created and also eliminated danger. The lofty ideal might never be reached. The Tigers were not in a funk. They were not in a fog. This was their identity. This was their rhythm. This was their version of perfection.

This was their walk on the wild side. Clemson appeared content to continue flirting with disaster, but they had to know that, sooner or later, her jealous boyfriend, agony, would show up. And that he would bring his best friend, regret.

Clemson and disaster agreed to see other people on November 5 against Syracuse. Clemson set dates with execution and ease. Swinney emptied the bench in a 54–0 rout. They moved up to No. 2 in the CFP rankings. Then Clemson called disaster again. Agony answered the phone.

*C-L-E-M-S-O-N-I…*

No, no one wanted to bother uttering that jettisoned term. It did not need to be resurrected. There are so many other —*ing* words that fit better.

Try *deflating*.

With six seconds remaining in Clemson's 10th game of the season, Chris Blewitt, the place-kicker for the unranked, 5–4 Pittsburgh Panthers, lifted a 48-yard field goal through the uprights behind Death Valley's west end zone. He lifted Pittsburgh to a 43–42 victory and the Panthers off their feet in exuberant disbelief.

He also appeared to puncture the promise of Clemson's season, disrupt a plan for playoff redemption, and divert a hopeful run toward a national championship.

The unexpected loss could have prompted one to revive the dubious label of *Clemsoning*, defined as the tendency to falter against perceived inferior foes in pivotal moments. Reinserting that term into the lexicon would be the natural contrivance, considering the circumstances, but Clemson's performance stirred several synonyms.

Try *puzzling*.

Clemson's pass defense chose the wrong time, and the wrong opponent, to deviate from its sound, stout, and steady character. Through its previous nine games, Clemson allowed only one pass that covered more than 40 yards. Pitt quarterback Nathan Peterman completed three passes that covered at least 44 yards. Through its previous nine games, Clemson compiled a defensive pass-efficiency rating of 93.2, the third best figure in the FBS. Peterman recorded an efficiency rating of 174. Through its previous nine games, Clemson allowed five passing touchdowns. Peterman threw five that Saturday.

Try *mystifying*.

Clemson's offense wore an equally peculiar disguise. It abandoned balance and converted temporarily to an all-aerial attack. Watson attempted 70 passes. He completed 52. He amassed a school and ACC record 580 passing yards. However, three of his passes landed in the arms of Pitt players, including two near the end zone. Clemson rushed on merely 25 snaps. In the fourth quarter, when it needed to sap the clock, Clemson netted a loss of three rushing yards. Clemson recorded its sixth game with more than one turnover but its first game rushing for fewer than 100 yards.

Try *foretelling*.

Clemson had trifled with fire all season. It could have been burned at Auburn. It could have been burned against Louisville. It should have been engulfed against North Carolina State. Propelled by the hybrid fuel of resolve and luck, Clemson accelerated through the flames and sped toward perfection.

Yet luck is not a sustainable energy source. Clemson may have survived, even against more talented teams, but eventually, resolve must be mixed with diligence and precision. The Tigers encountered a hazard they could not avoid. They drove into a predicament out of which they could not navigate. They slowed down long enough for their mistakes to catch up to them.

Try *embarrassing*.

The Tigers once again left their fortunes in the hands of their adversary. They left the decision on the foot of a foe. They left control of their destiny to chance. And they were left to accept the results.

It was *debilitating*. It was *demoralizing*. It was *alarming*. But it was not *Clemsoning*. It was *befitting*, and Clemson spent a night with its national championship chances *pending*.

Then the CFP Selection Committee was *forgiving*. Fate appeared to be operating directly out of the handbook for compassionate parenting.

A frustrated father hustles his son into an empty room. Tears well in the young boy's eyes. He knows a spanking is imminent. He knows he deserves it. He closes his eyes, clenches his fists, and braces for the impending pain. The father raises his large hand and swings it forward.

Gently.

He places his palm softly on the child's shoulder, nods, and leaves the room without a word. Relieved, the son wipes the sweat from his temple and vows never to repeat that crime. He appreciates the pardon. He is certain there will not be another one.

Clemson deserved a spanking for its letdown against Pittsburgh. It deserved swift punishment for its uncharacteristically porous defense and untimely turnovers. It deserved the loss and deserved to slide in the standings.

But Father Fortune was merciful. Clemson felt a gentle touch on its shoulder instead of a belt on its bottom. Despite the loss, Clemson slipped merely two spots to No. 4 in the CFP rankings the following Tuesday night. Clemson entered the weekend positioned to secure a playoff spot with a favorable remaining schedule. No one anticipated a home loss to Pittsburgh, but after that disappointing defeat, many anticipated a plummet. Out of the top four and possibly out of contention.

However, Clemson was immediately bailed out by its peers. A few hours after Clemson sulked back into its locker room, Michigan and Washington, then ranked Nos. 3 and 4, respectively, also suffered their first losses. From grace, Clemson did not fall alone. From its benchmark, Clemson did not fall far at all.

Clemson built goodwill with wins against Auburn, Louisville, and Florida State. At that point of the season, Clemson, Alabama, Ohio State, and Michigan were the only teams with at least three victories against teams ranked in the top 20.

Additionally, the playoff selection committee asserts that its primary consideration is a conference championship. Clemson could seal the ACC Atlantic Division title with a win that following week against Wake Forest. If it added another top 25 victory in the ACC Championship Game, Clemson would separate itself further from one-loss teams with less impressive résumés, like Louisville, Washington, and West Virginia.

The relief of clemency may not fix the minor deficiencies in Clemson's defense. It may not have restored balance to the offense or eliminated turnovers. Yet, if it was not clear before, the Tigers must have recognized unequivocally the penalties of inefficiency.

Father Fortune would not forgive a second slip. He would not swing with mercy. He would strike with admonition. Closed eyes and clenched fists could not dull the pain of a squandered second chance. The Tigers avoided the punishment they deserved. They wiped the sweat from their temple and vowed never to repeat that crime.

# 19

## LITTLE BROTHER

CLEMSON DID NOT want to rely on anyone else for assistance. It had already received enough charity from its peers to remain in the top four of the College Football Playoff rankings after losing to Pittsburgh. But in Week 12, the playoff was not the primary focus. A win at Wake Forest would seal the Atlantic Coast Conference Atlantic Division championship.

Clemson wasted no time revealing its revitalized attack. It bolted to a 21–0 lead before the end of the first quarter. The Tigers amassed 192 yards of total offensive in the first frame, while the defense limited Wake to an average of 1.8 yards per play. Clemson scored on four consecutive drives before its first miscue. Receiver Ray-Ray McCloud muffed a punt in the second quarter that disrupted the dominance. Wake recovered at the Clemson 27. Although the Tigers surrendered merely three yards, the turnover donated a field goal to the Demon Deacons.

Clemson turned the ball over on downs on its next possession. Wake responded and rolled 64 yards on six plays. The Deacs capped the drive with a one-yard touchdown plunge. Clemson's next four drives resulted in two three-and-outs, a four-and-out, and a turn-over on downs. The 28–10 cushion Clemson had built sufficed as the defense stifled Wake. Clemson compiled eight tackles for loss and inhibited Wake from reaching the end zone again.

Clemson shook its funk and manufactured a 13-play, 80-yard, 5:35 drive that culminated in a one-yard touchdown run from Wayne Gallman. The insurance score secured the 35–13 victory and the Atlantic Division title. Just before he hoisted the division trophy in the locker room, Swinney emphatically commended his players for their resilience, as they dismissed the previous week's disappointment.

"Life is about how you respond. I don't care what it is that happens," Swinney told them. "We talked about the opportunity that we had as a football team. How are you going to pick yourself up? How are you going to respond? Let me tell you something, you guys set the tempo in that first half. I'm so proud. I knew you were going to play well, but watching you guys come together and respond like we did, on the road coming off of a tough week, how you went back to work, that's what it's all about.

"It ain't about pouting. It ain't about pointing fingers. It's about getting better. It's about taking ownership, and it's about everybody doing what they've got to do. You guys have earned your way. Ain't nobody given you nothing. You've earned your way. You've been the best team all year, and you put an exclamation point on it."

The 2016 Palmetto Bowl was intriguing in every way except the game. South Carolina limped into the game with a 6–7 overall record in Will Muschamp's first season as head coach. The Gamecocks needed victories against East Carolina, Massachusetts, and Western Carolina to seal their bowl eligibility.

Both teams arrived at Death Valley already slightly salty after exchanging a few veiled insults in press conferences earlier in the week. South Carolina is a small state. News circulates quickly. Gossip travels even faster, especially when it is misconstrued.

Carolina linebacker Chris Moody provided the fodder that week. In a conversation with media members during which he also deemed Clemson "one of the top teams in the country" and complimented Deshaun Watson and Wayne Gallman, Moody attempted to compare Carolina's annual series with Clemson to a sibling rivalry.

"It's always excitement when you're playing your rival," Moody said. "It's like beating on your little brother."

Moody meant to relay how badly he and his teammates wanted to win the game, similarly to a driveway series of hoops. But by the time the quote reached Clemson players, the report was that Moody had cited that Carolina had won five of the last seven in the series and that Carolina was the elder, more powerful sibling who would lock the younger one in the linen closet.

Under the helmet and between the white lines, there is little room for context. And when a team sits at the top as long as Clemson had by then, the Tigers had to take their slights where they could get them, even if they had to stretch for them. Clemson has been conditioned to max out their effort regardless of the opponent or stakes. The Tigers did not need any added incentive. But a perceived insult does add a little juice around the game, and it makes the victory celebration significantly sweeter.

Clemson hammered the Gamecocks 56–7. Watson completed 26 of 32 pass attempts for 347 yards and six touchdowns. Mike Williams caught three of those touchdowns. On the second, he carried a South Carolina defender seven yards into the end zone. He finished with six receptions and 100 yards. Gallman rushed for 112 yards and a touchdown.

In an abbreviated evening, senior linebacker Ben Boulware led Clemson with seven tackles. He also notched two sacks and forced a fumble. He also relished in the most lopsided victory in the rivalry since Clemson's 51–0 rout in 1900. Clemson improved to 68–42–4 in the Palmetto Bowl series.

"On our end, it's like Daddy giving his son a whupping," Watson said. "We run this state. The longtime record since Game 1, it speaks for itself."

During Clemson's final drive, Swinney gave the fans additional time to savor the victory. He called two timeouts to grant the seniors a curtain call for their final game in Death Valley. That also ruffled the Gamecocks' feathers.

"I feel like they kind of disrespected us at the end, holding the ball and doing all that showboating." Carolina safety D.J. Smith said. "I feel like it wasn't really classy, but it is a rivalry game. It's going to stick with all of us, and we're going to remember."

Boulware wanted the Gamecocks to remember. He was certain to clarify the status of the rivalry for anyone confused by Moody's analogy. "South Carolina, they always have been and always will be the little brother of this state," Boulware said. "I don't have to play them anymore, so I don't have to be nice to them anymore. South Carolina's always the little brother. They always will be. So it is what it is. It kind of just annoyed me because we were being super respectful giving credit where credit was due. They were trying to disrespect us, saying our offensive line was finesse, saying we were the little brother. We were trying to be mature and respectful of the whole situation.

"We knew they weren't in our league. We knew at every position, they couldn't compete with us. We proved that. I think they were just running their mouths. They were trying to play mind games with us and get in our heads. That's South Carolina. So it doesn't surprise me. I know they were saying they played at Florida, so they were prepared for this environment. Hell no, they weren't. Go watch their game against Florida, the stands weren't even full. They can say they were ready for the environment and they knew it was going to be loud. No, the hell they weren't. They definitely will have a good future, but they weren't ready for Death Valley."

Before the season started, Swinney advised his team to keep the first weekend in December clear on their calendar. He planned another trip to the ACC Championship Game. At that time, the reservations were set for Charlotte, where the event was held the previous six seasons. But Clemson was forced to alter those travel plans.

The ACC joined the succession of sports organizations that pulled events from North Carolina in response to House Bill 2, the state legislation that restricted cities and counties from legislating protections based on sexual orientation and gender identity. The bill also stipulated that citizens must use the public restrooms and changing facilities that correspond to their biological sex.

The "bathroom bill" ignited a fiery backlash. Musicians moved their concerts. Major organizations relocated their conventions. Major corporations abandoned plans to build facilities in the state. The NBA moved its All-Star Game from Charlotte. The NCAA moved the men's basketball tournament events from Greensboro. The ACC, which is headquartered in Greensboro, North Carolina, demonstrated its opposition to its home state by moving its marquee championship events.

Clemson president Jim Clements served as the chairperson of the ACC Council of Presidents. The council met in Clemson in September and voted to move the football championship game from Bank of America Stadium.

"The ACC presidents engaged in a constructive, wide-ranging, and vigorous discussion of this complex issue," Clements said when the move was announced. "The decision to move the neutral site championships out of North Carolina while HB 2 remains the law was not an easy one, but it is consistent with the shared values of inclusion and non-discrimination at all of our institutions."

The massive loss of revenue prompted North Carolina legislators to readdress the bill. Many organizations, including the ACC, were satisfied and announced that they would return their events to the Tarheel State the following year. That reconciliation did not help Clemson's team and fans, who were counting on a short trip to Charlotte for the title game.

Two weeks after it announced plans to move, the ACC reached an agreement to relocate the title game to Camping World Stadium in Orlando, Florida. In Charlotte, the event could have been a day trip—a short drive up, a tailgate, a night game, and a short drive back home. However, a trip to Orlando required a bit more planning. Only the most ambitious and most caffeinated fans would attempt that round in a single day, including the game. Those with the means to fly still would risk fees for refundable flights.

The ACC held its first five conference championship games in Florida—from 2005 to 2007 in Jacksonville and 2008 and 2009 in Tampa. Charlotte hosted the game each year from 2010 to 2015 and was contracted to stage the game until 2019. The ACC's return to Florida was not an inconvenience for all Clemson fans. Clemson alumni in Orlando welcomed another "home" game. Clemson's last visit to Camping World Stadium was during its 40–6 thrashing of Oklahoma in the 2014 Russell Athletic Bowl.

This time Clemson faced Virginia Tech, who broke into the CFP rankings at No. 25 after closing the season with a 9–3 overall record. Like Swinney, Virginia Tech's Justin Fuente notched a division title in his first full season as head coach. Swinney was not surprised. He was familiar with Fuente before he arrived in Blacksburg. In 2009 Fuente was the offensive coordinator at Texas Christian. He directed eventual NFL quarterback Andy Dalton in a tough 14–10 victory at Clemson. Two years later, Swinney considered Fuente for his vacancy at offensive coordinator before hiring Chad Morris. The next season, Fuente became head coach at Memphis. In 2011 Memphis finished with a 2–10 record. Memphis finished Fuente's third season 10–3. Fuente has not won fewer than nine games in a season since.

"I just had a lot of respect for the job he had done and watched him closely," Swinney said of Fuente. "Really, just a great guy. He and I became friends, kept in touch, and the next year he got the Memphis job, and we just kind of stayed in touch in that regard. I would shoot him just an encouragement text from time to time or he might send me one and then we talked a little bit about some recruiting. I had a couple players who had an opportunity who we had recruited here and for whatever reason were looking for another place to go, so I reached out to him a couple different times on a couple different players who had opportunities to go and play for him.

"Again, good, healthy relationship, and then got a chance obviously to spend some face time with him once he got into this league and we had some of our spring meetings and stuff. But just a great guy, heck of a football coach, and he's going to do a fantastic job at Virginia Tech."

The friends battled fiercely in Orlando. Clemson led 21–14 at halftime and pulled away with a pair of touchdowns in the third quarter. Virginia Tech did not close the deficit to fewer than 14 points until 5:43 remained in the fourth quarter. The Hokies opened their final drive from their own 40-yard line trailing 35–28 with 4:03 remaining. They marched to the Clemson 23 before the Tigers stiffened. On third-and-6, Clelin Ferrell and Christian Wilkins dropped quarterback Jerod Evans for no gain. On the next play, linebacker Kendall Joseph hurried Evans' throw and cornerback Cordrea Tankersley intercepted the pass at the 14-yard line. It was Tankersley's second interception of the game, his third of the season. Joseph led Clemson with 11 tackles, including one for loss.

Watson completed 28 of 34 passes for 288 yards and three touchdowns. He also rushed for 85 yards and two touchdowns. It was Watson's ninth game of the season in which he accounted for at least 300 yards of total offense. It was his final pitch to Heisman Trophy voters.

While Watson awaited his invitation to the Heisman ceremony, Clemson celebrated its secured invitation to the College Football Playoff, while raising another ACC championship trophy. Clemson won the consecutive conference titles for the first time since 1987 and 1988.

"Twenty-eight years, guys, since Clemson's won back-to-back titles," Swinney told his team in the locker room. "That's a long time, No. 1. I was playing. No. 2, it's hard to do. We were all brought here on purpose, with a purpose, for a purpose. We're all here for a moment like this."

The ACC was founded in 1953, when Clemson, Duke, Maryland, North Carolina, North Carolina State, South Carolina, Virginia, and Wake Forest withdrew from the Southern Conference. That season, Maryland quarterback Bernie Faloney completed 31 of 68 passes for 599 yards, five touchdowns, and seven interceptions. In this century, those numbers might get a quarterback benched. Then, they made Faloney a Heisman Trophy finalist. Faloney finished fourth in Heisman voting that year. No ACC player finished that high again until Virginia quarterback Shawn Moore in 1990.

From 1953 to 2016, merely nine ACC players finished in the top four of Heisman voting. Four ACC players won the award. The first three were all from Florida State—Charlie Ward in 1993, Chris Weinke in 2000, and Jameis Winston in 2013. In 2016 the ACC was represented by two Heisman finalists. Louisville quarterback Lamar Jackson and Watson were among the five players invited to New York City for the trophy presentation.

That season, Jackson passed for 3,390 yards, 30 touchdowns, and nine interceptions. He also rushed for 1,538 yards and 21 touchdowns. Watson passed for 3,914 yards, 37 touchdowns, and 15 interceptions. He rushed for 529 yards and six touchdowns.

Frame the debate any way you want. Consider victories. Consider impact. Consider leadership. Consider entertainment. Vote for the most valuable player. Vote for the most outstanding performer.

Either way, anyone who watched the 2016 season closely and objectively could acknowledge that the two best players in college football competed in the ACC. Talent across the league steadily improved. Schools once considered afterthoughts attracted coveted coaches. The ACC was more than a basketball league.

It may never match the championship lineage of its neighbors in the Southeastern Conference. The SEC produced eight of the previous 10 national champions. At that point, the ACC claimed six through its entire history. Again, Florida State contributed three of those, in 1993, 1999, and 2013. Georgia Tech won in 1990. Clemson won in 1981. Maryland, led by Faloney, won in 1953.

For much of its 25 seasons in the league, Florida State was the ACC's lone flag bearer. Expansions added Virginia Tech, Miami, and Pitt, but none of those programs maintained their dominance or prominence from the Big East. Swinney helped Clemson finally join Florida State on the national stage. Their annual rivalry essentially decided the conference championship and position in the College Football Playoff race. Clemson and Florida State elevated the standard for the league. Although they certainly were not there yet, programs like Louisville, Virginia Tech, Miami, North Carolina, Duke, and Pitt were attempting to follow.

That season, the ACC earned a 3–1 record against the Big Ten and a 6–3 mark against the SEC. One of those losses was Louisville's regular-season finale against Kentucky, which many thought pulled Jackson toward the back of the Heisman pack. Nevertheless, the ACC was discarding its reputation as the Almost Competitive Conference. It had not yet climbed to the top of the Power 5. Virginia did lose to Richmond in 2016, but the ACC was far from the doormat it once was. And it showed no sign of regression.

Nine ACC teams were ranked in the top 35 of the 2016 ESPN recruiting rankings. Only the SEC had more teams. From 2005 to 2016, the ACC produced 449 NFL Draft picks, second only to the SEC, which produced 519. The ACC compiled a collection of coaches who could recruit and maximize talent. Aside from tenured leaders Dabo Swinney and Bobby Petrino, new additions Mark Richt, Justin Fuente, Pat Narduzzi, Dino Babers, and Bronco Mendenhall could change the status of their programs and change the perception of the entire league.

Perhaps soon, a closely contested ACC game between Clemson and Syracuse could be assessed like the nail-biters in the Big Ten and SEC. It would be considered a showcase of conference depth instead of a lackluster blunder for the perceived power. Jackson and Watson claimed seats in New York City and signified pending progress for the league. Jackson hoisted the Heisman Trophy that night. Although disappointed, Watson had his eyes on another piece of hardware.

Clemson sealed the No. 2 seed in the College Football Playoff standings. The Tigers traveled back to University of Phoenix Stadium in Glendale, Arizona, to face Ohio State in the Fiesta Bowl. Watson was no longer concerned about that bronze statue. He was ready to chase gold.

Clemson dismantled Ohio State for a 31–0 victory. The Tigers outgained the Buckeyes 470 to 215 in total offense. Ohio State converted merely three of 14 third-down attempts, missed two field goals, and netted 88 rushing yards. Defensive end Clelin Ferrell led Clemson with three sacks. The Tigers amassed 11 tackles for loss that pushed the Buckeyes back 51 yards. Clemson defensive backs Cordrea Tankersley and Van Smith each snagged an interception off quarterback J.T. Barrett. Clemson also broke up five passes.

"There's no magic calls," defensive coordinator Brent Venables said. "These guys had to line up and get off of blocks and tackle and cover and play all three phases and complement each other. You have a night like that when you do the little things right."

It was Clemson's second shutout in a bowl game. The first was against Illinois in the 1991 Hall of Fame Bowl.

"We didn't really have any illusions they wouldn't score a point. We just wanted to have one more than them," Swinney said. "Coach V and our staff, nobody works harder at preparing, but then our guys and how they bought into it, they were highly motivated and excited to go play the game. We knew we had a lot to prepare for and thankful that we had a little extra time, but it all goes back to preparation and buy-in and commitment from those players."

On the other side of the bracket, Alabama pounded Washington 24–7 in the Peach Bowl. Clemson earned another shot at the king.

# 20

## ORANGE CRUSH

IMMEDIATELY AFTER the victory against Ohio State in the Fiesta Bowl, Dabo Swinney said publicly that he had no preference on whom his team met in the College Football Playoff National Championship Game.

"I just wanted to have an opportunity to go," he said, "whoever gets there, gets there."

Swinney was being honest. The opponent was immaterial to the opportunity. Whether it was Washington or Alabama, Clemson would be required to exert the same effort in preparation and performance. But the competitive fire inside Swinney burned for another chance at Alabama. Sure, Clemson could avenge the previous loss, but Swinney also felt the natural rite of passage for his program would be through the Crimson Tide.

"Alabama has been the standard. There's really no argument to that," Swinney said. "Sooner or later, if you're going to be the best, you've got to beat them."

Approximately three months after their previous clash, Swinney told Alabama coach Nick Saban that they would meet again in Tampa, and he was not referring to a vacation. Saban was not surprised by Swinney's accuracy.

"What Dabo has done with his program there, it is one of the top college football programs in the country. They do an outstanding job of recruiting. They do an outstanding job of coaching. They do an outstanding job of developing players. I can't tell you how much respect we have for the job that they do," Saban said. "I think it's reflected in the way they play on the field, the success that they've had, the consistency in performance that their team has shown, whether it's offense, defense, and in every phase of the game."

The Tigers savored another opportunity to dethrone Alabama. Perhaps no one savored it more than Mike Williams. He never sat down that morning during the College Football Playoff Media Day. It was three days before Clemson's rematch with Alabama. He was in high demand for the entire hour. He graciously flashed his wide smile for national television cameras, a horde of writers, and a crowd of zealous fans.

"It's just special," Williams said as he took a break from signing autographs. "It means a lot. It's just a special moment. Just being here now, being able to play. It's special. I'm soaking it all in."

Williams did not share this same experience with his teammates the previous year. The neck injury he suffered in the 2015 season opener forced him to miss the remainder of the season. All he could do was watch the five-point loss to Alabama.

"To not get a chance to play and be a part of it, that was tough, because you don't know if that opportunity will ever come back," Swinney said that morning. "I'm very happy for him that he gets to play in this game and be a part of this moment, and hopefully the confetti will rain down on him when it's over."

Williams led Clemson through the first 14 games with 90 receptions, 1,267 yards, and 10 touchdowns. Williams could have matched those figures the previous season, but he also earned an honor that he would not have achieved that year. A degree. Williams graduated that December with a bachelor's in sociology.

"Maybe if I didn't get hurt, I wouldn't be here right now. I guess God wanted me to get my degree," Williams said with a laugh. "Everything happens for a reason."

Clemson compiled 554 yards and 40 points against Alabama in 2015. The Tigers hoped adding Williams to the operation would instantly increase that output and change the outcome. He caught his first pass on the first third-down snap on Clemson's first drive. But it was a three-yard gain that left Clemson with fourth-and-1 at the Alabama 41. After a timeout, Swinney elected to pursue the first down, but running back Wayne Gallman was stopped for no gain. Alabama scored on the ensuing possession. Bo Scarborough rushed for a 25-yard touchdown.

Both defenses tightened. On the next five possessions, the teams combined for 61 yards on 29 plays, an average of 2.1 yards per play. Alabama receiver ArDarius Stewart opened the next drive with 25-yard run. Scarborough closed it with a 37-yard touchdown run. Clemson trailed 14–0 with 7:42 remaining in the half.

By that point, the Tigers had compiled 79 yards of total offense with an average of 2.9 yards per play. Receiver Deon Cain improved that rate drastically on the next possession. Cain caught a high pass from quarterback Deshaun Watson behind the line of scrimmage and carved through the Crimson Tide defense for a 43-yard gain. It was welcome redemption for Cain, a Tampa native who was suspended during the 2015 bowl run. It was welcome relief for Clemson's offense. The Tigers advanced to the 8-yard line with two passes, a 26-yarder to tight end Jordan Leggett and a five-yard gain from Williams. Watson finished the drive on an outside designed run. He bobbled the snap, sprinted to the edge, tip-toed along the sideline and twisted into the end zone.

Clemson trailed 14–7 at halftime. The Tigers did not allow Alabama to convert a third down in the second quarter. Watson passed for 130 yards in that frame. But the offensive revival was dulled on the fourth snap of the third quarter. Running back Wayne Gallman took a wide handoff to the right but was stuffed at the Clemson 34-yard line. Alabama linebacker Ryan Anderson stripped the ball from Gallman, collected the fumble, and sprinted toward the end zone. Receiver Hunter Renfrow swiftly turned and darted ahead of a pack of Alabama blockers and dove to trip Anderson at the 16-yard line. Through its previous 14 games, Alabama's defense scored 11 touchdowns, including six interception returns, and five fumble returns. Considering Clemson surrendered 17 interceptions and nine fumbles through its previous 14 games, the Tigers heeded the threat of a scoop-and-score or pick-six.

"That was one thing we stressed the whole game," Leggett said. "If they do have a fumble recovery or pick off a ball, we've got to get them on the ground and let them go play offense against our defense."

Renfrow's effort saved four points. Clemson's defense denied Alabama a first down and forced a field goal. Clemson drove to the Alabama 43 before being stopped on third-and-1. The Tigers lined up like they were going to attempt the fourth-down conversion, but Watson clutched the snap and popped a pooch punt that was downed at the 5-yard line. Alabama opened its next possession with its backs lined up in the end zone. Clemson capitalized on the field-position swing and forced a three-and-out. Clemson opened the next drive one yard further than the previous drive ended. Four plays later, Watson zipped a pass to Renfrow as he broke free across the middle. Renfrow sprinted toward the right corner of the end zone, planted at the 10-yard line, cut sharply upfield, and tangled the feet of an Alabama defender. The 24-yard touchdown trimmed the margin to 17–14 with 7:10 remaining in the third.

A frightening refrain returned for Clemson. Tight end O.J. Howard logged five receptions for 208 yards and two touchdowns in the teams' previous meeting. He slipped behind Clemson's coverage again for a 68-yard touchdown. Watson completed five of six pass attempts on the ensuing drive. He tossed a four-yard touchdown to Williams on an aggressive rub route.

The teams combined for two first downs over the next five possessions. Watson broke the stalemate with a 17-yard pass to Leggett followed by a 26-yard pass to Williams. Watson rushed around the edge for 15 yards and leaped toward the end zone. He was ruled out of bounds at the 1. Gallman capped the drive with a touchdown plunge. Clemson claimed its first lead, 28–24, with 4:38 remaining.

Alabama quarterback Jalen Hurts completed two of his first three attempts on the next drive. Then he shot a pass behind the line of scrimmage to Stewart, who gathered and unloaded a 24-yard pass to Howard that advanced the ball to the Clemson 30-yard line. On the next play, Hurts dropped back and looked downfield. As Clemson's defense penetrated the pocket, Hurts quickly tucked the ball, escaped through an opening, and sprinted through the middle of the field. He slipped two tackles and skipped into the end zone. Hurts put the Crimson Tide back on top 31–28, but Watson was unfazed. He simply looked at the clock.

After C.J. Fuller returned the subsequent kickoff 20 yards, the Tigers took over at their own 32-yard line with 2:01 remaining.

"I saw the two minutes and one second on the clock, and I just smiled, and I just knew. I told myself, *They left too much time on the clock*," Watson recalled. "We prepared for moments like this all the time. It was just another opportunity for us to show what we're about, just on a bigger stage. God put us there for a reason. I just told my guys, 'Hey, let's go be legendary.'"

Watson opened with a short pass to Leggett for five yards. He lofted the next pass down the sideline to Williams, who soared above the draping defender, hung in the air, and clutched a 24-yard reception. Watson zipped the next throw to Artavis Scott four yards behind the line of scrimmage. He lateraled the ball to Gallman, who wove through traffic for a six-yard gain. Watson scrambled on the next play, avoided a sack, and pushed forward for a yard. On third-and-3, he tossed a short pass to Renfrow across the middle for six yards. On the next snap, Watson spiked the ball to stop the clock with 19 seconds remaining.

Clemson had advanced into Greg Huegel's field-goal range, but Swinney did not want to settle for the tie. On the next play, Watson muscled the ball toward Leggett, who contorted and stretched to snag the 17-yard pass at the 9-yard line. Watson misfired on the next throw but tested the Crimson Tide in the end zone again and drew a pass-interference flag. Clemson lined up at the 2-yard line with six seconds remaining. The ball was on the right hash. Gallman stood on Watson's right side in the backfield. Williams split out wide alone on the left of the formation. Leggett was tight on the line to the right of the tackle. Scott was flanked wide. Renfrow was slotted on the right hash.

"Coach Swinney wanted a running play, but I told him, 'Let's pass it,'" Watson recalled. "I told him to put the ball in my hands, and that's what we did."

Watson widened and pumped his hands to signal for the snap. Jay Guillermo snapped the ball cleanly to Watson, who darted immediately to his right. Scott launched left and collided with cornerback Marlon Humphrey. The tussle essentially created a basketball screen that diverted Tony Brown's pursuit of Renfrow as he cut right sharply toward the pylon. Watson snapped a pass into Renfrow's chest. Renfrow rocked back in the end zone, absorbed a hit from Brown and rolled on his back for the touchdown.

The Clemson sideline exploded in exuberance along with the large section of Raymond James Stadium that was covered in orange. Renfrow popped off the crowd and flipped the ball casually to an official. Watson stretched his arms as he glided jubilantly back to the sideline.

"We knew we were in a situation where we felt like we had points," said co–offensive coordinator Tony Elliott, referring to the play the staff calls "Orange Crush." "We had six seconds. It was a sprint out. Either it was going to be there, or you throw the ball away. Call timeout. Have two seconds left. Kick the field goal. Go to overtime.

"We're a fast-paced team, so scoring in a minute or two is nothing new to us. Guys just made huge plays, and what you saw was the heart of our team, the heart of Clemson."

One second remained on the clock. Huegel added the extra point, then recovered the onside kick. Watson took the snap and kneeled to exhaust the clock. Clemson edged Alabama 35–31 and seized the national title. Watson stood still, soaking in the moment. Pandemonium ensued. Swinney pointed to the sky, acknowledging his father, Ervil. Swinney was certain he smiled proudly as his son hoisted the College Football Playoff National Championship Trophy.

Swinney was overjoyed by the accomplishment. He was touched by how they achieved it. "To me, that moment, that epitomizes what our program is all about. You've got the five-star quarterback throwing the game-winning touchdown to the walk-on wideout."

Hunter Renfrow grew up in Myrtle Beach, South Carolina, with three brothers, two sisters, and too many cousins to count. But occasionally, Hunter could not find a partner to toss the football to him. "One of my favorite stories of Hunter was when he was about eight or nine," Hunter's mother, Suzanne, said. "I was in the kitchen cooking, and he came in and he had his little shoulder pads on. I said, 'I didn't know you were playing football. Are all the boys over here?' And he said, 'No, I'm playing with the trees.'"

The Renfrows had a cluster of seven oak trees in their front yard. When he could not find a partner, Renfrow would toss the ball high into the air and see how many trees he could ricochet off of before he caught the ball. "He'd stay out there for an hour and just play with the trees. That's just Hunter," said Suzanne, who frequently substituted in for those oaks when she had time. "I loved playing with my kids in the backyard," she said. "I would throw balls to the kids and particularly to Hunter. I could not throw a straight ball, baseball or football, so he would always have to dive after them to get to them."

"That's why I became a decent receiver," Hunter said, "because I'd have to go and retrieve my mom's balls when they were all over the place."

"God can use anything," Suzanne said with a laugh. "He can even use a mom that's a terrible athlete."

Hunter developed quick reflexes and soft hands, but, by the time he reached Socastee High School, he had developed into a dynamic option quarterback. He stood slightly under 6′ and weighed slightly more than 160 pounds.

"I was out there every day with him and watched him compete," said Hunter's father, Tim Renfrow, who played football and baseball at Wofford College in Spartanburg, South Carolina.

During his senior season at Socastee, Hunter rushed for more than 1,400 yards and 19 touchdowns. He tossed eight touchdown passes without an interception. But no scholarship offers from major programs trickled in to the Renfrows' mailbox. He did draw interest from Wofford, Furman, and Appalachian State.

But Hunter wanted to attend Clemson.

"I knew even coming in as a walk-on, even if I got hurt and couldn't play anymore, that I'd enjoy going to school there," Hunter said. He attended camps at Clemson and attracted an offer as a preferred walk-on. He returned from his visit without informing Swinney that he would like to join the team.

"I remember just thinking, *I know this is where he wants to go. I wonder why he didn't tell them he was coming?*" Suzanne recalled. "My husband just said, 'I think he's just concerned about putting that burden on us with tuition.'"

While appreciative of his concern, Suzanne and Tim encouraged Hunter to follow his heart. "We said, 'We want you to know that we want you to go wherever you feel like God's leading you to go,'" Suzanne said. "And within two minutes, he was on the phone with Coach Swinney saying, 'I'm coming to Clemson.'"

Renfrow arrived on campus in 2014. He served on the scout team but quickly impressed his new teammates. "He's just one of those guys who came in and went to work," Watson said. "All the guys on defense were saying, 'Hunter's going to be special.'"

"I mean, I'm at practice every day, and he's the best player, period," said Swinney, who offered Hunter a scholarship the next year during August camp. Hunter shared the news with his parents the same way he flipped the ball back to the official—casually.

"We were on the phone, and Hunter called to talk like any other day," Tim recalled. "He didn't say much, but right before he hung up he said, 'Oh, by the way, I got a scholarship today.' Of course, we were happy financially. That always helps, but more than anything, he had a goal to go there and get a scholarship. We want our kids to be successful and we want them, when they set goals, to be able to reach those goals."

Hunter worked his way into the rotation and finished 2015 with 33 receptions, the fifth-highest total on the team. He started the final eight games of 2016. He compiled 26 receptions for 289 yards and five touchdowns through his first four CFP games.

"He won't talk a lot about it, but deep down in Hunter, he loves a challenge," Tim said, "and he wanted to prove to himself that he could play at that level."

"He's tough as nails, maybe surprises people a little bit from time to time," Swinney said. "It's just amazing to me. If we lined all of our managers up [beside] him, he'd be about the 10th guy you'd pick to be Hunter Renfrow."

Alabama certainly knew who Hunter was. He amassed 10 receptions, 92 yards, and two touchdowns in Tampa.

"It's been such a journey for me," Hunter said. "It's like I got knocked out in the third quarter, and this was all a dream."

"Just bloom where you're planted. Be about the right things," Swinney said. "The theme of this whole playoff was 'Chasing Greatness.' That's what was special about that moment, to give hope to a lot of people out there, that greatness is for everyone."

Confetti continued to shower Raymond James Stadium as the team gathered on the stage to celebrate the victory. ESPN's Rece Davis cycled through the captains for a series of television interviews. Once he arrived at Ben Boulware, Davis did not need his microphone.

Boulware gripped his fists, tightened his shoulders, and dug deeply into the soul of every Clemson fan. He roared and released three decades' worth of frustration, three decades' worth of unmet expectations, three decades' worth of tenuous optimism. His proclamation resonated from that stage to those majestic hills in Upstate South Carolina.

"It's coming home!" Boulware blared.

After 35 years, the wait was lifted. Clemson claimed its second national championship. The chorus of cheers rolled steadily from euphoric Tigers. Streams of joyful tears flooded the stands. Fans clung to each other in disbelief, wondering if the moment they just witnessed actually happened.

For so long, it was the Tigers' goal. It was their motivation. It was their hope. But it never was their time. There was always at least one game, one injury, one mistake, one play that forced Clemson to wait until next year. But through patience and persistence, the Tigers finally reached that lofty goal—and raised that elusive gold.

Boulware, the fiery linebacker, signified the grit and resolve of Clemson's community and the program. He was named the defensive MVP after compiling six total tackles, including two for loss and a vicious hit that dislodged the mouthpiece from an unsuspecting Alabama receiver. In his honorary national television interview and afterward in a crammed locker room, Boulware refused to revel in his personal accolades or in the achievement of this single team. He used that platform, instead, to acknowledge the foundation on which Clemson constructed its championship program and the loyal community that shared its success.

He credited the players who preceded this senior class. Those who cultivated a culture of accountability. Those who elevated the standard of effort. Those who opened this lofty pursuit but never quite managed to complete it.

"It's just very satisfying for our community, our university, and our fans," Boulware said. "For our forefathers, the Tajh Boyds, the

Stephone Anthonys, Grady Jarretts, and C.J. Spillers. For us to put the finishing touches on it and come out with a national championship, it's a very satisfying feeling just to bring it home for our family."

Tajh Boyd, the former All-America quarterback, served as Clemson's honorary captain for the title game. He also was in that crammed locker room, triumphantly celebrating the championship he, his teammates, and his own predecessors facilitated.

"It's special to see where it's grown. With this team, these players, all the leaders they have and Coach Swinney spearheading that, this is special," Boyd said. "People have been waiting around here for a long time. There have been some great teams to play here at Clemson, but only two have won the national championship."

Few observers anticipated this moment when Swinney was promoted to head coach. He was a modest wide receivers coach, with a plethora of clichés and acronyms but without a proven pedigree of leadership and success. He recruited well. He hired well. He directed well. He managed well. And when he encountered adversity, he responded well.

He set a vision that seemed unrealistic, and then he forced it into reality. He helped Clemson elbow its way into an elite neighborhood. He constructed an immaculate new home for Clemson football on campus, and now he had a shiny new housewarming gift.

"When I came to Clemson as an assistant, I truly saw the greatness and potential," Swinney said. "It's not just for this team. It's a credit to all my teams, all my players. What they did was meant for them at that time, but this was meant for this team. This was this team's responsibility. This was this team's mission, and there was really only one lid left on the program, and that was to win the whole dadgum thing."

This moment reached further back than Tajh Boyd and Deandre Hopkins. It reached further back than C.J. Spiller and Da'Quan Bowers. It reached back to 1981. It reached back to all those who relished that glory but wondered when they would ever relive it. It reached a hearty community, filled with teachers and textile workers, executives and students. It reached fans of different ages, ethnicities, interests, and backgrounds, who would have never even exchanged a glare before but may now exchange an embrace, as they all wrap their arms around that memory.

They believed when there was nothing on the roster to substantiate their confidence. Their loyalty was rewarded. Their devotion was affirmed. That was their goal. That was their motivation. That was their hope. And on that enchanting night, that was, finally, their time.

# 21

# HOME

IN LESS THAN A DECADE as Clemson's head coach, Dabo Swinney cultivated a culture of family, faith, fervor, focus, and fun. The $55 million football complex Clemson opened in January 2017 captures that culture completely. The Allen N. Reeves Football Complex sprawls across 142,500 square feet and integrates seamlessly with the preexisting indoor practice facility and practice fields. The complex includes a grand lobby showcasing the CFP National Championship trophies and the Waterford crystal footballs on the 1981 and 2016 Coaches' Trophies. There is a replica of the Hill and the Rock, a bowling alley, an arcade, a barber shop, and a nap room.

The massive dining wing includes a biometric scanner to help players monitor and adjust their nutrition. The weight room covers 23,000 square feet. One area near the lobby is dedicated only to displaying Clemson's Nike gear. It includes three rotating mannequins sporting the Tigers' uniform combinations.

Swinney even ordered a slide to provide a quick, fun alternative to walking from the second floor to the ground level. Outdoors, there is a fire pit, an artificial turf Wiffle ball diamond, a sand volleyball court, a horseshoe pit, a nine-hole miniature golf course, and a covered regulation basketball court.

The immaculate facility exhibits the standardized exorbitant extravagance in the college football arms race. However, the building was not dreamed, designed, and constructed simply to pander to players and recruits. Swinney desired a building that reflects the personal growth and academic excellence he demands. It is a demonstration of his boundless ambition. Swinney has repeatedly expressed his apprehension to paying players a salary. Education rescued him from a generational cycle of pain and poverty. It allowed him to enhance the lives of his entire family. He believes strongly in the transformative power of education. He rejects anything that he believes would threaten its significance.

"Nobody ever talks about the value of an education when you get into that stuff," Swinney said. "These players are getting a whole lot. It's the best it's ever been, and it certainly can still be improved."

Swinney suggested collegiate administrators could make "common-sense" changes like allowing travel allowances for players' families and possibly even exploring adjustments in the use of players' names, images, and likenesses.

The discussion of loosening the NCAA constraints that prohibit players from capitalizing on their personal brand is often erroneously, or conveniently, lumped in with the debate on schools paying athletes actual wages. These conversations concern two unconnected revenue streams, and one of them does not even run through the schools. A tiny percentage of college players will excel as professionals in their sport. For all others, their time in college is the height of their football career, and thus, the peak of their popularity.

Quarterback Tajh Boyd could serve as a powerful lead plaintiff for this case. His NFL career was curtailed, but during his tenure as the face of Clemson football's resurrection, he could not monetize that marketability. There were no endorsements or paid autograph sessions. He could not secure speaking engagements or host instructional camps. Boyd flourishes in many of those ventures now, blossoming as a businessman in Greenville, South Carolina. But obstructive and obsolete NCAA rules forced Boyd to leave plenty of money on the table.

Meanwhile, the NCAA permits coaches to earn millions from endorsements, speaking honorariums, merchandising, and other

revenue streams. Most of them even have new cars and other benefits written into their contracts. Federal lawsuits are being pursued
to examine the contradiction and possibly correct the incongruity.
Although those potential funds would be separate from the universities and in addition to the scholarship compensation package,
there are still dangers that a free and fair market will lead to more
manipulation, exploitation, and corruption than what is already
rampant in college athletics.

Swinney fears that, if monetary compensation becomes the top
enticement in college athletics, not every influencer in the indus-
try will continue to honor the duty of educating these young men
and women. Those who oversee the money can easily overlook
its impairments. The proliferation of academic fraud, in addition
to the mishandling of domestic violence, sexual assault, and other
deplorable scandals support Swinney's trepidation.

Swinney believes football instruction, recruiting, and roster
composition constitute a very small fraction of his duties. He feels
responsible for developing his players holistically. Toward that
aim, in addition to the opulent amenities in the Reeves Complex,
Swinney also dedicated space, personnel, and resources to the
PAW Journey program. It employs one his signature acronyms—
Passionate About Winning—and focuses on preparing players for
life after football.

Players sacrifice so much of their time, bodies, and mental health
for the game. Universities generate millions of dollars from that
sacrifice. They owe these students a genuine education. And if they
cannot cut them a slice of that revenue pie, they at least owe them
the training, guidance, and encouragement that will equip them to
obtain their own pie after graduation.

Jeff Davis was an All-America linebacker and captain on Clemson's 1981 national championship team. "The Judge" terrorized
offenses for 175 tackles that season. As a player, Davis made a living
dismantling opponents. He returned to Clemson in 1999 to build up

young men. Davis served as field director for Call Me Mister, a program that recruited and trained African American elementary educators. He later accepted a position leading athletic fundraising to help Clemson build up its facilities. During that time, Davis' office was across the hall from Swinney's. As the two developed a rapport, they realized they both shared a common belief system. Not only because Davis is an ordained Christian minister, but they both believe in the power of education. The day after athletic director Terry Don Phillips named Swinney the interim head coach, Swinney returned to Phillips to request the creation of a new position: associate athletic director for football player relations.

"I said, 'I need Jeff Davis,'" Swinney said. "He is passionate, truly passionate, about impacting their lives."

Davis makes it easier for parents to entrust their children to Clemson. He is a surrogate father, a confidant, a demanding mentor who holds players accountable but also offers compassion and understanding. He has endured the battles these players face, on and off the field. He promotes integrity and character but also equips players with life skills they can carry with them for a lifetime.

And he can achieve all of that with simple chats. He speaks with clarity and gravity. One cannot leave his office uninspired. Yet, formalized in the PAW Journey program, Davis' vision for personal and professional guidance elevated the standard for college athletics.

"I'm grateful for my experience at Clemson. I'm grateful for the resources that were provided," Davis said. "But I understood that had I known some other things and been taught some other skills before I left Clemson, my impact could be even greater. I want our young men to leave here prepared to compete in the marketplace at a high level. I want them to be aware of their skills. I want them to be aware of their core values, so they can be productive members of society."

The mentorship the program provides, the community service projects it organizes, the corporate partnerships it maintains, and the resources it provides are more valuable than a commercial with a local dealership. They will last longer than a scholarship stipend check. What is the point of providing additional money to athletes if no one will ensure that they know how to manage it wisely? All players deserve that care, so all coaches should care.

"When you walk into our new facility, the first thing you see is the PAW Journey," Swinney said. "We want that to be the front door of our program."

"We're sending a message," Davis said, "that nothing is more important than how we develop you as a man."

PAW Journey transcends graduation rates and other NCAA metrics. Those measurements reveal an adherence to minimum guidelines for eligibility, and Clemson is ranked in the top 10 in those measurements. However, those metrics do not measure the lasting impact of sculpting good fathers, good colleagues, good citizens. That immersive education changes lives.

It also stimulates success on the field. Recruits are coveted for their talent. A program that also genuinely cares about their well-being is attractive, and sadly Clemson remains among the exceptions in college football in that regard. But that approach has helped the coaching staff attract top tier talent each year. Talent is the primary prerequisite for success on the field. Clemson intends to build leaders, but winning also remains an objective. Swinney has proven that a program can achieve both, at the highest level.

"One of the things that I really want for our players is, I want them to know that they can come to Clemson and not just score touchdowns and be an All-American on the football field," Swinney said, "but they can be an AD at Clemson. They can be an offensive coordinator, a defensive coordinator. Tony Elliott, who played for me, is our offensive coordinator, and calls the plays, does an unbelievable job, and I think that's a great message to those guys."

After cutting the ribbon to open the new complex, Swinney drove a few miles to Daniel High School to watch one of his recruits sign a letter of intent. "I have been recruiting this kid for 18 years and paid his mother a lot of money," Swinney said with a laugh. Swinney was at the hospital when this player was born—in Birmingham. Will Swinney, signed with his father's team as a preferred walk-on.

"Just proud of him. He's a good young man," Dabo said. "I've never in all my years recruited a young man who was more driven and worked harder to achieve his goals and dreams. He's a great example. He inspires me and his mom all the time just by watching how he works."

Will was 10 years old when his father was named Clemson's head coach. He frequented practices and kept charts on the sidelines during games. As he matured, Will developed close friendships with Clemson players, including a *Sports Illustrated* cover boy.

"I'll come home, and Hunter Renfrow will be at the house, and I'm like, 'What are you doing here?'" Swinney said. "Well, he and Will are great friends."

Like his father, Will is an undersized but scrappy receiver. He also is a sure-handed holder for place-kicks. Will aimed to secure a spot in the battery, and he knew his personal connection to the head coach would not grant him any shortcuts. He would not have accepted one.

"When we're at home, that's my dad. We don't ever really talk about football, it's just life," Will said. "When I'm at school, it's never really too hard for me. He's still my dad but I just view him as my coach."

Clemson recruited another Daniel High player heavily.

Daniel linebacker Jake Venables committed to Clemson in December 2016. He will join the Tigers in the fall of 2018. That provided some incentive for his father, defensive coordinator Brent Venables, to remain in Clemson for at least a few more years. Speculation stirs around the longevity of his tenure each off-season when the coaching carousel turns. But Brent Venables is more likely to leave the profession altogether than leave Clemson.

Bob Stoops' retirement from the University of Oklahoma in June 2017 sent shockwaves through college football. They rippled to Pickens County, South Carolina. Brent Venables coached on Stoops' staff before joining Swinney at Clemson in 2012. Their relationship began long before then.

"He recruited me to Kansas State," said Venables, who joined Stoops on Bill Snyder's staff as a graduate assistant in 1993 after that all-conference season. He earned a full-time role in 1996, when Stoops left to join Steve Spurrier's staff at Florida.

"I was hired full-time certainly because of Bill Snyder, but not without Bob Stoops urging him that, 'This is our guy,'" Venables said. "So I've known him intimately and his family. I spoke to him the day he retired. There's finality to it. All the emotions he was going through I shared, probably on a much smaller level."

Stoops retired at 56, a decade before he could draw Social Security benefits but much younger than other luminaries were when they hung up their whistles. Frank Beamer was 69. Spurrier was 70. Bobby Bowden was 80. Snyder was still K-State's coach in 2017 at 77.

Venables professed deep, sincere appreciation for his job. He enjoys influencing the lives of countless young men while participating in a game he loves. Yet he also values his family and his own health. He is committed to the demanding process of his profession. But not for life.

"Today, if you ask me, I'm a mid-fifty kind of guy," Venables, 46, said of his projected retirement age. "It's not an easy thing to manage, the rigors of a long season. I'm not asking for pity whatsoever. I'm lucky to do what I do. I'm definitely not putting the cart before the horse, but I want to be able to have options, like we all do. At some point, you'd like to enjoy your family more. That's why you work as hard as you do."

A family-friendly atmosphere attracted Venables to Clemson. Swinney schedules time for wives and children to join the staff for dinner on campus. He has adjusted speaking engagements to ensure he can attend his children's school events, including those Friday night games at Daniel High, whether Clemson is facing Kent State or Notre Dame the next day.

Proper perspective is important in any profession. Venables identified what he values most—family, a pleasant work culture, and winning. He does not allow anything to compromise those things. He revealed his disdain for supporters who credit him too much for the defense's success and critics who contend his satisfaction in his current position indicates a lack of ambition.

He remained among the top-five highest-paid defensive coordinators in college football, yet he asserted that he has never been concerned about salary. He will never chase a job to chase a raise. He developed his fiery focus simply because he never wants to be fired.

"I was a young coach, and this older veteran coach had had 30 jobs in his career. He said, 'There's only two kinds of coaches, y'know. Those who have been fired or those who are gonna be fired,'" Venables recalled. "I sit there like, 'I'm not getting fired. Why would you say that?' I remember just thinking, *You're crazy! I'm going to do a great job, because, if I do a great job, I don't have to worry about that.*"

Thus, you will not catch Venables tracking the coaching carousel. He will not review the *USA Today* database to compare his pay. He will not extend his career past the expiration date. And whether he coaches for 10 more years or 10 more minutes, he will not waste any of it.

"I try to make sure I maintain humility and appreciation and thankfulness for what I do have. I just want to be great at what I'm doing," Venables said. "You work to live, hopefully, not living to work."

Venables and Swinney's entire staff received raises in February 2017. Clemson increased total staff pay for the on-field assistants by $775,000. Venables signed a one-year extension that would pay him $1.7 million.

"This is something that has been incredibly important to Dabo over the last three to four years," Clemson athletic director Dan Radakovich said, "to make sure our coaches who do such a great job are compensated at a level commensurate with their output."

The Clemson Board of Trustees compensation committee also approved salaries for new assistants Todd Bates and Mickey Conn. Defensive tackles coach Dan Brooks announced his well-earned retirement shortly after the national championship. Defensive ends coach Marion Hobby accepted a job in the NFL with the Jacksonville Jaguars. Conn served as defensive analyst the previous year. Swinney promoted Conn, a 1995 Alabama graduate, to assist Mike Reed with defensive backs. He hired Bates, a 2005 Alabama grad, to coach the defensive line.

When Swinney sat down with reporters in July during his annual media golf outing, Bates recalled the extended amount of time he spent in the high school waiting rooms. Although he scheduled appointments, he sat while others strolled directly into the office. Bates spent the previous three seasons as the defensive-line coach at Jacksonville State University in Alabama. His program competed in a national championship game in 2015. It never lost a conference game during his tenure there.

However, Jacksonville State does not play in a Power Five league. It is the flagbearer for the Ohio Valley Conference in the Football Championship Subdivision. Bates would always arrive on time for recruiting visits. He was prepared for each meeting with high school coaches. But regardless of what was written in the appointment book, if a coach from a major Football Bowl

Subdivision program popped up, Bates' meetings could easily be postponed.

"You've got to just sit and wait your turn," Bates said with a laugh.

Bates is on the other side of the exchange now, and thus he more easily gets on the other side of the office door. Representing a national champion can open entrances more expeditiously.

"Well, it was good to be on the other side of that," Bates said, recalling his first recruiting trip wearing the Clemson logo. "I still try to be as organized as you can be, and respect everybody's time, because it's all about relationships. I've never been the type of guy to put my chest out because of what level I'm on or where I am."

Bates' humility, creativity, and thoroughness could equip him to replace a pair of coaching luminaries who fortified a stellar reputation as recruiters and instructors. Hobby and Brooks spearheaded the development of former standouts Vic Beasley, Kevin Dodd, Grady Jarrett, and DeShawn Williams. By consolidating the defensive line roles for the first time since 2004, Swinney exhibited confidence in Bates' ability to compensate for Hobby and Brooks' departure. Yet Bates never intended to replace them.

"Those are legends," Bates said. "The biggest mistake you can make is to try to do exactly what they did. You've got to put your thumbprint on it. You've got to be you. That's going to be enough."

Bates starred as a defensive end at the University of Alabama from 2001 to 2004. He played two seasons in the NFL with the Tennessee Titans before opening his coaching career at high schools in Alabama and Mississippi. He landed his first college position at Idaho State in 2011 and ventured to Jacksonville State two seasons later.

There is a stark talent discrepancy between the Championship and Bowl Subdivisions. Major programs have the resources to attract high-caliber players in abundance. Bates inherited All-Americans Christian Wilkins and Dexter Lawrence and rising stars Clelin Ferrell and Austin Bryant.

"You've got guys here who can do exactly what you say. Everybody at the FCS level may not be able to do a technique that you've learned in the NFL," Bates said. "I couldn't have walked into a better situation. They helped make my transition that much easier, because of how mature they are as a unit and what they've already accomplished. They're not afraid of heights. They've climbed the mountains. When I first got here, of course, they knew the playbook better than I did. I humbled myself and asked them sometimes, because I got some concepts mixed up."

Bates will not need long to master the playbook if he maintains the dogged demeanor his new colleagues observed.

"He's got a lot of pride. He's intelligent. He's a hard worker," Venables said. "He's a relationship guy. He brings passion and enthusiasm every day. He's got an upbeat, positive attitude that can bring the best qualities out in your players."

Bates writes a blog, crafts personal messages, and even composes poetry to motivate his players.

"He cares about their well-being. He cares about how they are as young people," tight ends coach Danny Pearman said. "He's always trying to cut the edge with anything to motivate them. From that standpoint, I think he's an excellent fit for us."

Bates believed Clemson was a desirable destination long before Hobby and Brooks departed. He visited previously to coach during Swinney's summer camps. "I believe success comes down to the circle and the soil you're in," Bates said. "You've got to know where you can thrive. I knew from the time I came to visit Clemson that this would be an atmosphere where I could thrive and grow to the maximum."

On August 25, 2017, the compensation committee awarded Swinney an eight-year, $54 million contract. Swinney received a $1.5 million signing bonus. With an average base salary of $6.75 million per year, Swinney became the third-highest paid coach in college football behind Alabama's Nick Saban, who earned $11.1

million in 2017; and Michigan's Jim Harbaugh, who earned $7 million. Swinney is one of only four active head coaches who have won national championships. The championship run also earned Swinney $1.53 million in incentive bonuses.

"What he's done with our program has been incredible," Radakovich said. "He means so much to our athletic department, to our university, to our community. He and Kathleen are just incredible ambassadors for the institution."

Swinney climbed a long way from the $800,000 he earned in his first season, and a long, long way from eating SpaghettiOs. He and Kathleen built a new home in Clemson, twice the size of that dream manor in southeast Birmingham. Like his new football operations complex, Swinney wants to build a mansion on the foundation of family, faith, fervor, focus, and fun. A structure that will remain in the Clemson family for generations.

"Anybody can build a building," Swinney said, standing in the complex's cafeteria. "This is a home. You can go stay at the Ritz Carlton, but if they treat you like crap, you ain't gone be happy. This is a home, and a home is made from the inside out with the people who live there. We've got some unbelievable people here, but this was the home built with vision. This was a home built with love, with passion, with care, with attention to details, and a clear understanding of Clemson."

# 22

## ATTACKING NATIONAL CHAMPIONS

THE FIRST TASK in the pursuit of a second consecutive championship is to forget about the first one. Clemson needed to tuck it into the attic for four months. The Tigers had another road trip planned, and they did not need to pack 2016.

Clemson aimed to become the second school to reach the College Football Playoff in three consecutive seasons. The only other team to achieve that feat is Alabama, Clemson's nemesis during its previous two visits.

Alabama is an outlier. A rare dynasty in this period of parity. The Crimson Tide won four of the previous eight national championships. Alabama is one of merely four schools that claimed or shared consecutive national titles through the previous 50 years.

Alabama has mapped this route. Nick Saban, off the top of his head, can write a list of every item to pack. Momentum is not one of them. Coaches and players certainly can retain lessons from previous seasons. They can recall scenarios and situations to reshape their strategies. Experience is the most effective teacher. Ignoring those opportunities to teach and learn is irresponsible.

Yet past success provides no magic thrust. Clemson can include the national championship trophy on its admissions literature to attract more applicants. The trophy is tangible evidence of excellence that coaches can show recruits. And beyond the abstract application, the trophy is simply a stunning, elegant piece of décor adorning the lobby.

However, that national championship does not grant a head start for the next season. Clemson is not defending a title. That would indicate that they were still holding one. Repeat champions realize that one must start back at the beginning. They must work with the same hunger and diligence that fueled their first ride. The 2017 season was not a defensive driving course. It was another endurance race.

"We're not defending nothing. We're the attacking national champions," defensive end Clelin Ferrell said. "We might have the belt, but this team didn't win that belt. It's up to us to go back and get another one if we want one."

Conventional conjecture suggested Clemson was no longer equipped for that journey. The Tigers lost the legendary quarterback, the first-round receiver, the most reliable runner, the top tackler, the defensive captain, and the two most seasoned defensive position coaches.

Deshaun Watson earned his degree in education in less than three years. He was selected in the first round, 12$^{th}$ overall, in the NFL Draft and joined a fellow Clemson legend, wide receiver DeAndre Hopkins, with the Houston Texans.

The Los Angeles Chargers selected receiver Mike Williams seventh overall. Cornerback Cordrea Tankersley was drafted in the third round. Running back Wayne Gallman and defensive tackle Carlos Watkins were drafted in the fourth. Tight end Jordan Leggett went in the fifth. Clemson also lost All-American, first-team All-ACC, ACC Defensive Player of the Year, Jack Lambert Award winner, and CFP National Championship Game Defensive MVP Ben Boulware.

Center Jay Guillermo and safety Jadar Johnson, who also earned first-team All-ACC honors, also graduated. All-ACC wideout Artavis Scott departed early as a junior and signed a free-agent NFL contract.

Teams lose starters every year. Players graduate. That remains the objective of college. The number of departures was not the issue. It was the caliber of those players. These were generational players. One could make a reasonable argument to declare Watson, Williams, and Boulware among the greatest players at their respective positions in the history of Clemson football.

Those losses induced many forecasters to project Clemson behind rival Florida State in the drive toward the ACC title. The afterglow of the national championship and the unavoidable reality of those losses conciliated many fans. They contently set a non-playoff New Year's bowl as a satisfactory goal. They were aiming too low.

Clemson advanced to this elite class before Watson delivered that game-winning touchdown to Hunter Renfrow. Swinney applied for membership into this club all the way back in 2009. When Ohio State, Oklahoma, Florida State, LSU, and even Alabama attempted to deny Clemson entry, the Tigers kicked in the door.

Clemson stretched its recruitment net wider. Coaches were dominating the Carolinas, Florida, and Georgia. Then they began infiltrating hotbeds in California, Texas, and Ohio. Wherever Clemson coaches visit, regardless of how obscure that corner of the country is, Clemson's reputation precedes them. And through the previous seven years, that reputation has been positive. As long as Clemson continues to recruit at a high level, it will compete on the field at a high level. Talent turns good coaches into tenured coaches.

The previous two campaigns proved that, to return to the playoff, Clemson would need a challenging yet conquerable schedule and a little luck. Clemson replaced stalwart stars throughout the starting lineup with gifted, but inexperienced prospects. Clemson needed to navigate the learning curve quickly without driving its playoff hopes into a ditch.

The schedule presented several hazards in four foes that were ranked in the preseason Coaches Poll—No. 13 Auburn, No. 17 Louisville, No. 22 Virginia Tech, and No. 2 Florida State. Clemson opened No. 5. Each of those highly touted opponents presented an opportunity to impress the CFP selection committee. If it dropped one of those games early, Clemson would have enough track left to recalculate its course. That is the fallacy of the ranking system and the selection process, but Clemson has steered through it well.

In 2016 luck kept Clemson between the ditches. The Tigers avoided catastrophic injuries. Their lone loss was perfectly timed. A short potential game-winning field goal missed inexplicably. Persistence positioned Clemson for good fortune. Champions do not rely on it, but they certainly capitalize on it. Clemson was equipped to optimize its opportunities in 2017. That started with its new starting quarterback.

Kelly Bryant had revealed flashes of his dynamic ability, but he was relegated to obscurity in the shadow of Deshaun Watson. To some degree, Bryant was going to be doubted regardless. He could have a strong arm, dazzling agility, sharp instincts, and sprinter speed. He still was not Watson, and that diminished many outsiders' opinions. Bryant has all of those tools. He just had not had the opportunity to showcase them. He never desired to be Watson. He was content and confident being "Kelly B."

Bryant lettered in football and basketball at Wren High School, less than an hour's drive from the Clemson campus. Bryant suffered through lingering stomach pain during February 2014. It forced him to sit out of the first half of a basketball game. He did not immediately come back out after halftime, so his football coach, Jeff Tate, went to the locker room to check on him. He found Bryant hunched over, vomiting blood.

Fearful that it was more than the virus that had infected many of his classmates, Bryant's parents, Russ and Deborah, escorted him to the Children's Hospital of Georgia in Augusta. An MRI of his abdomen revealed an abscess the size of a softball blocking his lower intestine. If the Bryants had waited much longer, the abscess could have burst and infected Kelly's entire body. Doctors removed the blockage in emergency surgery and diagnosed Kelly with Crohn's

Disease, a chronic inflammatory condition that causes abdominal pain and anemia. Kelly recovered for a month in a hospital in Anderson, South Carolina. He was placed on a restrictive liquid diet. He withered from 205 pounds to 160.

Doctors performed a colostomy to divert Kelly's large intestine to a stoma. Thus, when he left the hospital in March, he needed a colostomy bag until the affected part of his lower intestine healed. Kelly wrapped the bag in bandages to conceal it under his clothes. He wore it under his tuxedo during his junior prom. He even wore it during spring football practice.

Kelly worried that his illness and subsequent weight loss would prompt major programs, including Clemson, to withdraw interest. However, Clemson extended a scholarship offer. Kelly Bryant committed to the Tigers that April. He spent that summer catching up on his schoolwork and restoring his weight. He trained tirelessly with personal quarterback instructor Ramon Robinson to refine his passing. He also underwent a second surgery to reverse the colostomy.

Scars remain on his abdomen. He has been forced to alter his diet. Symptoms occasionally surface. Those are the reminders of this trial, of his toughness, of the precious privilege of playing. Those reminders muffle the cacophony of doubters and detractors. Compared to Crohn's Disease, criticism was nothing.

Each year during training camp, Swinney places a chair in the front of the team room. He opens the floor for any player to share anything with the team. Bryant accepted the chance before the 2017 season. His teammates may have noticed his scars in the locker room, but few of them knew the story behind them. Bryant astounded his teammates with details of his ordeal. The tale provided a new perspective on Bryant's gregarious, playful nature. A man who can laugh so liberally after such a trial would not be shaken by a blogger. He would not be rattled by a defensive end. A man with that resilience, that toughness, and that resolve would be a leader.

Bryant flourished in his first start. He completed 16 of 22 passes for 236 yards and a touchdown in a 56–3 rout of Kent State. He also rushed for 77 yards and a touchdown. Bryant was not the only new starter who thrived in his debut.

Will Swinney won the holder role. He had spent much of his childhood on the sideline each game, charting plays for his father and making absolutely certain that he stayed out of the way. The white paint marking the bench bounds might as well have been an electric fence. Will was so conditioned to stay off the field that after Clemson scored its first touchdown, he hesitated slightly before running to his spot.

"My whole life, I'm used to staying back on the sideline," Will said. "When we scored and I'm running on the field, I'm like, *Am I supposed to be doing this right now? Oh, my gosh, this is happening?*"

Will settled into his spot and completed a clean first game. Kelly's sturdy legs and Will's steady hands remained critical to Clemson's success through the subsequent weeks, when defenses loosened their coverage and uncertainty crept into Clemson's place-kicking competition.

Auburn visited Death Valley on September 9. It backed off its secondary and contained Clemson early. Merely five of Bryant's 19 completions covered more than nine yards. Three of those were on the masterful drive Bryant manufactured to close the half. Trailing 6–0, Bryant completed six of eight passes for 79 yards. He rushed for 12 yards, including a three-yard touchdown. Clemson took the air out of the ball in the second half. It rushed on 68 percent of its snaps. Clemson ran a total of 67 plays.

"Welcome to 1988," Swinney said with a smile. "That's what it felt like out there."

Perhaps the best way to neutralize Clemson's defense for four quarters is to eliminate halftime. Invariably, against the toughest challenges and after the roughest starts, defensive coordinator Brent Venables spends the intermission concocting a remedy.

Clemson allowed Auburn to manufacture a seven-minute, 47-second scoring drive on its first possession. Auburn quarterback Jarrett Stidham had ample time to balance his checkbook while standing in the pocket. Clemson capitalized on the condensed area in the red zone to limit Auburn to field goals.

But the Clemson defense was not its typical, disruptive self.

Then, after halftime, Venables put on his chef's hat and cooked up a pungent brew of blitzes and perplexing coverages. The adjustments tore the lining out of Stidham's pocket. Clemson notched three sacks in the third quarter, and Auburn averaged 0.6 yards per play.

Clemson continued its dominance in the final frame. It closed with 11 sacks and 14 tackles for loss. Auburn gained 74 yards in the first quarter, 23 in the second. Clemson surrendered merely 20 yards through the second half. It was another remarkable dismantling for Venables. It was the perfect primer for his next challenge.

Louisville's junior quarterback Lamar Jackson had the Heisman Trophy. He had the gaudy statistics. He had the incessant highlight reel. He was the brightest star in college football, but when he faced the attacking champs in Cardinal Stadium on that Saturday night in September, a rising star outshined him.

Bryant amassed 316 passing yards through Clemson's first 11 drives, more than double the amount of yards Jackson gained through his first 11 possessions. Bryant completed six of nine attempts on third down for 99 yards. He finished 6-for-7 on third-down attempts in the previous game against Auburn.

Clemson contained Jackson and left Louisville with a 47–21 win. Jackson mystified a few Clemson defenders with juke moves, but Bryant produced more meaningful highlights. He lofted a 79-yard touchdown pass to Ray-Ray McCloud. His 38-yard touchdown strike to Deon Cain was negated by offsetting penalties.

Bryant also rushed for 26 yards and two touchdowns. He closed the evening midway through the third quarter with 342 yards of total offense, merely eight yards fewer than Louisville's entire team netted by that point.

Obviously, the variables were not controlled. Jackson faced Clemson's deep defense. The Tigers' front seven tore through Louisville's offensive line like it was perforated. Clemson flustered Jackson and repeatedly flushed him out of the pocket, and the back end of Clemson's defense kept him contained, at least enough to limit his scrambles to first downs instead of touchdowns.

Clemson linebacker Dorian O'Daniel fooled Jackson with crafty coverage, snagged an interception, and returned it for a touchdown. Jackson nearly threw another interception on his ensuing attempt, but it slipped through Kendall Joseph's fingers.

Bryant was not perfect. He struggled through a stretch of erratic throws. He sailed a series of short passes over the heads of receivers. He was nearly intercepted on one of the turnaround throwback screen passes Clemson's offensive coordinators adore. Yet Bryant rebounded and exhibited the resolve and poise that made him more than a placeholder. His star was ascending, and he took his team up with him.

In the next game, against Boston College, Clemson fans discovered another rapidly rising star. Freshman running back Travis Etienne rushed for 113 yards on nine carries. He scored two touchdowns, including a 50-yarder in the fourth quarter of the 34–7 drubbing. Etienne notched an 81-yard scamper the previous week. He was beginning to make a name for himself, although folks in Upstate South Carolina did not quite know how to pronounce it.

Etienne is a native of Jennings, the seat of Jefferson Davis Parish in southwest Louisiana. Even in his neck of the bayou, his name can be "E-tee-in" or "Eh-tee-in" or "Eh-te-enn" or the Cajun pronunciation, "A-chan." His name is like gumbo. It is a standard but varies based on the part of the state. The Creole cooks in New Orleans toss in tomatoes. Cajuns use fowl. Vegetarians use spinach and mustard greens.

Regardless of what is added, every gumbo starts with a roux. It is a blended thickening agent for sauces and stews. It is the foundation upon which every delicious mouthful of gumbo is constructed. Gumbo embodies the myriad cultures that compose Louisiana. Heritage, economics, and dialects distinguish groups throughout the state. Tradition is the roux that brings those groups together.

Etienne was Jennings' roux. Before he rushed to stardom at Clemson University as a freshman running back, Etienne was a unifying, thickening agent in his hometown. "Football fits this community, because it's people who grind, people who fight through tough times," *Jennings Daily News* sports editor Kevin Bruchhaus said.

A railroad track runs through the heart of Jennings, a physical reminder of its sectored past. Events and tragedies occasionally threaten to revive that past. "It's a good community. There's wonderful people here all over the place, but there was some issues with some murders and crime. Maybe a little racial divide at times," Bruchhaus said. "But Travis was kind of a community hero. Everybody, regardless of where they came from, what color they were, what their background was, every question you heard around town was, 'What is Travis going to do this week?'"

Each Friday, the answer was the same—"Something we didn't see last week."

Etienne started three seasons for Jennings High School. With dexterity that defies physics and a smile that defies his doubters, he compiled 8,864 total yards and 115 total touchdowns. "We went every Friday night, because we didn't know what we were going to see. What acrobatic move was he going to make on somebody going at a speed nobody else could go at?" Jennings radio announcer Charlie Williams said. "You just couldn't take your eyes off the field."

"Football, that was his gift that God used," Travis' mother, Donnetta Etienne said. "It changed a lot of how they see the area, how they view the area. It made our community whole. Travis became like a community kid. He was the hope and the light for the whole community."

The love and support he received in Southwest Louisiana guided Etienne in South Carolina. The toughness he learned in that hearty town carries him through the line of scrimmage and against any adversity he encounters off the field.

Etienne combined with Bryant and sophomore Tavien Feaster to lead Clemson to an average of 237.3 rushing yards per game through the first six contests of 2017. That was 68 yards more than Clemson's rushing average in 2016. Clemson proceeded to victories at Virginia Tech and against Wake Forest and climbed to No. 2. At that juncture, Florida State had fallen to a 1–3 record and dropped out of the top 25. FSU quarterback Deondre Francois suffered a season-ending injury in the opener against Alabama, and the Florida State defense had not played up to its preseason praise. Clemson could empathize with its Atlantic Division foe much better after visiting Syracuse on October 13.

A Friday the 13th game night did not scare Clemson. Feaster rushed for a touchdown on the Tigers' opening drive. Alex Spence missed a 35-yard field goal attempt on Clemson's next drive, and the next four possessions ended in punts. Conversely, Syracuse scored on three of its first six possessions. Clemson safety Tanner Muse scooped a fumble and returned it 63 yards for a touchdown, but Syracuse led 17–14 with less than a minute remaining in the half.

Bryant attempted to mount a hurried drive before the break, but Syracuse forced Clemson into third-and-10 at the Clemson 45. In the previous game against Wake Forest, Bryant had rolled his ankle as he was tackled awkwardly on a red-zone run. He toughed through pain to play in the Carrier Dome, but he did not appear as elusive or explosive as normal.

He collected the next snap and dropped back three yards. He planted, stepped up in the pocket while scanning the field, then clutched the ball and tucked it as Syracuse defenders closed in.

Bryant slipped through an opening up the middle, but defensive lineman Chris Slayton reached out and clobbered down on the bridge of Bryant's nose. Slayton grappled Bryant as he attempted to spin and slammed him fiercely to the turf. Slayton jumped to his feet to celebrate the third-down stop. Bryant did not move. He remained motionless for a frightening period. Team doctors eventually got him to his feet and helped him off the field. Bryant suffered a concussion and did not return.

Redshirt freshman Zerrick Cooper replaced Bryant. He completed 10 of 14 attempts but for merely 88 yards. Clemson won a field-position battle in the third quarter. After stalling on its opening possession of the second half, Will Spiers booted a 50-yard punt that was downed at the 1-yard line. Clemson halted the ensuing drive at the 14-yard line, and a 28-yard punt gave Clemson the ball in Syracuse territory. Clemson gained 29 yards on seven plays, but Spence pushed through a 30-yard field goal to tie the game at 17.

The Clemson defense faltered again on the next drive. Syracuse quarterback Eric Dungey scrambled for a 45-yard game and then followed with a 30-yard touchdown pass two plays later. Etienne answered with some microwave offense. His 52-yard touchdown sprint evened the game at 24–24 with 6:16 remaining in the third quarter. An offensive pass-interference penalty and a Clelin Ferrell sack thwarted Syracuse's next possession. Clemson responded to the stop with an eight-play, 20-yard drive. The Tigers settled for a 38-yard field-goal attempt to reclaim the lead and preserve their perfect season.

Spence entered the season as the backup place-kicker, but All-ACC starter Greg Huegel tore a knee ligament on September 20 during practice. In a routine two-minute drill, a teammate rolled into Huegel after a kick. Huegel was ruled out for the season. Spence, a redshirt junior from Florence, South Carolina, attempted no field goals in a game before the 2017 season. He converted one of his first three attempts in relief of Huegel. The misses were both from beyond 40 yards, so Spence was granted grace before the Syracuse game.

With 45 seconds remaining in the third quarter, Spence set his back foot on the 33-yard line. Will Swinney put his knee down on the 28. He snatched the snap and planted the ball. Spence stepped into his kick and bounced as he watched it sail...terribly wide left.

Syracuse regained possession and drove 68 yards in 16 plays. The marathon resulted in a 30-yard field goal. After getting the ball back, Clemson advanced to the Syracuse 41 before being stopped on third down. Trailing 27–24 and facing fourth-and-6 with less than seven minutes remaining, Swinney ordered a fake punt from Spiers. His pass floated waywardly, and Syracuse reclaimed possession with 6:10 remaining. The Orange converted three third-down conversions then downed the ball three times to seal the upset victory.

Dejection and disbelief seethed on the sideline. The Tigers' season was blemished. Their playoff hopes were in jeopardy. Their defense inexplicably lapsed. Their quarterback was injured. In that crushing moment, the situation appeared dire. But Swinney placed things in the proper perspective before he even left the field.

He has not needed to display it much through the past three seasons, but Swinney values grace and class in defeat. He revealed that virtue during the customary postgame, head coach handshake at midfield. Swinney embraced Syracuse coach Dino Babers and told him, "I'm happy for you...I'm so happy for you." Swinney later visited the Syracuse locker room to congratulate the victors personally.

"That's one of the classiest things I've seen in my life," Syracuse linebacker Zaire Franklin told David Hale of ESPN. "To have been knocked down like that and have the humility to come talk to us, that was cool as hell."

The Tigers arrived back in Clemson at approximately 5:00 AM on Saturday. The Friday night game and the ensuing open date allowed Swinney to take a trip home to Alabama to celebrate the 25th anniversary of the 1992 national championship.

"I wasn't real fired up about going," Swinney said, referring to the logistics of the trip after the painful loss and the late return trip. "We got a few hours of sleep and caught a plane to Tuscaloosa."

But once he arrived in Alabama, reunited with his teammates, swapped stories, and spent some quality time with his coach, Gene Stallings, the loss to Syracuse never crossed Swinney's mind. It was lost in nostalgia. "It was great to be with my teammates and especially to be with Coach Stallings," Swinney said. "It was awesome, really. Just what the doctor ordered."

Alabama held the commemorative ceremony before the Crimson Tide's game that day. Swinney left Bryant-Denny Stadium shortly afterward and was back in Clemson before halftime. Clemson enjoyed an open week before its next contest. That provided the staff ample time to regroup and reassess. But the Tigers never spend the open week locked in the office or secluded in the practice facility. They utilize the additional time to go out and have some fun—serving their community.

The stairwell to success is lined with mirrors. The climb requires a narrow focus. Folks often look only at themselves and can easily neglect to reflect on others. Selfishness is a necessary additive to ambition. It fuels personal growth and resists the viscosity of contentment. However, too much of that additive dilutes its potency. Then ambition becomes combustible.

Self-improvement does not require self-absorption. But humility and altruism are not intrinsic attributes. No one is born into philanthropy. Giving is an intentional habit. It must be encouraged, just as strongly as achievement.

Swinney established charitable service as a tenet of the program. Through nine seasons, he has compiled a staff that has diligently recruited and developed players. The consistent, guided effort transformed Clemson into a perennial power. Swinney has been equally diligent in promoting the team's commitment to community.

Less than a week after the loss at Syracuse, Clemson players volunteered with the Golden Harvest Food Bank to fill children's backpacks and boxes with food. They then distributed the goods to 300 families.

Since Swinney took over the program, the Tigers have conducted at least one community service project each year during the bye week. Shortly after players stand shoulder to shoulder on the field to celebrate a championship, they stand shoulder to shoulder at a worksite in a quiet Upstate neighborhood. There are no television cameras or confetti cannons. There is only the opportunity to change someone's life.

The Clemson team has partnered with Habitat for Humanity to construct several homes for deserving families. "Building a house for a single mom with three kids who don't have anywhere to stay, that's really deep," tight end Milan Richard said. "We can come out there and put three walls up in one day. That's life-changing."

Clemson scouts character as keenly as speed and strength. Many players arrive with an understanding of benevolence. Yet Clemson's recent climb to national eminence extends the reach of their compassion and intensifies the impact of their service.

"To understand the type of influence that we as football players have on others is something that really hit home for me here," Richard said. "Clemson right now, where we are as a program, we can impact the world, just based off one day and the simplest things that we do every day."

# BUILT TO LAST

GEORGIA TECH was the perfect opponent to aid Brent Venables in restoring Clemson's defense after a disappointing performance. Tech's pesky triple-option offense requires intense focus, discipline, and cooperation. Venables challenged his unit to remain sharp on their keys and execute the scheme as expected.

"Everybody wanted to anoint the defense as the best ever. Who's to say who's who and what's what? I'm one to say we haven't done anything yet," Venables said that week. "I just despise putting the cart before the horse."

His charge was a reset button. Clemson swarmed the Yellow Jackets. On Tech's third possession, Clemson slipped and surrendered a 65-yard run. The Tigers regrouped and limited Tech to a field goal. Outside of that blunder, Clemson limited Tech to 1.7 yards per play in the first half. Nothing changed after halftime.

Leading 24–3 with 6:48 remaining in the third quarter, Clemson's defensive linemen grew impatient as Tech huddled. With the music blasting through the stadium, the linemen broke into an impromptu dance routine. They "Swag Surfed" to the delight of the crowd until Tech lined up. Then, the Tigers took on an old-school vibe. They popped and locked the Yellow Jackets. Clemson surrendered 17 yards in the third quarter. Georgia Tech did not score again until Venables mercifully pulled his starters. The Tigers got their swagger back. They got their field general back too.

It was one part sincere uncertainty, one part cunning gamesmanship. Swinney shed little light on Kelly Bryant's health earlier that week. Kelly maximized the open week with rest and rehab. However, Swinney would not divulge details on his progress. His only prognosis was that Kelly would "be ready to roll."

It was an ironic idiom, considering the initial injury, a rolled ankle, but it became an accurate assessment. Fully recovered and completely refreshed, Kelly shuffled through warmups with no brace, no bulky tape, and no hitch in his silky stride. He completed 22 of 33 passes for 207 yards and two touchdowns. He opened the game comfortably with a pair of quick catch-and-release passes. Deon Cain converted the second into a 38-yard score.

During the second drive, Kelly rushed for gains on a designed run and a scramble. Yet it was not the positive plays that dispelled the uncertainty of his health. It was a six-yard loss. On his seventh snap, Kelly darted right off an option read and nearly beat Georgia Tech safety Corey Griffin around the edge. With a desperate reach, Griffin grabbed Kelly by that left ankle. Kelly twisted slightly to loosen Griffin's grasp but tumbled to the soggy turf.

Kelly popped up with vigor and without ceremony. He was fine, and through the duration of the game, he was himself. He maneuvered fluidly in the pocket, rolled out, and delivered accurate throws on the run. He tucked the ball and avoided occasional pressure. He challenged defenders physically in the open field. He steered Clemson to three touchdowns in the first half and celebrated each score with the trendy soaring chest bump. He bounced with the same "K-Boogie" swagger that signified his smooth transition to the starting role.

Clemson did not need to soften its offense. Offensive coordinators Tony Elliott and Jeff Scott did not limit quarterback runs. Kelly carried the ball on 101 of the 424 snaps he logged through the first seven games. He notched 10 carries through his first 35 plays against Georgia Tech.

That frequency did not wane, despite the series of rattling hits Bryant absorbed. He is too confident to jump out of bounds and too ambitious to slide. He logged 49 carries through Clemson's next three games against FBS foes. The option is a permanent fixture in Clemson's offense. Running is a requisite task of the quarterback. With his speed, discernment, and toughness, Bryant flourished in that scheme. He netted 67 yards on 12 carries against Tech. Bryant was not Clemson's engine. He was the entire 18-wheeler pulling the trailer. Now that his front tire had been repaired, Clemson was ready to roll again. Through North Carolina State, Florida State, The Citadel, and South Carolina.

With a clean sweep through the remainder of the regular season, Clemson ascended to No. 1 in the CFP rankings. After knocking off Clemson on October 13, Syracuse did not win another game. Clemson sealed another Atlantic Division championship and set a date with Coastal champion Miami in the ACC Championship Game.

Miami charmed college football fans that season with an extravagant tradition. A South Florida jeweler crafted 900 sapphire stones in the shape of the Miami logo. He attached the pendant to a thick, 10-karat gold Cuban link. It became the Turnover Chain.

Miami defensive coordinator Manny Diaz stored the chain on the sideline until a Miami player recovered a fumble or snagged an interception. The chain was then draped over the honoree's shoulder pads and flashed for television cameras. It was an ostentatious incentive for Miami's defense and a symbol of solidarity for Miami's fans. Yet, on December 2, it was fodder for Clemson's jokes.

The offense protected the football. The defense protected the end zone. Clemson crafted a chain of turnovers and secured its own jewelry—another ACC championship ring. The Turnover Chain's lone appearance occurred in the first quarter, when Clemson receiver Tee Higgins inadvertently tripped teammate Ray-Ray McCloud as McCloud attempted to field a punt. The ball ricocheted off McCloud's shoulder. Trent Harris recovered the muffed kick at the Clemson 37-yard line. The chaining ceremony was brief. Miami's ensuing possession was as well.

Clemson stalled Miami in six plays. The Tigers snuffed out a horizontal pass play on third down and repelled the Hurricanes for a seven-yard loss. The drive ended in a missed field goal. Miami did not drive beyond the Clemson 40-yard line again until the fourth quarter. Clemson limited Miami to merely 64 yards through the first half. Miami averaged 2.5 yards per play and converted two of eight third downs.

Clemson compiled six tackles for loss, including four sacks. Clemson cornerback Ryan Carter and linebacker Kendall Joseph each grabbed an interception. Linebacker Dorian O'Daniel also recovered a fumble. Conversely, Clemson's offense did not surrender a possession to the Hurricanes. Clemson mastered Miami with its own opportunistic focus.

"Everybody talked about Miami and the turnovers, but our guys have been pretty good with turnovers too," Clemson coach Dabo Swinney said that night. "We were at our best."

Spence nailed a 46-yard field goal with 10:14 remaining in the third quarter. After the calamity at Syracuse, Swinney opened the place-kicking competition and even invited a walk-on, Drew Costa, to audition for the job. Spence would not yield. He rejected his competitors and retained his role. He converted five of his next six field-goal attempts.

"After the Syracuse game, I was hurting pretty bad. You never want to let your teammates down like that," Spence said. "I always knew I could do it. I just had to put my mind to it and refocus on my process. The only thing I really care about is how my teammates feel. I always want to be there for my teammates. It was good to kind of bounce back and be able to be consistent and help them win and not have to worry about being a burden."

The Tigers overpowered Miami 38–3. They dominated the line of scrimmage while toeing the line between confident and cocky. They waved their hands dismissively after pass deflections. They pointed jokingly after false starts. They mimicked Miami's chaining ceremony after sacks.

Their dominance backed up their bravado, and they boasted another ACC championship. In the locker room, after the game—and before the dance session—Swinney handed a replica Turnover Chain to O'Daniel. He stepped aside as Carter gripped a pair of oversized scissors. O'Daniel positioned the chain in a dramatic stance. Carter cut the chain and ignited a delirious celebration.

The margin of victory was startling, but the defense's performance should not have surprised anyone. It was Clemson's customary performance during the final four weeks of the season. Veteran players peak, like defensive lineman Christian Wilkins, who manhandled Miami's linemen to disrupt countless plays. Newcomers emerge, like linebacker James Skalski, who filled in flawlessly for Joseph and Tre Lamar while they nursed injuries.

Venables composes complex schemes, but the Tigers utilized no mystifying gimmicks. They simply emphasized discipline, awareness, toughness, and tenacity. More often than not, they raced to the right spot and executed their assignments when they got there.

This unit infused exceptional talent with consistently sound fundamentals. That method endures. It is the standard that carried Clemson to three consecutive ACC titles and three consecutive College Football Playoffs.

And for the third consecutive year, Clemson was pitted against Alabama. This time in New Orleans at the Sugar Bowl CFP Semifinal. Swinney returned to the Superdome 25 years after he won the national championship there with Alabama. And less than a year after he visited the dome with Watson for the Manning Award presentation.

"That was kind of a fun moment back in the spring. I remember we landed, and I was messing with Deshaun. I'm like, 'Hey, man, that's where it went down right there. That's where we beat [Miami] in the 'Natty,'" Swinney recalled. "So literally, 25 years earlier I was in that stadium and just won a national championship. And now here we are, we had just won a national championship.

It was kind of a surreal moment. That's when I realized that was one of the playoff sites. So I took a couple pictures and turned it into a reconnaissance trip. I had a little fun when we were in spring practice and kind of told the guys, 'Hey, I checked it out. And, you know, if we do what I think we can do, this is where we have a chance to get to.'"

Swinney and Alabama coach Nick Saban shared a stage at the College Football Hall of Fame in Atlanta for the College Football Playoff press conference. Before they fielded questions, Saban posed a simple question to Swinney.

"He was asking me if I was staying for the show after the press conference," Swinney recalled, alluding to the College Football Awards Show during which the winners of the prestigious individual trophies were revealed. Swinney had stayed for the show during the previous two years. Deshaun Watson won the Davey O'Brien Award, presented annually to the top quarterback, in each of those seasons. Tight end Jordan Leggett was a finalist for the John Mackey Award the previous year.

However, no Clemson player won any of those major individual awards in 2017. Among the four teams selected to the playoff, Clemson was the only one without an award winner. That gave Swinney less incentive to stay for the awards show, but it gave him a great response to Saban's question.

"I was messing with him," Swinney said with a grin. "I was like, 'No, we didn't have anybody good enough to win any of these awards this year. It was kind of a rebuilding year for us.'" Swinney could carry that satisfying grin then, but he was not smiling prior to the season, when he was asked the same question ad nauseam in interviews, teleconferences, and casual conversations.

Swinney repeatedly dismissed the preemptive excuse that Clemson would endure a rebuild. He asserted that the Tigers' standard would not slip. He continually exhibited confidence in the emerging players. The questions kept coming. Swinney's answer never changed. He simply needed 13 games to convince everyone outside Clemson's locker room.

Too polite to mock his inquirers with "I told you, so," Swinney could sit with that satisfied, sarcastic grin. Back on the same stage. In a chair many prognosticators prematurely designated for Florida State. In a position to match a feat only two teams achieved through the previous 35 years: consecutive national titles.

Clemson would be the only team to repeat as champion over that span with a different starting quarterback. Nebraska had Tommy Frazier in 1994 and 1995. Alabama had A.J. McCarron in 2011 and 2012.

Clemson had Deshaun. Clemson had Kelly. Clemson had a new identity. Clemson had a chance.

Kelly Bryant is the most explosive runner Clemson has enjoyed at quarterback since Woodrow Dantzler. He facilitated Clemson's improved ground attack. With emergent running backs Feaster and Etienne, the Tigers averaged 204.1 rushing yards per game. Clemson closed the season over that 200-yard benchmark in two of the previous 16 years.

Kelly recorded his three highest efficiency ratings against FBS competition during the previous three games. He flourished simply by remaining himself. He relied on the plethora of playmakers and dominant defense Clemson compiled. Playing within his comfort zone helped him frequent the end zone.

"Proud of Kelly," Swinney said. "That's really all we recruited him to be, was just to be him. We didn't recruit him to be Deshaun or anybody else. Just come be the best version of you. That's why we thought he could come in here and be a great player for us."

The game was portrayed as a clash between the schoolyard bullies and the class clowns, the guys grinding in their blue-collar shirts against the guys dancing around with their shirts off. Alabama purportedly approached the game with a businesslike attitude. And Clemson allegedly traipsed playfully around the French

Quarter. Neither depiction was accurate. They were hyperbolic reaches from fans and media members who encountered players around the Big Easy. New Orleans is a much smaller city than the other sites in the playoff, including Tampa and Phoenix, where Clemson and Alabama met the previous two years. There was no way to isolate teams from the speculating public and also facilitate the fun the players deserve on a bowl trip.

Alabama players were more straitlaced in their interview sessions. Clemson players were more animated. They were simply behaving according to their personalities. They were also reflecting the personality of their respective coaches. But the discrepancy in their personalities did not necessarily indicate a discrepancy in focus.

"If you get beat, you get beat," Swinney said. "It ain't going to be because we didn't prepare well or show up with the right mindset. It's not going to be because our guys had fun at a press conference or whatever. I don't buy into that mess."

Many critics erroneously suppose Swinney's willingness to joke in press conferences and dance in locker rooms signifies that he is less meticulous or demanding than Saban. They believe because Saban does not joke or laugh in public as often means that he is less beloved by his players than Swinney.

"Obviously, Dabo is a big kid at heart. He put a slide into the new facility," Ferrell said. "The imagination he has, he dreams like us and thinks the way we think. But, at the end of the day, he knows what it takes to get there and the discipline it takes to get there. He's not a pushover and letting his players do what they want to do. He's going to put them in the right position and hold you accountable. You can do nothing but respect him and run through a wall for him."

Folks love neatly arranged storylines, regardless of how overblown they are. But pitting fun against focus added another wrinkle to the epic Clemson-Alabama trilogy. It convinced more than

72,000 viewers to fill the Superdome on New Year's Day for another blockbuster, but they did not see the show they expected.

The previous two Clemson-and-Alabama clashes were decided by a total of nine points. In the third installment, Clemson did not score nine points. The Crimson Tide defensive line rolled around, over, and through the Tigers. Clemson appeared to be attempting to stop an 18-wheeler with a door wedge. Clemson allowed an average of two sacks per game through its previous 13 outings. Alabama ripped the threads out of Clemson's pocket and stuffed Kelly Bryant for five sacks. Clemson had not allowed more than four sacks in a game since 2013.

That figure does not account for several snaps in which Bryant escaped instant penetration. Alabama deflected and intercepted two of Bryant's short passes. The Tide converted those turnovers into touchdowns. Alabama clogged Clemson's rushing attack. Through the first three quarters, Clemson averaged 1.8 yards per carry. Clemson did not advance past the Alabama 25-yard line until 3:39 remained in the game.

Conversely, Alabama stymied Clemson's defensive front. Ends Ferrell and Austin Bryant and tackles Christian Wilkins and Dexter Lawrence were often engulfed by the Tide's offensive line. Through the first three quarters, Alabama netted 119 rushing yards, seven more than Clemson's previous average allowance for an entire game. Alabama converted seven of its first 16 third downs. They dominated with the defiant swagger Clemson embodied through the season.

The Tide was more physical and more disciplined. It executed the explosive, entertaining plays that made the previous two games box-office blowouts. Clemson simply could not match the Tide on screen. And this simply became a blowout. Alabama dismantled the Tigers 24–6.

Swinney preemptively and rightfully combatted the predictable excuses and explanations that began to circulate late in the third quarter, after Mack Wilson returned an interception for a touchdown and lifted Alabama to the 18-point advantage.

*They weren't focused. The coaches weren't prepared. Kelly Bryant was not ready. There were too many injuries. This was supposed to be a rebuilding year, anyway.*

None of those stances hold any merit. None of that nonsense mattered. Clemson did not lose because it sauntered along Bourbon Street, caught second lines Uptown, or clowned at media day. The coaches were not distracted. Bryant was not overwhelmed by the moment.

Clemson lost because Alabama was better. Alabama performed better. It does not mean they prepared better. The confidence that carried Clemson through the ACC did not suddenly vanish. Bryant did not suddenly become the incompetent placeholder his critics denigrated in August. The coordinators did not forget how to coach. And appreciative fans did not forget what the team accomplished. Another 12-win season. Another ACC title.

Many of those appreciative fans lined the road to the Reeves Complex to welcome the team back home. They knew it was a regrettable performance, but it was not the first threequel that failed to produce the excitement of the previous two films. The box-office flop stuck with Swinney, his staff, and his players. They returned to Clemson determined to revive their championship franchise.

After a few weeks passed, rays of perspective peeked through those clouds of disenchantment. The Tigers could peer out a window and look back on all they had accomplished. They still enjoyed the majestic view from the top tier of college football.

Clemson designed a ring to commemorate its third consecutive ACC championship. Phrases are inscribed on each side running parallel to the finger. On one side it reads, "Built by Clemson." On the opposite side it reads, "Built to Last."

With a plethora of a talent, a culture of commitment, and a standard of excellence, Clemson is equipped to endure. The Tigers will continue to reload and continue to compete at the highest level. Clemson was not simply renting space among the college football elite on a month-to-month lease. That boy from Pelham moved his family to the fancy neighborhood and put down roots. Dabo Swinney constructed a program on sturdy principles—faith, family, forgiveness, fortitude, and above all, fun. Those traits are timeless. They never go out of style.

Neither does winning.

# ACKNOWLEDGMENTS

THIS ADVENTURE in storytelling would not have been possible without the unwavering support of my wife, Parthenia Luke Robinson. Your encouragement and sacrifice through this process was truly a blessing. You are the epitome of compassion, diligence, ambition, love, and endurance. I thank God for you every day. When I was facing fourth-and-16, you were the daring pass that helped me convert a first down.

I am grateful for my children, Zoe and Elijah, who remained understanding and uplifting. Your love and creativity are infectious. You two will always be my greatest motivation in any endeavor.

As much as I enjoy crafting stories, I never envisioned that I would write a book. I was always daunted by the undertaking, but I thank the folks at Triumph, including Josh Williams, Noah Amstadter, Alex Lubertozzi, and Adam Motin, for making this an enjoyable and exhilarating first ride.

I am eternally indebted to Tim Bourret for urging me to continue this project and for his aid and insight through my career. Additionally, I thank the entire Clemson University athletic department, including Sam Blackman, Joe Galbraith, and Dan Radakovich, for their continued assistance through this and countless other projects.

I appreciate Dabo Swinney's consistent candor. He has always been magnanimous with his time, and despite his rising stature, he has remained grounded in his roots of respect. I am grateful for the countless stories you have shared, for the unique excursions and unforgettable experiences the team has facilitated and for the annual serving of Kathleen Swinney's Krispy Kreme casserole.

I appreciate Tajh Boyd and Eric Mac Lain for their welcoming spirits and colorful insight during their tenure as players, during their transition into laudable men, and especially during the composition of this book.

I thank Katrice Hardy, Jim Rice, and the leadership team at the *Greenville News* for supporting this venture, and my current and former colleagues on the Clemson beat, Scott Keepfer, Bart Boatwright, Marcel Louis-Jacques, Ed McGranahan, Willie T. Smith III, and Bart Wright. Without you, this book would have remained nothing more than an idea.

To Sandy Dickson, Cindy Hill, Cara Pilson, Peter Gilbert, Chris Sheridan, Chris Zaluski, and Ann Bell, and my fellow storytellers in the Wake Forest University Documentary Film program, I appreciate your patience, understanding, assistance, and guidance through this creative process.

To my family, Jackie and JoAnn Robinson, Patrick and Angelia Luke, Adonna, Ramon, Oren, Patrick Jr., Ebony, Jessica, Khalila, Zarian, Tyler, Jaylen, Cameron, and Landen, I appreciate your continued support, encouragement, laughs, and love.

Take care,

Manie.